The
Shy Child

ALSO BY PHILIP G. ZIMBARDO

SHYNESS: WHAT IT IS, WHAT TO DO ABOUT IT

THE PSYCHOLOGY OF ATTITUDE CHANGE AND
SOCIAL INFLUENCE

PSYCHOLOGY AND LIFE

ALSO BY SHIRLEY L. RADL

MOTHER'S DAY IS OVER

HOW TO BE A MOTHER—AND A PERSON TOO

OVER OUR LIVE BODIES

THE INVISIBLE WOMEN

Philip G. Zimbardo is a social psychologist at Stanford University and co-director of the Stanford Shyness Clinic. He is the creator/narrator of the popular PBS-TV series "Discovering Psychology."

Before her death in 1991, **Shirley L. Radl** was a journalist and author.

The
Shy Child

A Parent's Guide to Preventing
and Overcoming Shyness from
Infancy to Adulthood

Philip G. Zimbardo

and
Shirley L. Radl

MALOR
BOOKS

This is a Malor Book
Published by ISHK
P O. Box 381069, Cambridge, MA 02238-1069

© 1981, 1999 by Philip G. Zimbardo, Inc.

First published by McGraw Hill Book Company, 1981
Second edition published by ISHK, 1999

Zimbardo, Philip G.
    The shy child: a parent's guide to preventing and overcoming
shyness from infancy to adulthood / Philip G. Zimbardo and Shirley
L. Radl.
        p.   cm.
    Originally published: New York : McGraw-Hill, c1981.
    Includes bibliographical references and index.
    ISBN 1-883536-21-9 (pbk.)
    1. Bashfulness in children. 2. Parent and child.   I. Radl,
Shirley L. II. Title.
BF723.B3Z55 1999
849'.64--dc21   99-29796
                                                              CIP

This book is dedicated to our children,
Adam, Zara, and Tanya Zimbardo,
Lisa and Adam Radl,

And to our students, both shy and not

ACKNOWLEDGMENTS

We must first thank our research assistants, Diana Dahlgren and John Buckner, for the outstanding job they did for our study of shy preschoolers. They approached the work with enthusiasm, dedication to the problem, and a genuine caring concern for shy children. Throughout our two years of working together with them, they gave us many insights into the mystery of shyness.

Next, we thank the teachers at Palo Alto's Bing Nursery School and the Binet-Montessori School of San Francisco for all their help, support, sharing of information, and enthusiasm for developing this guide for parents and teachers. Also, the teachers and counselors at Green Gables Elementary School, Jordan Middle School, and Cubberly High School in Palo Alto were generous with their time and insights and made every effort to help us learn what we needed to learn from their students and themselves. We thank them.

However much information is gathered, the enormous task of putting it all together in readable form remains. Aiding us in the fundamental stages of this effort were Avy Nielsen and Rosanne Saussotte, who not only typed draft after draft, but helped us in a range of ways that gave order to the chaos we created. Not only their work, but their generous and loving support is deeply appreciated.

In the "advanced stages" specialists of a different order were needed. The first to put us on the right track was our agent, Rhoda A. Weyr of the William Morris Agency. A most exacting taskmaster, from the beginning, Rhoda ran us through a rigorous course, demanding only the most concise and the best we could offer, compelling us to be as thorough and as thoughtful as she knew we could be. In the "final stages" we relied very heavily on our editor, Gladys Justin Carr, and her associate, Gail Greene. We thank them for their patience and their guidance.

Finally, after three years of working harmoniously together, despite the myriad of crises, large and small, and the times when we wondered if we would ever really put that final period on this book, we express our gratitude to each other—for the support, understanding, affection, and reinforcement, given generously and reciprocally, whenever it was needed.

CONTENTS

CHAPTER ONE

Unraveling the Mystery
of Shyness

Perhaps the last thing in the world parents think about when anticipating the birth of a child is whether the child will be shy. We pray that the baby will be healthy and normal, and when he or she arrives, we count the tiny fingers and toes and set out on the incredible journey that is parenting. We keep height and weight charts, record milestones of first words and steps, buy books to encourage early reading—and now we even buy little computers to get our soon-to-be math whiz kids on their way.

The emphasis on motor development, language skills, and learning has tended to divert the attention of parents, teachers, and even child psychologists away from the social and emotional growth of the child. It is only recently that professional "child watchers" have come to realize the serious effects of ignoring or taking for granted the so-called "normal" development of social responsiveness and emotional health in children. As an article in the *Sage Foundation Report* stated, "Despite the growth of developmental research over the past 20 years, the study of social and emotional development in children has continued to lag behind research on other aspects of development."

We usually wait until *after* some problem behaviors appear—when the child is "too shy"—to realize that there is need to be concerned. For some parents and teachers the concern is minimal as long as the child is well behaved, quiet, and follows the rules. Indeed, shyness may be seen as desirable to those adults who believe "silence is golden," "children should be seen and not heard," or "obedience to authority" is the highest rule. Fortunately (for our children), not all parents and other grown-ups to whom they are entrusted see it that way. One parent might react with embarrassment to his or her child's shyness when, for instance, the child responds to another adult's attention by running and hiding behind mother or father and hangin ; on for dear life. And then there are parents who share the view of the concerned mother of a six-year-old who wrote the following letter:

I have a six-year-old daughter who is extremely shy, and who has an extremely poor opinion of herself. Her excessive shyness has caused her a great deal of discomfort in peer as well as adult relationships. She has been placed in pre-first instead of first grade because of her inability to deal confidently with others of her own age. She adapts with extreme difficulty to new situations. I am afraid she will be consistently placed in the lower class grouping because of her emotional makeup.

She does not relate to the outside world easily, she holds so much inside and reacts in such a frustrated way. She can be a lovely, sensitive child, but I'm so afraid she'll find the world a hostile place unless someone can help her.

−Excerpted from a letter to Dr. Zimbardo

Not unlike many parents who have written to us or spoken with us, the mother fears that shyness may be ruining her child's life, and she's looking for answers before it is too late.

It is apparent that anything that makes your child unhappy, such as being unpopular, not feeling comfortable around peers, and being unable to communicate thoughts effectively or to express feelings directly, is a health hazard. As we shall soon discuss, these are but a few of the negative consequences that shyness imposes in its silent mission to destroy the human connection.

Now for the good news. After studying shyness for the past nine years by surveying thousands of people of all ages and backgrounds in the United States and eight other cultures; conducting in-depth interviews with shy youngsters, their parents, and teachers; observing shy children in classrooms of every grade level from preschool through college; and performing systematic experimental research that compared the behavior of shy to not-shy people, we have discovered not only the range of its consequences, but also what causes shyness, and what can be done to minimize, overcome, or prevent it. This pioneering investigation of our Stanford University Shyness Research Project has begun to reveal what lies behind the many masks of shyness. In the Stanford Shyness Clinic (along with Meg Marnell and Rochelle Kramer) we have developed different means—strategies and tactics proven effective—of helping shy people cope with the many personal problems that shyness poses.

From the researcher's point of view, shyness is a fascinating phenomenon. It is at the very core of what it means to be human; where individuals make contact with each other—or where they fail in their efforts to become social beings. Charles Darwin, writing in 1890, observed that shyness is often recognized by blushing, which is "the most peculiar and the most human of all expressions." From an analytical perspective, shyness makes us keenly aware of freedom and its constraints. Indeed, shyness can be thought of as a self-imposed loss of basic freedoms, much as incarceration denies prisoners their rights to freedom of speech, association, and acting in one's own best interests. The more we learn about the dynamics of shyness, the more the myths fall by the wayside and curious paradoxes emerge, such as the bottled-up rage in the good, shy "pussycat" boy who makes headlines as a mass murderer—the first naughty deed of his life.

But the detached perspective of the researcher gives way to the pain that we feel as parents when we watch a shy child desperately wanting to be accepted by other children yet not knowing what to do to gain their approval, or else too frightened to take the risk of trying to reach out to them. They may feel as Anna did. She writes:

During my adolescence I was so shy that at age nineteen I became emotionally ill and needed professional help. Growing up is painful at best, but excruciating for the shy. When others could not understand the reason for my lack of zest for life, I knew all along that my shyness was the real problem. I was terribly envious of anyone who seemed comfortable with people. Anyone who could express their thoughts and feelings verbally . . . not only I but all those near and dear to me, suffered immeasurably because of this illness—which has lasted for sixty-four years!

The silent prison of shyness can be a nightmare for shy students who have not learned "to work and play well with others" or to recite in class what they have studied and know well. A first-year law student with a 3.94 college Grade Point Average (GPA)—4.0 is perfect!—had to withdraw before the first quarter was over not because of lack of ability or motivation but, as she says, "because I am so shy that I could not take sitting in class and hoping (praying) that I won't be called on." As a college student she could hide out in the back of large lecture courses performing spectacularly in multiple-choice exams, but when she had to strut her stuff in front of the law class, the quicksand of shyness sucked her under.

But this young student's fear is not all that unusual. In fact, it is *the* most common human fear, according to a recent survey of 3,000 U.S. residents. When responses were tallied to the question: "What are you most afraid of?" "darkness" came in twelfth, "flying" was eighth, "sickness and death" were tied for sixth place. In third place there was another tie among 22 percent of the respondents with "fear of financial problems" and "fear of insects and bugs." "Fear of heights" had a large vote of 32 percent, ranking it second behind the biggest fear of all, at 41 percent, "speaking before a group."

In our surveys, a comparable figure of 42 percent emerged when people were asked whether they considered themselves to be "shy." Thus about two out of every five people you meet think of themselves as shy. Many of those who are not shy now, however, reported being shy at some time in the past. About 80 percent of all those surveyed revealed that they are shy now or used to be shy. The majority of those who labeled themselves as shy go on to describe this disposition as "undesirable" and a "serious problem" that interferes with their lives.

It is, of course, possible to think of yourself as not being shy yet to have occasional feelings of shyness. The contrast is between the chronic shys who believe shyness is "in them," a trait, a part of their personality makeup that gets uncovered by other people, and the situational shys who believe that certain undesirable situations cause them to react in an unnatural, shy manner. For the situational shys, the fault lies in the nature of social situations that force them to perform, to feel on the spot, etcetera. As a first step in reducing the negative impact of shyness, we have helped those who suffer chronically by getting them to reevaluate their shyness as an often appropriate reaction to situational pressures.

In 1977 we began to zero in on specific age groups, and when we surveyed high school students we found that the incidence of shyness—about 40 percent—was the same as that in the adult sample. However, when we surveyed junior high school students, the figure jumped to over 50 percent, with the increase owing largely to the prevalence of shyness in a majority of adolescent girls. Shyness is a major symptom of the many problems of adolescence—especially those problems for females undergoing the transition from elementary-school girl to woman. We held a series of informal meetings with groups of these youngsters to better appreciate how shyness functions at this age. (Later, chapter 7, we shall discuss in depth why adolescents feel "all eyes are on them" and that their parents are always prying to find out their "real selves.")

When studying younger children, we don't find this split between the public self teenagers show the world and their private self revealed only to "dear diary" and the closest of confidants. In pre-teenagers what you see is usually what they are feeling and thinking.

A study of grade school children by one of our research team members, Trudy Solomon, found the same prevalence of self-reported shyness— 42 percent—as we have found repeatedly with adult samples. These 204 children, ages nine to thirteen, from Oakland and Richmond, California, schools, showed no differences in shyness between the sexes. There was a trend, however, for the extent of shyness to increase in children in the fourth to sixth grades. This result fits with other data we have on junior high school students that shows an escalation of shyness in adolescence.

When these grade schoolers were asked to rate themselves on five-point scales on a series of traits, such as active-passive and cold-warm, the shy students differed significantly from the not-shys in perceiving themselves to be: less friendly, more fearful, more passive, less sociable, more introverted, liking themselves less, and as less tolerant of others.

This last trait raises an especially important point for our understanding of the dynamics of shyness. One paradoxical consequence of shys being excessively concerned about being evaluated is their own tendency to be evaluative and critical of others. Although shy children are sensitive to external constraints that influence "problem behaviors" in other children, they are still likely to label that child in negative ways. Similarly, in a study with female college students, it was found that when shys were presented with case studies of a peer in trouble, they were less sympathetic, proposing to treat the peer's psychological problem by institutionalizing her rather than by working with her in a counseling, therapeutic relationship.

In an investigation of how teachers, parents, and elementary school children (ages seven and eight) evaluate shyness, researchers discovered some shy behaviors that were specific to the situation (of home or school) and others that were consistent across settings. The parents and teachers of 135 Iowa schoolchildren completed rating scales of the shy/nonshy characteristics of each child. The children gave peer ratings on tape-recorded stories of shy and not-shy behaviors.

Significant agreement between judgments of shyness in school and home settings was found for the following eight behaviors. Those who agreed that the presence of such behavior was indicative of a given child's shyness are noted next to that behavior:

1. conforming   *(Father/Teacher)*
                                 (Mother/Teacher)

2. timid   *Mother/Teacher*
                                 Father/Teacher
                                 Mother/Peer

3. easily embarrassed   *Mother/Peer*

4. soft voice   *Mother/Teacher*
                                 Mother/Peer

5. talks little   *Mother/Teacher*

6. rarely shares problems
   or ideas   *Mother/Teacher*

7. rarely initiates
   interactions   *Mother/Teacher*

8. timid when meeting
   strangers   *Mother/Peer*

It is interesting to note that fathers tended to be inconsistent in their ratings of shyness. They were in least agreement with any of the other three raters: mothers, teachers, children. Either they had a different definition or criterion for shyness, or they knew their child less well than did the other judges.

For our research on preschoolers we could not rely upon questionnaires and direct interviews with children. Instead, we used four different sources of information to discover what it means for a three-, four-, or five-year-old child to be shy. We (and our research assistants) observed a number of preschool class settings, then administered our Stanford Shyness Survey Questionnaire to parents and teachers for them to evaluate the shyness of their children and students. Finally, we devised a gamelike test of shyness to indirectly assess the preschool child's conception of shyness.

Parents, teachers, and research observers were in surprisingly close agreement as to which children were shy, largely because shyness is such a public event at this young age. The child hasn't yet learned how to conceal self-doubts and social anxieties with the kind of subtle strategies that often mask the older person's private self from public scrutiny. One-third of the preschoolers were judged to be shy children, although some were more shy in school than at home, while others were more shy outside of the safety base of school or home.

Our "Which puppet is shy?" game presented the child with two adorable hand puppets, one of whom was introduced as the shy puppet, the other as the not-shy puppet. In response to each of a dozen questions, the child pointed to the puppet that was the correct answer: for example, the one who "plays alone the most," "doesn't like to talk to other people," and so forth. While reserving the details of that study for a later discussion of how to help preschool-age children overcome their shyness, several general conclusions are important to state now. By four years of age (middle-class) children in our culture have a coherent conception of what it means to be shy; shyness is a negative state that inhibits social actions and interactions and restricts opportunities to have fun. The children can identify with the puppet who is "shy like them," but regardless of their own shyness, prefer to be like the not-shy puppet.

This research on shyness in children complements our earlier (and still ongoing) investigation of shyness in adults. One goal is a better understanding of how shyness develops—the forms it takes and the consequences it has. Another goal is to use that knowledge to help parents, teachers, and shy people intervene in ways that will undo the toll that shyness extracts. For those already shy, there is much that can be done to reduce its inhibiting effects and even to overcome it completely. The prevention of shyness will also be discussed in this book as part of a general program of personality development designed to encourage your child to be sociable, to enjoy people, to be able to take appropriate risks, to better accept failures, and to perform up to his or her own potential.

Before we begin to share ideas with you about how to help shy children at each of the four age categories we've studied—preschool, elementary school, junior and senior high school, and college age—let's first consider just what shyness is, the forms it assumes, the experiences that trigger it, and the ways it affects the lives of the young as well as their elders.

Shyness is . . .

Shyness is a mental attitude that predisposes people to be extremely concerned about the social evaluation of them by others. As such, it creates a keen sensitivity to cues of being rejected. There is a readiness to avoid people and situations that hold any potential for criticism of the shy person's appearance or conduct. It involves keeping a very low profile by holding back from initiating actions that might call attention to one's self. In three words, "reserved," "cautious," "suspicious," shyness was defined by Dr. Samuel Johnson in his 1804 *Dictionary of the English Language.*

Most of us do experience some degree of that kind of shyness *naturally.* It functions as a natural protective device—a sensible reserve that allows people to size up new experiences before rushing in. And in that reflective pause we try to determine what is expected, appropriate, and desirable to say and do, in such a place and at that time. This cautious approach is most evident when we encounter new people (especially when they seem dissimilar to us), or when we're in situations where the rules of the game are unclear or unknown. The most outgoing of children can be observed clinging to a parent, when a band of visiting relatives descends upon them with big, wet kisses. ("Whatsamatter, cat's got your tongue? Come over here and tell Uncle Louie what you're gonna be when you grow up! Don't be shy, I won't bite you!")

Hint of advice: Don't allow *anyone* to label your child "shy," not even you, his or her loving parent. Tell it like it is, as spokesperson for the child's rights: for example, "he needs a little time to get to know you better, after all he was only a few months old on your last visit."

Shyness, this "natural reticence," is most intense and pervasive in young children simply because so many situations are new and so many people are strangers to them. With maturation comes an expanded memory for faces, places, and how to act to get what they want and stay out of trouble. And in most cases, with experience, the child learns how to make "small talk" and to use other tactics for gradually reducing the unfamiliarity gap. The important point here is to try to look at the current situation from the child's perspective. When we do, it usually becomes obvious that something or someone in that situation is provoking the child's bashful reaction. Consider what an observer from out of space would conclude about the shyness of all earth creatures if the alien were to judge us by how little we talk to each other in elevators.

Shyness is a virtue, "a special grace to be celebrated" according to some philosophers, artists, and others who prefer solitude to socializing. They'd rather be alone, to think, write, paint, or commune with nature. If shyness is *chosen*, and found compatible with one's life goals, then being shy is just doing one's own thing with minimal social contact. There are those who are not shy who view shyness as desirable in others because it makes them act modest, unassuming, demure, and agreeable. However, it also makes such shys more easily influenced and controlled by not-shy exploiters. We have yet to meet one very shy person, whether he or she be four or eighty-four, who sees shyness as a personal asset. Rather, it is seen as an affliction, an unwelcome state of being that forces them to shrink back from life, sometimes all the way to isolation and loneliness.

According to the current psychiatric diagnostic manual, shyness is a social phobia, its essential feature "is a persistent, irrational fear of, and compelling desire to avoid situations in which the individual may be exposed to scrutiny by others. There is also fear that the individual may behave in a manner that will be humiliating or embarrassing."

Some people have a fear of spiders or snakes, others show a phobic avoidance of heights or airplanes. In the presence of the feared object, anxiety surges and threatens to overwhelm the person unless he or she flees through the nearest exit. But those with snake phobias can live in the city and phobics with fear of heights can live and work in one-story houses. Where do those with a "people phobia" go? They avoid anxiety-provoking people by going within themselves, by tuning out and turning off others. In doing so, they intensify their self-awareness and egocentric preoccupation. Furthermore, when most people become anxious, they feel vulnerable and don't want others to know it. The way they cope with such feelings is to isolate themselves until they can get their anxiety under control. But such isolation only serves to worsen feelings of shyness and deprives the person of opportunities to practice social skills.

Shyness tends to go hand-in-hand with low self-esteem. Although shy people may value some skill or special ability they may possess, most are their own worst critics. Paradoxically, one source of this poor self-image comes from the high standards shy people tend to set for themselves. They are always coming up short when the yardstick is measured in units of perfection. A case in point is Steve, a community college student who describes himself in these terms: "I'm six-foot-four inches tall, weigh two hundred pounds, and am reasonably strong, handsome, and intelligent. Therefore, one would expect me to feel competent, confident, and comfortable around others. But I don't. I feel inferior—physically and mentally to others, and I feel painfully incompetent and uncomfortable around them."

To help Steve and others like him, requires a lot of self-esteem boosting, which you will see can be readily accomplished with concerted effort. What is harder to alter is the second source of the shy person's low self-esteem: feelings of insecurity.

Ideally, the relationship between parent and child should enable the child to develop a sense of identity that is anchored in a firm belief in his or her own self-worth. Where love is not given freely, then love is given conditionally for doing the "right thing." Under such conditions, ego and self-respect are put on the line every time the child, and later the adult, takes some action. The message is clear: You are only as good as your most recent success, but never better than the sum of all your failures. Approval, acceptance, and love are thus seen as commodities exchangeable for "desirable behavior." And most frightening, they can be taken away at a moment's notice for doing the wrong thing. And saddest of all, the insecure, shy person accepts the loss as justifiable because he or she really didn't deserve to "make the team" or "get the raise," "get asked to dance," or "apply for a top job." Even after a number of setbacks, the love-assured person still keeps the faith in his or her own essential goodness and self-worth. Like a good baseball player in a slump or a top salesperson with a run of "misses," this individual accepts failure and rejection as an inevitable consequence of taking necessary risks, of competing, of reaching beyond the comfortable attainment of the sure thing for the challenge of uncertainty.

The next two chapters will deal specifically with this central issue in shyness by examining how some parenting styles can induce insecurity, while others can build a solid foundation of self-confidence that helps the child resist self-esteem assaults from peers and authorities outside the home.

Feeling Shy

What does it feel like to be shy? wonders the non-shy person. And shy people often wonder whether or not other shys feel the same things they do when the red alert, "shyness-is-at-hand" signal is sounded. Our in-depth interviews with shys and not shys reveal the range of reactions and intensity of feeling that go into the making of a shy person.

Some people experience only slightly shy feelings and are hesitant and uncertain in their social relations or are easily embarrassed. Some people are merely timid. But at the extreme end of the spectrum is a chronic fear of people which can keep a shy person from entering into any social encounter at all.

Fear!! The one word that appears again and again in discussions of shyness is "fear." The four most dominant fears are: fear of being negatively evaluated by others one encounters; fear of failure to respond in social situations (not knowing what to say or do, or becoming "tongue-tied"); fear of being rejected by someone who is liked or controls a desired resource; and fear of intimacy (having to reveal one's "real self" and "true feelings" to another person in private).

Such fears are typically accompanied by physical arousal in which the adrenaline shoots up, pulse increases, heart pounds, butterflies flutter around the stomach, perspiration flows, and a blush appears. Each of these symptoms of internal discomfort occurs in more than 40 percent of the shy Americans surveyed. While the shy body is churning, the shy mind is even more agitated. It is filled with unpleasant thoughts and sensations. There is an excessive degree of self-consciousness, overconcern for how poorly the situation is being handled and what kind of evaluation others are making, as well as free-floating negative thoughts.

I am living in a churning, painful anxiety of self-preoccupation, and I'm tired of it. Somewhere in me I know there is the capacity to be free, to laugh, to love (maybe even myself). . . . I have so much of what is supposed to make life good—a husband who loves me, two bright, promising children, a home in the country. I should be happy, but I'm nearly always miserable. I hide. I cower. I'm afraid of people. My profession (nursing) terrifies me. I avoid unpleasant confrontations at all costs.

In addition to their awareness of being fearful and aroused, many shy people are all too aware that they suffer deficits in social skills. They lack adequate verbal skills necessary to feel comfortable in conversations. They lack assertiveness skills to negotiate interpersonal conflicts and to initiate action in their best interests. Finally, they may be insensitive to the nuances of appropriate social behavior needed, for example, to get someone's attention, to interrupt effectively, to handle compliments, or to know when to strike before the iron gets too hot.

As parents, teachers, or supportive friends, we can have a considerable impact in turning shyness around. We do so by modeling appropriate social behaviors, giving the shy lots of practice in socializing, providing constructive, nonthreatening feedback that helps refine the shy person's social skills, and most of all by rewarding all attempts at trying to be a social being.

We have found that while some shys are obviously so, even to a casual observer, others have learned to conceal their inner torment from the most careful scrutiny. These two basic types of shy people, *shy introverts* and *shy extroverts* essentially generalize the experience and capture our interest. It is from these two types of shy people that we have learned the most about what it *feels* like to be shy, and we have seen that their feelings are quite similar despite the fact that their public selves are so dramatically different.

Shy introverts are those people whose shyness—like starched underwear—cannot be concealed. A shy student majoring in speech pathology describes the feelings and symptoms of extreme shyness most succinctly.

"I was doing research on stuttering. While reviewing passages describing the emotional trauma and juxtaposed feelings of the stutterer (the *desire* to speak, and the *fear* of speaking) I was constantly reminded of similar fears, anticipatory avoidance behaviors, and many other association factors involved in stuttering that I could apply to my own experience with shyness.

"I remember thinking, as I would read various avoidance characteristics, how similar these fears and anxieties are to my own.

"For example, I anticipate that I'm going to blush when I talk, therefore I enter a conversation with anxiety. When I actually speak, the anxiety has become physiological—my heart races, I perspire—then I think to myself that I must be blushing already; then I blush—even if I wasn't blushing before, or blush *more* if I was!

"This is so similar to the anticipation-anxiety-stutter behavior of the stutterer. In increasing my embarrassment because I'm blushing, I think I appear awkward to the listener and am making him or her feel awkward. Finally the whole situation snowballs into: 1) confusion on my part because by now I'm concentrating on my (hated) blushing, and 2) confusion and either impatience, no respect for what I'm saying (mumbling, by now), or pity—I can see it in their eyes just as a stutterer can see the pity, shock, or horror in the eyes of his listener—on the listener's part because they can see I am uncomfortable and unable to express myself (because all I want by then is to crawl into a hole!)."

In addition to the abject misery in this sort of situation, clearly, we can see that the shy person winds up on both the receiving and giving ends when it comes to rejection. Ultimately he or she is rejected, and somewhere in the whole process withdraws into shyness, thus rejecting whoever it might be who is attempting to listen or reach out. Not surprising then, is their reluctance to take risks, to try new things. Fear of failure (which can run the gamut from a difficult social encounter to learning a new sport) is so great that many shy children stay locked in place, never giving themselves the freedom to find out how well they might be able to perform socially, academically, or creatively. So they don't learn how in the only way one can—through practice, trial and error, and success.

Shy extroverts, on the other hand, manage to find the words in most situations, respond warmly to other people by smiling, laughing, making eye contact, giving compliments, and thus do a pretty good job of hiding their shyness from others. So successful are they, that often their best friends don't know that they experience many of the same sensations and fears that shy introverts do. Most of the time they are able to transcend their shyness and step into the role of the not-shy person. One rather vivacious eighteen-year-old described what it is like to be a shy extrovert this way:

"Many times in unfamiliar situations or when I'm with people I either don't know or hold in awe, my heart races so much I worry that people can actually see it pounding in my chest. My mouth goes dry, my hands get clammy, but all the while I manage to talk and smile because I certainly don't want anyone to know that I'm shy. I keep trying, and can usually put up a good front, because I really do like other people, and as uncomfortable as it can be, I like to be around them.

"Sometimes when I walk into a room full of people, not only do I tremble, but I actually get dizzy. Sometimes I decline a cup of coffee because I'm afraid my shaking will cause me to spill it.

"The most embarrassing thing I do is that when I'm introduced to new people, the first thing that happens is that I forget their names simply because I'm so preoccupied with what sort of an impression I'm making."

Shy extroverts are at their best when they can play well-rehearsed roles in clearly defined situations, and especially when they are in the driver's seat. Actors, politicians, college lecturers, reporters, TV talk-show hosts are more often of this breed than one would suspect. They create the illusion of "doing naturally" what takes a lot of practice and concentrated effort (and maybe a stiff drink or two). Their shyness expresses itself when they leave the stage, or the red recording light goes off and they, too, must deal with the spontaneity and unplanned give-and-take of everyday encounters with ordinary people.

Shy extroverts make us aware of a special aspect of shyness, the separation of public self from one's "real," private self. Carol Burnett steps into a variety of not-shy roles with a unique style that wins her top awards as an outstanding performer. But give her a defective product to return or a cocktail party filled with strangers and she is the first to admit her shyness bugaboo intrudes to make her uncomfortably awkward. Former President Carter and Rosalyn Carter have both testified publicly how much they disliked campaigning because they are both shy. The list of shys seems endless, each day we add one more shy celebrity to it, including John Travolta; the late Jimi Hendrix; Charlton Heston; Loni Anderson, who on TV is Jennifer, the sexy WKRP receptionist; and Michael Jackson of the Jackson Five who says he is shy in private but comfortable on stage. In an interview with Johnny Carson, Mike Wallace touched on the private shyness of this very successful, public person.

MW: There's a stereotype of Carson. You know there is.

JC: Well, what is it?

MW: It is icewater in his veins . . .

JC: I had that taken out years ago. I went to Denmark and had that done. It's all over now.

MW: Shy, defensive . . .

JC: Probably true. I can remember when I was in high school. If I pulled out my high school annual book and read some of the things. People might say, oh, he's conceited, he's aloof. Actually, that was more shy. See, when I'm in front of an audience, it's a different thing. If I'm in front of an audience, I can feel comfortable.

MW: Why?

JC: I'm in control.

MW: (*Voice over*) That's a key to Carson. Control. Professionally, he insists upon it. Socially, he can't demand it so he retreats. He's uncomfortable. And the fact is he is shy.

JC: There's Carson the performer and there's Carson the private individual and I can separate the two.

Origins of Shyness

Some psychologists point to a genetic component in shyness. Within the first week of life, babies appear to differ in their emotionality, some cry a lot and are easily distressed. In addition, young children exhibit temperamental differences in their sociability that may develop into rather fixed patterns of social behavior. Those with more "sensitive" nervous systems, the argument goes, would overreact to threats. Cautious approach to, and ready retreat from threatening social situations would then develop in these children as ways of coping with their greater degree of anxiety.

The supporting evidence for an inherited origin of shyness is indirect and not very conclusive. Babies do indeed differ in how emotional and socially responsive they are, but it has not been shown that those who *are* more "sensitive" become shy as children or adults, while their thick-skinned, smiling siblings become the assertive kids on the block.

Learned social experiences can shape most genetically determined patterns of behaviors. Smiling babies get smiled at, picked up, and fussed over more than do sullen or placid ones. Sociable children are more fun to be with because they are responsive to the attention they get. They get more social rewards and warm strokes because they give more to peers and adults.

Contained in the belief that there is a genetic component to shyness is the fairly widespread notion that shyness is inherited. Indeed, there is suggested evidence that shyness runs in families; at least one of the parents of a shy child is also likely to be shy. However, in those same families, there is as much chance that other children will not be shy. But the problem lies in the difficulty of separating the contribution of inherited predispositions toward shyness in a particular child from the learned consequences of family, school, work, and cultural experiences that are shyness producing regardless of the child's heredity.

From our research we've seen there are a number of different origins of shyness rooted in early childhood experiences, and, in how such experiences are perceived and interpreted by the individual. Some shy children report specific failures in social settings; difficulties in school; unfavorable comparisons with older siblings, relatives, or peers. Others, of all ages, suffer from the loss of usual social supports that results from frequent family moves out of the neighborhood or from sudden changes in social bonding due to divorce, death, going off to a new school, and so forth.

Where parents provide poor models from which to learn both the joys of being outgoing as well as some of the basic social skills essential to effective interactions, their "socially disadvantaged" children are likely to be more shy than not. This seems to be the case with children born in the United States whose parents are from cultures that downplay public displays of affection, emotion, and active discussion and debate between parents and children.

Sheer lack of experience in social settings contributes to shyness. Living in isolated areas or being raised in restricted environments that deny access to a variety of social experiences makes for awkwardness and fear of the unknown. For example, being alone with someone of the opposite sex is one of the most potent elicitors of shyness from adolescence through old age—but not among young children. The reason is obvious: People of different sexes are separated and kept apart by a host of societal devices prior to the onset of puberty. The other sex is thus not only "different," but an alien species about whom we know little. For some parents who want to keep the natural interest between the sexes at bay as long as possible (or until marriage unites them), the admonition is: "Better shy now than sorry later!"

It has repeatedly amazed us how many shy people can pinpoint the day, place, and culprit responsible for pinning the shyness label on them. Sometimes the child will adopt the label as self-descriptive because it must be so if authoritative dad or all-knowing teacher says so. Sometimes shyness will be accepted as preferable to other labels that might account for why the child did not respond appropriately, such as "lazy," "dumb," or "unloving."

Another factor that quite likely tips low self-esteem in the shyness direction: shame. The list of things over which one can feel shame is endless: unsatisfactory personal appearance, bad habits, peculiar family members (like a Billy Carter in the closet), to name just a few. Shame gives people something to hide, something over which to feel self-conscious. Which might come first, shame or shyness? Perhaps they arrive together. One woman told us that she had been shy all of her life and for as long as she can remember her grandmother always reprimanded her with the words, "Shame on you," or "You ought to be ashamed of yourself," for virtually any act of misbehavior or failure to perform well.

In any event, our research bears out that in the culture in which shyness is the most prevalent—Japan, with about 60 percent of those surveyed saying they are shy—shame is used as a tool for getting people to perform or behave the way society says they "should." Typically, the Japanese grow up with it deeply impressed on them that they are not to bring disgrace to the family—and "disgrace" may be seen in not performing well in school, making an error in a Little League game, or any failure at all. In this regard, there is an important comparison between the cultural values of Japan, and Israel—where shyness is least prevalent in any country we've studied. In Japan, failure falls entirely upon the shoulders of the person who erred, while his or her success gets credited to parents, grandparents, teachers, coaches, or Buddha. Such a system suppresses individual risk-taking and solitary initiative.

Israeli children typically experience exactly the opposite child-rearing practices. Any success is attributed personally to the individual, while failures are externalized, blamed on inadequate teaching, unfair competition, prejudice, or whatever. There are rewards for trying to achieve something as well as for its attainment, with few, if any, sources of punishment for failure. The Israeli child has nothing to lose by trying and everything to gain. So why not take a chance? The Japanese child who has little to gain from trying and much to lose, holds back, defers, and passes up the chance.

In our culture, children raised under parental values that approximate those of the Japanese, will avoid situations of uncertainty or novelty and take few chances in social settings. These, as we have seen, and will discuss again later, are hallmarks of the shy person's approach to life.

We believe that shyness is, ultimately, caused by a combination of feelings of low self-worth, labeling, and shame. And when all of these factors are present in the extreme, the consequences can be devastating. An example can be seen in Sarah, a college student who traveled from Oregon to Palo Alto in an effort to get into Stanford University to be near the Shyness Clinic (which she felt was her last hope).

When we first met Sarah, she sat in the office with her shoulders protectively slumped forward, her head down, her long hair covering her face, and not only did she not make eye contact, she kept her eyes closed. When we asked her to tell us about her shyness, she muttered that she couldn't. We continued to try to prod her into talking to us, but she would only mumble, sometimes incoherently. Finally, because we were getting nowhere, we suggested that she talk into a tape recorder, and left her alone in the office. Playing back the tape, which took Sarah nearly an hour to falteringly record, this is what we heard:

"I'm wasting tape. . . . (*four full minutes of silence*)

"It's very hard for me to make eye contact with people because . . . because . . . all my life it's been hard to communicate with people, you know, make eye contact with them . . . my mother, you know, says . . . it's the way my personality was. . . . And growing up not having a friend, you know . . . any really good friends.

"The reason I make very little sense to people . . . when I look at people . . . I can't think straight and I really can't talk very well. I feel nobody would like me because I don't, you know, have very much going for me. . . . I'm not loud, not vivacious . . . and I don't know if I can do anything that well . . . be an asset to other people.

"It's just that I can't . . . I just feel that I . . . that . . . I can't get my thoughts together. . . . I'm nervous . . . like now, you know, and I'm not making very much sense. I feel like a damn fool. . . . I wonder if there's any hope for me. I'm trying. I made an ass out of myself coming here to Stanford trying to get help. I can't go on like this. Part of me wants friends and the other part of me is frightened. . . . I don't know if they'll accept me. . . . I don't think I'm worth accepting. Because you know . . . I've decided to fight . . . for a change . . . for something. I've never done it before in my life. . . . I just hope it will work out for me.

"I'm feeling a little more relaxed now. . . . I'll try to make more sense.

"All my life growing up and having an older sister who was very extroverted . . . it was very hard to grow up under that. Everybody always praised her . . . it made me feel inferior. Then having to have a brother who's the same way . . . makes you feel like you're sandwiched in between the two of them. Kinda weird. Then having a father who abuses . . . I could never feel secure in that house because he'd come home and be in a violent mood . . . he didn't even have to be drinking when he'd get violent . . . when he drank, he'd get more violent. I never felt secure. He was always saying, you know, I was no good, that I should never have been born, that I was an accident . . . and he didn't want a second child and then *I* came along. My father never let me forget that.

"My mother . . . she was better in that she always tried to make me feel welcome in the house. [But it still sounds like Sarah was at best a guest.] She always felt that I shouldn't be blamed for . . .

"The teachers were, you know, always picking on me. When I was in elementary school I always had one or two really good friends. . . . One teacher . . . she used to ask these really bitchy kids to make friends with me. I couldn't respond to them. They were so nasty all the time. The teachers always used to single me out . . . because I didn't have many friends. I was always being sent to the school psychologist."

From this, and from subsequent conversations with Sarah (which gradually we were able to ease her into), it was obvious that Sarah's self-esteem had been destroyed. And yet, the home environment was only *one* factor in the making of Sarah's debilitating shyness.

Other important factors, Sarah told us, included having to

wear thick glasses and ugly orthopedic shoes—and "walking funny"—all of which made her feel extremely inferior and self-conscious. And after Sarah started school, her first-grade teacher made it a practice to draw attention to her problems with her feet by forcing her to get up in front of the class and "walk right," which provided her classmates with a "comedy act," and Sarah a jeering audience. In a very classic experience, Sarah graduated from being the family scapegoat to being teacher's scapegoat, a role she was to play many times over the years.

Certainly Sarah's parents set her up, but the important thing to remember when looking at the role they played is that *they had many accomplices.*

Far less guilty parents than Sarah's blame themselves if their children are shy. While it is obviously true that shyness can sometimes be traced to the home environment, there are, as we have thus far seen, other causes.

Those most vulnerable to shyness, we have found, are children who relate well to adults but not to their peers, gifted children, only children, children mature beyond their years, those who live in isolated environments (rural and unsafe urban areas), nonathletic boys, and others who see themselves as significantly different. And we have found that shyness often surfaces when parents divorce or when some other crisis occurs in a family. Being put into a highly competitive, achievement-oriented college setting can weaken all but the best laid foundations of self-worth. Many college students report becoming more shy as a consequence of being a residential student at a top-flight college.

Shyness Elicitors

Just as there is a diversity of origins that predispose someone to be shy, there are many specific situations that precipitate the shyness reaction. The kinds of people and social settings that trigger the shyness response can be summarized as follows:

Other people (in order of their potential to trigger shyness)
1. strangers
2. authorities by virtue of their knowledge
3. members of the opposite sex
4. authorities by virtue of their role
5. relatives and foreigners
6. elderly people (for the young)
7. friends
8. children (for older people)
9. parents
10. siblings (least of all)

The underlying principle appears to be that shyness is elicited most by those who are perceived as different, relatively powerful, controlling desired resources, or familiar enough to be critically evaluative.

Situations (in order of their potential to trigger shyness)
1. where I am the focus of attention—large groups, as when giving a speech
2. where I am of lower status
3. requiring assertiveness
4. new, in general
5. where I am being evaluated
6. of vulnerability (need help)
7. one-to-one opposite sex interactions
8. social, in general
9. where I am the focus of attention—small groups
10. part of a small, task group

Shy people begin to worry when they have to perform in unfamiliar situations where they are the object of attention and critical evaluation by others whom they perceive to be dominant or demanding.

Such circumstances arouse some anxiety in even confidently assertive people, but they recognize the anxiety as a cue to exert more effort in order to manipulate the environment to make it work for them. Similarly, an athlete interprets the flow of adrenaline just before the contest begins as excitement and "getting up" for the challenge rather than as anxious concern over prospects of failing. Shyness tends to be maintained by the biased ways we have learned to interpret our reactions to situations that we often distort. Thus, a major strategy for treating shyness consists of restructuring those thoughts so that they lead to constructive coping actions instead of the paralysis of inaction.

What Shyness Can Do

Shyness does lots of bad things to people, young and old.

• It makes it difficult to meet new people or enjoy potentially good experiences.

• Shyness prevents people from speaking up for their rights and expressing their own opinions and values. The shy are more conforming and less likely to challenge oppressive rules and authorities.

• It limits positive evaluations by others of one's real personal strengths.

• It encourages self-consciousness and excessive preoccupation with one's reactions, to the exclusion of concern for others.

• Shyness makes it hard to think clearly and communicate effectively, thus causing learning difficulties in schoolchildren.

• Negative feelings such as depression, anxiety, low self-esteem, and loneliness typically accompany shyness.

• Shy people are more dependent than others on, and vulnerable to, peer pressure, which, in the instance of young people, makes them susceptible to pressures to smoke, drink, use dope, be unwillingly promiscuous, and even to join cults.

• Shy people tend to bottle up their emotions, which not only can deprive them of the warmth and intimacy with others we all need, but can also lead them to suppress their anger until they explode—sometimes violently.

• Shy children are reluctant to ask questions, seek clarification, or ask for help in school when they need it.

• Shy people of all ages are frequently misunderstood. As the poet Tennyson noted, *"Shy she was, and I thought her cold."* They may be seen as disinterested in what someone may be saying to them, or unfriendly, or untrustworthy for not being able to look other people in the eye. If also attractive, the shy are judged to be condescending and rejecting of others.

• When the symptoms are functioning at full throttle, the shy person may remember past experiences with embarrassment and worry in anticipation about future goofs. The present—at least the social present with its chance to enjoy the moment—becomes virtually nonexistent. Nearly 10 percent of the shy are shy even when they are alone.

• With all of this self-preoccupation, shy people don't tune in appropriately to what is happening at the time and, thus, often don't hear accurately. A good example of this is that shy people frequently forget a person's name immediately after being introduced to someone new. And the inability to concentrate on the present and accurately keep track of who is saying what, makes it difficult to think clearly or express oneself effectively.

• Friendships with one's peers are not only pleasant, but research has shown that they are vital to the emotional growth and health of a child. When shyness prevents children from having friends—which it can do—it is then damaging to a child's emotional health.

Our primary concern is to help you to minimize the effects of shyness that may keep your children from reaching their full potential as human beings. Even when children are only moderately shy, they still miss out on valuable social experiences. And, when shyness is really severe, living in that psychological prison can ruin a life.

Sarah is just one example of how much can be done for shy

children. She not only made it through the interview with the Admissions officer, but she has been accepted as a transfer student to the university of her choice. And for the first time in her life she has a number of friends whose caring about her has taught her to smile, to look into their eyes, and to enjoy life and reach for something more. She's still quite shy, but she's not the same painfully shy student who came all the way from Oregon for help. To use her words, "After I was here for two weeks my whole life started to turn around because I found people who cared about me." Yes, it turned around because people cared enough to help Sarah make that happen for herself and because of her own inner strength.

Sarah is an inspiration to all of us—parents, teachers, concerned humans—to do whatever we can to help our children conquer shyness.

CHAPTER TWO

A Parenting Style
to Combat Shyness

Parents who have several children often wear as many parenting hats as there are children. One mother of a family of fourteen children, for instance, described herself by saying, "I'm fourteen different mothers." However, there are three basic parenting styles that parents generally build on, and each has a different impact on children. Psychologist Diana Baumrind describes those styles essentially as follows: The *permissive* style "has as its goal giving the child as much freedom as is consistent with the child's physical survival"; the *authoritarian* style "values obedience as a virtue and believes in restricting the child's autonomy"; the *authoritative* style "attempts to direct the child's activities in a rational, issue-oriented manner." After studying the effects of these styles of parenting on 150 children, Dr. Baumrind concluded that of the three, the authoritative style was the most effective.

When looking for a possible connection between shyness and parenting styles, we see that the authoritative style is most likely to create feelings of security and self-confidence in a child and hence is the most effective in combating shyness. For a deeper understanding of the reasons behind this, let's take a closer look at all three of these basic parenting styles and what they do to promote or hinder the development of a socially responsive child.

Contrary to popular belief, permissiveness doesn't contribute much to a child's sense of security. It has been found that often permissive parents are casual about everything from an infant's crying that signals a need for comfort or care, to setting down guidelines for a child's behavior as he or she grows older. Permissive parents are sometimes benignly neglectful and inconsistent, and they may convey to their children a sense that they are unconcerned. Recalling her own permissive upbringing, one college student told us, "It wasn't that my parents were mean, and they certainly weren't strict. I don't think they really cared because they just couldn't be bothered. I grew up feeling I wasn't very important or worth bothering about, which I think is one reason for my shyness."

At the other end of the spectrum are authoritarian parents, who are also neglectful when it comes to showing affection and caring. They too will let a child cry instead of giving loving comfort—out of a mistaken fear that responding to a baby's cries to be held will result in "spoiling." From the beginning, even though they may see to all of their children's actual physical needs and give them plenty of attention when it comes to discipline and guidance, authoritarian parents don't pay much positive attention to their children. They go quietly about their job of parenting, and they don't comfort and cuddle them, don't read to them, talk to them, or play with them very often. Authoritarian parents tend to be very concerned that their children's "good" behavior will reflect well on them. They often are more concerned with the evaluation of outsiders than they are with those of their family. While they may sincerely believe that by being stern and tough they will, for example, "make a man" of their boy, they may be doing just the opposite. As child development specialist Eleanor Maccoby of Stanford University says, "Two ways to make a child overdependent are to ignore him and handle him roughly. . . . It is withdrawal of affection, insensitivity, unresponsiveness, and rejection that can lead to dependent behavior." When a child's needs for affection are not met, they remain unsatisfied, resulting in feelings of insecurity that may contribute to dependence on others.

The connection between authoritarianism and shyness is clear in this description by one shy student. "Good behavior was everything to my mother, who always worried about appearances. She was very strict and she wanted us to be quiet, polite, and well behaved. She was always very tense and never very demonstrative. But she was long on discipline. I think she was so busy trying to create perfect children that she didn't have time to be affectionate. I have no memory of ever being held, but instead one of a mother grimly doing her job.

"Her strictness and her demands for perfection made me nervous and made me feel I could never live up to her standards—never be quite as good as I should be. I've always felt sort of inferior and very self-conscious."

An authoritarian parenting style is more likely to be characteristic of a father's approach to his children since this style is better tailored than the others to masculine sex-role stereotypes as well as to traditional values of the "work place." Its emphasis is on the product not the process; feelings are relegated to a back burner because they often get in the way of efficient task accomplishment. Control, power, status, and authority are the means used to achieve explicit goals. Cooperation, negotiation, and democratically shared participation in setting of goals and means to achieve them are *not* part of the authoritarian approach to getting things done.

But what happens when a child incorporates such values into his or her approach to other people? Survival of individuals and groups requires flexibility, ability to deal with uncertainty, decision-making that integrates diverse inputs from other people, and always some willingness to bargain and accept compromise. For the authoritarian, these "social-political" strategies and tactics appear as unnecessary hassles and barriers rather than as part and parcel of interactions among less than perfect human beings.

In a study with college students we found a significant relationship between shyness and a tendency to endorse authoritarian values. This finding fits with our analysis of the nature of shyness in the previous chapter, where we saw that avoidance of novel, unstructured social situations is typical of shy people, as is their better functioning when given a specific role to play in a well-defined social relationship. But the way of the world is often along unmarked paths, with fuzzy trail markers and ever-changing guides.

The middle ground between these two extremes is, obviously, the authoritative style, which, according to Dr. Baumrind's studies, finds the parent very much in control, yet very nurturing. The authoritative parent is affectionate, has a realistic grasp of what a particular child is capable of at a particular stage of development, and both talks and listens to his or her child. That parent will modify rules and decisions when situations change or there is persuasive evidence (sometimes offered by the child) to do otherwise.

Before you wring your hands in despair that you have been too permissive, too much of a dictator, or have caused your child to be shy, take heart. Remember that there are a number of forces that can cause a child to be shy and keep him or her that way. Psychologist Dr. Louise Bates Ames of Yale University's Gessell Institute of Human Development told us, "While the home environment is an important factor in the psychological development of a child, it is but one. Other influences consist of school, church, a child's relationships with other adults, and most decidedly, with the peer group, and inborn personality traits."

But most parents, she continued, "have a deep basic dread that they are somehow damaging their children. But the fact is, conscientious parents probably cause *themselves* more anxiety worrying about this than they could ever visit upon their children.

"Naturally," she reminded us, "if parents are very harsh, indifferently permissive, or terribly inconsistent in dealing with their children, the chances are the children may be damaged. But such parents tend not to worry about this, while paradoxically, conscientious parents *do*—and that they care so much tells me they are the *least* likely to cause any harm.

"Parenthood is probably the most difficult job in the world, and I think it's a miracle that parents do as well as they do. And most do very well indeed."

So, yes, you may have made some mistakes—mistakes that may or may not have contributed to your child being shy, but *do* remember that other forces in your child's life exist that also play a role. And recognizing mistakes, you can stop making them.

Before going on to describe (and prescribe) what a parent does who wants to contribute positively toward the development of a socially outgoing, emotionally responsive, not-shy child, a caveat is in order. *You* might have to face up to some changes in yourself. You will have to modify certain ways of dealing with others in the presence of your child—if you are shy, domineering, overly dependent, too self-sufficient, or hypercritical. And you may have to be willing to act as a "social change agent" to alter the whole social-emotional atmosphere in your home to create a setting which is not conducive to shyness. This might mean eliciting changes in your spouse or other adults living at home or visiting regularly, as well as in siblings. Shyness is not like a child's hearing disorder that you can correct with a hearing aid, it is analogous to a motor disability which requires structural changes in the home setting.

Let us now take a closer look at some of the *basic* elements found in the parenting style (authoritative) most likely to combat shyness.

Touching

Because the relationship between shyness and insecurity cannot be minimized, the importance of touching to a child's basic security cannot be minimized either. Numerous studies bear out what is obvious to us. One study, for example, was conducted by Mary Salter Ainsworth of the University of Virginia. She and her associates have been examining mother-infant relationships for the past ten years, and they have found that children whose mothers are responsive to their emotional needs—the need to be touched and cuddled—as well as their physical needs tend to be very secure, or, put in more analytical terms, "securely attached." Typically, the mothers held the children a great deal from the very beginning and responded to their babies' cries by picking them up and giving comfort.

While there may not be a direct relationship between the amount of physical affection a child receives and shyness, we believe a connection exists, not simply because touching and security go hand in hand (so to speak) but because of what some of our shy students have told us. One young man, now twenty, told us that he had no memory at all of his parents ever hugging him, or having ever sat on his mother's lap. And one young woman said, "I used to ache for my parents to hug me. I'd see my mother hold my little brother, and I'd try to get her to hold me too, but always my father would shoo me away, saying, 'Don't be a baby.' I couldn't have been more than four years old at the time."

This need to be touched and loved by no means disappears at *any* age. It may be better if you started out touching your child from birth, but the good news is, *you really can start any time.* As one father, divorced from his son's mother, and since remarried, told us:

"My son, now fifteen, was very undemonstrative as a young child. He never showed any affection to any relatives—not even to his grandmother. I think it had to do with the fact that his mother and I were going through all these problems, so he wasn't seeing affection there. Then about four years ago, we were sitting watching TV, and my second wife, Jane, purposely put her arm around me, and then around my son in a most loving way, and started saying, 'He's my *big* baby.' Teasing and touching, what she was saying was that not only can we hug and touch in this house, but we want to. Since that time, when he's staying with us and he comes down to breakfast, he kisses her good morning, kisses me, kisses the baby. And he's a teenager! Now he was twelve years old before he was like this. I love it. I kiss him back. And he loves that."

So, even if you haven't done it in the past, touch your children, kiss them, hold them, and demonstrate your love for them.

And don't be afraid to let the little ones crawl in bed with you and cuddle. Or, at least, to all cuddle together on a weekend morning. It's really too bad that some parents, inhibited by general cultural narrow-mindedness, miss out on this way of giving and experiencing closeness. Some, we know, are even afraid to let their children in their beds when the children have nightmares.

Fear of eroticism does get in the way of expressing affection, both in "the family bed" and out of it, however. Parents need to realize that it's natural to feel a certain amount of sensual pleasure in touching (and even looking at) their own children. So long as that sensual pleasure is platonic, there is no need to be reserved in expressing affection. As one mother told us, "The love you feel toward your child is the purest and the truest." If that is *your* feeling, go with it.

Touching, by the way, is a good way to get a zany child to calm down. When you think one is begging for a spanking because he's bouncing off the walls, he may be begging for a touch of another order. Try patting and touching him or her on the hair, the arms, the shoulders, the back, the legs. And when children are "out of control," a tight bear hug and a kiss when they settle down will do wonders when punishment won't.

Psychologist James Prescott presents a rather convincing case for the hypothesis that physical pleasure actively inhibits physical violence. "It is clear," he argues, "that the world has only limited time to change its custom of resolving conflicts violently. . . . [To do so] we can work toward promoting pleasure and encouraging affectionate interpersonal relationships as a means of combating aggression."

The power of touch to help people feel connected in a meaningful way to the human community not only affects shyness but, according to James Lynch, author of *The Broken Heart*, it plays an important role in disease and maintenance of health. Lynch asserts that when a person is isolated from the touch, trust, and tenderness of fellow human beings, chances of sickness and disease increase. "There is a biological basis for our need to form human relationships," he concludes from his research. "If we fail to fulfill that need, our health is in peril."

Talking

It has been found that when mothers talk to their babies, when those babies become children, they are more verbal than those whose mothers just went quietly about their business taking care of their infants. Even if a child is too young to understand the language then, talking, reading stories, and singing will all help to set your child's sociability program in motion. And when that child first starts talking to you, the basis for keeping the lines of communication open will be whether or not you listen and respond.

Some basic rules for further keeping the lines of communication open are:

• Allow your children to express themselves freely; encourage them to give their opinions—to tell you what they dislike or like—about everything from what you've just served for dinner to a relative they aren't crazy about. Why is a particular book or cartoon character their favorite, what did they dream about last night?

• Allow your children to express anger. This is especially important since most shy people have difficulty handling anger. When your children are allowed to express it in nonde-structive ways, they are less apt to bottle it up—and more likely to stand up for their rights and be assertive instead of shy.

• Encourage your children to talk about their feelings in a direct way, to be able to say "*I* feel sad," or happy, or whatever.

• Invite your children to talk to you, but don't force them.

Quite possibly the greatest barrier to conversation between family members is television watching, which is an isolating activity. It can, however, be turned into an opportunity for parents who would like to talk to their children more, but don't really know what to say to make conversation. When watching some shows together, for example, you can mute the commercial breaks and talk about what's going on: You can ask a child what he or she thinks the characters are doing and why they behave the way they do. Often, even on "Sesame Street," there are complex processes taking place which may be beyond a child's level of understanding—for instance, double entendre, individual words used, concepts of give-and-take. And if you ask a child how a particular situation or character makes him or her feel, this encourages a child to make self-statements—"I think," "I feel"—which shy people don't do very often. Recent research has shown that watching an educational program such as "Sesame Street" is effective in improving the child's intellectual abilities only if a parent also watches and discusses the program with the child.

Finally, most parents assume that their children know they love them, but children need lots of reassurance. They need to be *told* "I love you," and told it often. "But they know it even if I don't say it outright" is the usual response parents (especially fathers of older children) give us.

A recent profile on Henry Fonda, an actor who appears so direct, honest, and loving in most of his screen roles, reveals what the shy Henry Fonda is really like. According to the author and drama critic, Leonard Probst, Fonda says he is "painfully, painfully shy. . . . The worst torture that can happen to me is not to have a mask to get in back of. I first committed myself to acting when I discovered it was therapy for a very self-conscious young man."

Of special interest to us was Fonda's difficulty in enjoying his children as fully as he wanted to—until recently. He admitted candidly: "It is only in the last two years that I have been able to say 'I love you' to my children! Isn't it awful not to be able to kiss and hug and say 'I love you'? Of course I have loved them since they were born."

How did this loving father of Jane and Peter Fonda get turned around at the late age of sixty-nine? His children had to take the initiative for changing the script. As Peter explained: "We started this on the phone. I took the blatant position of saying, 'I love you.' That was four years ago [1974]. Henry's first response was a choked remark, ending in a garbled 'good-by.' But I wouldn't let him off the hook. As time progressed he was bound to respond to me. But the first 40, 50 times were the full choke-up, tears, not knowing how to respond." (*San Francisco Chronicle*, November 8, 1978.)

We are reminded by this touching tale with its happy ending of playwright George Bernard Shaw's analysis of shyness and the need to communicate feelings of love. In Shaw's *Candida*, the romantic, shy poet Marchbanks, who is secretly in love with the heroine, Candida, confesses:

I go about in search of love; and I find it in unmeasured stores in the bosoms of others. But when I try to ask for it, this horrible shyness strangles me; and I stand dumb, or worse than dumb, saying meaningless things: foolish lies. And I see the affection I am longing for given to dogs and cats and pet birds, because they come and ask for it. It must be asked for: it is like a ghost; it cannot speak unless it is first spoken to. All the love in the world is longing to speak; only it dare not, because it is shy! Shy! Shy! That is the world's tragedy.

Love Your Child "Unconditionally"

There is more behind the advice, often given, that parents need to make sure they convey to a child that while they don't particularly like what a child may do at times, it is the *behavior* and *not* the child that is being disliked at that moment. Put another way, what parents are being advised to do is to make sure that their children always know that their parents' love for them is constant—that is, *unconditional*.

Deep inside, most likely the love you feel for your children *is* unconditional. But ask yourself whether you may behave in ways that obscure that fact from your children. How many times has withholding love been your ace in the hole? How many times did you know you could add a little love or take some of it away to get your child to behave in a desired way—to pick up his or her toys, to take out the garbage, to be home on time, or to go to bed? *Or, to be quiet?* One shy person told us that her shyness grew out of being quiet: "I must have been about three years old," she said, "when I figured out that I could get strokes from my parents for being quiet. So, I was quiet. A nice, quiet child."

Remember that it has been found that shy people often invest every social performance with their most cherished possession—their ego. When their request is denied, or an approach not reciprocated, they conclude, "She doesn't like me"; "He thinks I'm not good enough"; "They don't want me around." Somehow, they have mistakenly learned to equate what they do or don't do—how they act—with their very essence: their self-worth and identity. Instead of focusing on how they might alter their request next time, or reasons for its refusal that have nothing to do with them personally, they jump to the egocentric conclusion: "*I* have been evaluated negatively and *I* have been rejected."

Part of that erroneous way of thinking comes from having learned at home that they are loved and respected *conditional* upon how they behave. What they add to the equation is: "How others respond to my behavior thus indicates what they think about me and whether or not I am a desirable person."

We feel strongly that *behavior* may be undesirable (thus not acceptable or even disciplined), but your child should never be made to feel he or she is an undesirable person.

Discipline with Love and Understanding

All children need limits to feel secure. And we not only want our children to be secure, but we want them to be socially acceptable outside the home as well. Thus, we don't want them to be "bratty" or act without regard to the needs of others.

Since the reason for discipline is to effect desirable behavior, it's useful to discuss parental perceptions of what is and what isn't just that. Many parents, psychologist Dr. Fitzhugh Dodson told us, think their children are misbehaving when "in reality, they are behaving like *children*." These parents, says Dodson, author of *How to Parent* and *How to Grandparent*, expect their children to behave like adults and they are shocked and frustrated when they don't. So take a look at your expectations of your child's behavior, and don't assume misbehavior, for example, in a two-and-a-half-year-old when he or she is simply acting like one.

Excessive discipline (especially if it is unfair or abrasive in intensity) may influence shyness in any number of ways.

(a) Discipline is often based on the assumption that the child is at fault and thus he or she needs to change. The child who believes parental authority is "just" accepts the discipline as deserved and himself or herself as "bad." Self-esteem, a core component of shyness, thereby is lowered.

(b) Fear of authority may generalize and lead to inhibitions in the presence of all authority figures. Authorities, as we've seen, are a major elicitor of shyness. Shyness occurs not out of respect for authority but out of the shy person's fear of its power over him or her.

(c) In other data we've collected, shy college students admit to a greater fear of losing control and worry more about others gaining control over them than do their not-shy classmates. Control is a central concern of parents who discipline severely, and our shy students grow up to both fear and worry about control—getting too much and having too little of it.

(d) People are disciplined, not situations. Often the truth of the matter is found by examining the *context* in which the behavior occurred: Others may be responsible, or elements in the situation may be the real culprit. For example, one girl complained to a boy's mother that her five-year-old mild-mannered, shy son hit her "for no reason at all." As it turned out, the girl had been taunting him, calling him a cripple. The boy was indeed crippled and wore heavy leg braces. While he shouldn't have hit the girl, it's easy to understand why he did. With that in mind, ask for your child's version of any infraction of one of your "must-follow" rules before meting out any punishments. In addition, always inquire of the plaintiffs what were the (extenuating) circumstances surrounding the deed in question. Was the child inattentive in class because he had completed the lesson and was bored? Were children forced to compete for a limited resource and the competition got out of hand?

Shy people themselves tend to underplay or even ignore the relevance of situational forces that may be determining their own behavior or that of others toward them. Their thinking has been narrowly routed toward persons-as-causes. There is much psychological research to support the conclusion that to change behavior it is necessary to identify and change the external conditions that maintain such behavior. But it is hard for shy people to change even when they are highly motivated to do so precisely because they fail to appreciate that their reactions are being caused by elements specific to the situations they are in and not just by their shyness.

Discipline must be a private matter. Whatever disciplinary action is taken, it ought to be taken in a manner that preserves a child's dignity. It should be done privately and whatever behavior elicited the discipline should be held as confidential. The use of public reprimands and the shame it often creates in the child is counterproductive to stopping the undesirable behavior and, in the bargain, fuels the embers of shyness.

In a study of the spontaneous use of punishment by schoolteachers, two children from each of five classes were observed for a five-month period. These children were "unruly" in class and were loudly reprimanded by the teachers in front of the rest of the class. These public reprimands did little to squelch the disruptive behavior. However, when the researchers got the teachers to switch to "soft" reprimands, that only the child could hear, the disruptive behavior decreased sharply. To demonstrate convincingly that public shame of the child was ineffective compared to personalized discipline, teachers were asked to give loud reprimands again for several weeks, then soft ones in the final weeks of the study. Discipline behaviors escalated when the reprimands were loud again, and went down when they were made low.

Dorothy McCorkille Briggs, author of *Your Child's Self-Esteem*, advocates what she calls "Democracy in Discipline." The democratic disciplinarian, she tells us, recognizes a child as a separate person, and not as either an extension of the parent or a possession. And as a separate person, a child, like the rest of us living in a democracy, wants to have a voice in the issues that touch his or her life. She has observed that "frequently adults confuse democratic discipline with overpermissiveness. Sharing power is a far cry from giving it away. *Democracy doesn't mean withdrawal; overpermissiveness does.*"

Briggs also notes that authoritarianism lasts only as long as the authority figure is present. We agree. We all know children who go wild once they are out of their parents' range of control. But we must add that we've also seen children so cowed by authority that they are too shy to rebel even when it's safe to do so. They grow up to have shy egos that are too overcontrolled;

they can't ever let go for fear that they will lose all control. They have internalized the values and the restrictive rules of their jailer, who now keeps them locked in their prison of shyness.

The more rules parents and teachers use to "run their shop," the less they will use positive incentives and praise. Since rules set the standards of what is expected, a child who obediently follows all the rules is "only doing what is expected"—so no rewards follow, usually. But violation of the rules always entails trouble, blowing the whistle, "calling the cops," and punishment. It's a no-win situation for people who live in such rule-controlled environments. For those who are shy or on their way to becoming so, it means they have little practice in handling praise and compliments—and grow up as shy adults still unable to graciously accept what they desire so much.

Perhaps one opportunity for children to practice handling praise (as well as encouraging good behavior) may present itself when children *don't* break the rules. Parents can, for example, balance the admonishments with appropriate praise for following the rules. You don't have to go overboard and say to your seven-year-old, "It's wonderful that you didn't steal anything today," or "How nice, you didn't kick your sister in the head," but when children put their toys away, get home on time for dinner, or do their homework without being told, a simple word of praise can be most reinforcing.

Teaching Tolerance

Prejudice can contribute to shyness because to the extent that it exists in the home, it lets children know that even people they love think about classes or types of people in evaluative terms. This tells them that people tend to negatively evaluate others simply on the basis of what they are. This reinforces the impression of the shy child that the world is a judgmental place where people stand ready to judge *them*, and as a result, they become reflexively self-conscious or fearful of other people who are in positions to (mis)judge them.

So, by your example, teach your children to be charitable. Teach them also to give others the benefit of the doubt by viewing mistakes in light of circumstances instead of owing to someone's ineptness. Wonder aloud with them what might have caused someone to commit a deviant act or what motivation could have led to an inexplicable change in someone's behavior. Where mistakes are due to ineptness, show how failure teaches us the necessity for practice, forethought, and planning next time around—and sympathy, not sarcasm, for the one who has failed. Sensitivity to the feelings of others must be part of the shy child's golden rule if others are expected to be sensitive to his or her tender feelings. This means parents and older siblings should avoid ridicule, hypercritical evaluations, and name calling—even of enemies and wrongdoers.

Sticks and Stones May Break Their Bones, But Labels Last Forever

Most parents are acutely aware that they should avoid *negative* labels such as "stupid," "lazy," "dumb," and avoid saying such things as "You're worthless, you'll never amount to anything," because they undermine a child's self-image. So, when you are tempted to use such labels, keep in mind the relationship between shyness and a child's self-esteem, and thus avoid a shyness program that may be in force.

Special caution should be used when labeling a child in front of his or her peers. This was brought home to us when the mother of a three-year-old girl told us that she had called her daughter "a bad girl" in front of her playmates. The very next day, the mother heard her daughter's friends say they didn't want to play with her because, "You're bad. Your mother said so."

In the Stanford Shyness Clinic, a constant theme that runs through every client's history and that becomes a major target for therapeutic change is name calling of oneself. We have come to think of self-esteem in the simple terms of the ratio of the number of good things people say about themselves to the number of times they put themselves down. High self-esteem people are liberal in giving themselves praise where it is deserved, but frugal in dispensing self-blame unless it is clearly warranted. Our low self-esteem, shy clients say little of themselves that is positive, but they'll find their negative in the haystack every time. Treatment consists of first having them record, over a week or two, each time they notice they are saying good or bad self-evaluations. They do so by starting with a fixed number of small objects (coins, paper clips, matches, and so forth) in one pocket or a purse then transferring one object to another place each time they notice a good thing they've said of themselves. They discover it's not a very moving exercise initially. Then they must say *"Stop"* to themselves as soon as they monitor those put-downs: "I was dumb to expect . . . *Stop"*; "My hair is so ugly today . . . *Stop"*; "Of course, I screwed up, it's just like me to . . . *Stop."* Next, the negatives are modified to provide constructive feedback, which means what could be done differently next time. "I should have expected that reaction from him, so next time . . . Good"; "I didn't ask the question I wanted to because I hadn't thought it out fully, tomorrow I'll be the first to ask whether . . . Good."

When good self-statements exceed bad ones, self-esteem goes up and one source of shyness goes down the tubes.

Building Trust

If shyness is a people phobia, what can we do to cut through that fear of people? Enable the child to be more trusting of others, is one part of the answer. Children trust more if they are trusted. They trust others when they have a learned history of experiences that add up to a view of human nature that says, "People tend to keep promises they make to me; when they don't there is usually a sufficient reason. People tend to respect my privacy, my possessions and shared secrets; people I care about are willing to disclose secrets about their fears and frustrations, hurts and hopes."

Self-disclosure builds trust, trust is essential for intimacy and intimacy is vital for acquaintances to blossom into close friendships. And, as we learned in the last chapter, not even shy extroverts are comfortable in intimate situations. "I can't believe anyone would love me if they knew the real me," is the refrain of their song. You as a parent should get as close as you can to knowing the "real self" of your child and showing you love and respect it—and so will others, if allowed to get close. Of course, there are times and there are people out there in the cold, cruel world who will lie, cheat, deceive, and act fraudulently toward us and our children, but they are in the minority and soon get exposed for what they are. Children who do not learn trust from their parents at an early age, we believe, may be unable to ever really trust anyone else completely—even their own spouse and children.

Paying Attention to Your Child

A typical response from a parent who is told that paying attention to a child is important might be, "But I *do* pay attention to my child. In fact, every two minutes it seems, he's asking me a question, and he not only expects me to drop what I'm doing to see to some need, but I do. What more can I give?"

Many children do *seem* to want 110 percent of your attention all the time. Some *actually* do and from the moment you open your eyes in the morning until they close theirs at night, they could consume you. There is a way for you not to be consumed and also a way for your child to receive the attention he or she craves, and the sort that will reinforce his or her self-esteem. To achieve this, you need to understand why some children are so demanding.

Child psychologist Dr. Annye Rothenberg heads up the Child-rearing Education Program at Children's Health Council in Palo Alto, California, and she says that it is natural for children to be demanding—to be interruptive—partly because they have a different internal time schedule than adults. "Children have short attention spans," she told us, "while adults have longer ones, and they don't understand that adults need time to think things through, time to read a complete sentence, or just time to be alone while they are doing something. Children simply are not sensitive to the adult needs of their parents, and they themselves have needs and hundreds of questions." They also live in a time zone of an "expanded present" where past and future take the back seat to the here and now.

This means that you do have to respond to a child's demand for attention, but you do so by explaining why you can't satisfy that demand *now* but will at a set time soon (after you've completed your current task). Teach the child how to politely interrupt your ongoing behavior with an "excuse me" or "may I interrupt?" And to wait for your reply before rushing headlong into the urgency of the moment.

If the specific request for action can't be fulfilled, the general request for attention usually can. Sibling rivalry that develops over a newcomer in the home is usually traced to a sharp reduction in the level of attention to which the older child has been accustomed. "Baby needs me now, later for you, Sonny" is momma's message. It need not be so. For example, while nursing her newborn, Phil's wife would still play games with her four-year-old daughter who said outright, "You have so little time for me and so much for the baby." The child was mobile even if mother was not, so hide-and-seek was one solution. During the count to ten, the child would run and hide somewhere within calling distance and come out when discovered. "Are you under the sink? in the hall closet? on top of the washing machine?" called the mother. Daughter responded with a gleeful "Yes, I am" when her hiding place was found, and ran to another hiding place for the next round.

Often, however, even intelligent parents can be insensitive to a child's eye view of what attention is needed. A good illustration of this occurred when we went to a party given by a couple who were both college professors. Shortly after we arrived, they were telling us about these strange-looking bookcases they had that started at about four feet off the floor. They explained that they had a young child and as he grew they had to keep moving the books up higher and higher because he, if they were in reach, would rip them to pieces. Finally, they said, they had realized that he was doing this because the books were competing with him for their attention. It seems his parents spent nearly all of their free time reading, and when he interrupted them, they would say, "Go away, we're reading." At this, the child would start ripping up the books.

While these parents had this insight about why the child was ripping up their books, they didn't translate it into the idea that they might solve the problem by giving him some minutes of undivided attention or explain, beyond saying that they were busy, why they couldn't always give it, and then tell him *when* they would talk to him or play with him—and then *do it.* Nor did they, like many parents, realize that children are going to get attention one way or another, and may feel compelled to take it a piece at a time possibly over several hours.

Frequent rivals for a child's attention besides siblings and books for parent-teachers are TV, the morning paper and the telephone. Be aware of how often you are totally tuning out your child's needs for attention. Try to minimize long or repeated time-outs and to let the child know when you will return to the reality the child is dealing with. As any single working parent knows, even with limited availability it is the good quality of the time you spend close to your child that counts more than the block of time you happen to be around the child.

Other children also benefit from your attention to them. Most adults treat their friends' children who answer their phone calls as if they were telephone operators. "Put your dad on, tell him it's Morris." Try talking to them for a minute or two, asking how they are, what they are doing, whether they've seen the new *Superman* or some appropriate movie, and so on. You will soon discover that you've made a new lasting friend who will grow up to like and respect you, in part because "you're different from other grown-ups who are so businesslike and never are interested in us kids." You might also hint to your adult friends that this lesson should extend to how they relate to your children.

Showing attention to others, asking personal questions, reflects an interest in them that is flattering and usually appreciated. During an appearance on the "Phil Donahue" show, our Phil interrupted Donahue's questions with one of his own: "Are you shy? I'd like to know and I'm sure your fans would." Before Donahue answered "Only at cocktail parties," he confessed to being pleased one of his guests was concerned about him since it was rare that any of them ever showed they were. Even superstars need our attention sometimes—so does your embryonic superstar.

Summing Up

If you now think your parenting practices may have contributed to your child's shyness, this is relevant only to the extent such practices may be keeping him or her shy, and if that's the case, you'll want to make some changes. To that end, ask yourself the following questions:

• Am I too permissive or too authoritarian with this particular child?

• Do I *show* my love enough? Does this child need more touching and hugging?

• When was the last time I really talked to this child? When was the last time I really listened to what he or she had to say?

Do I set an example by being communicative? Am I keeping the lines of communication open by letting him or her know he or she can talk to me? Do I encourage free expression?

• Do I discourage *excessive* isolating activities such as TV watching and (constant) reading?

• Do I give this child some undivided attention each day?

• Do I do those special things, such as making a fuss over birthdays, that make children feel special?

• Do I inspire in my children the sort of confidence that lets them know they can count on me and trust other people?

• Am I teaching this child to be tolerant of his or her shortcomings by teaching him or her to be tolerant of others? Do I teach the child the value of individual uniqueness?

• Do I discipline in such a way that it preserves my child's dignity, while giving him or her a sense of security?

• Does my discipline carry with it a message of caring and understanding?

• Do I let my child know that I'm an "unconditional lover"?

• Are my expectations of my child's behavior realistic? Or do I expect him or her to behave as an adult, rather than as a child?

CHAPTER THREE

Strategies for Minimizing Shyness

It is not all that unusual these days for parents to have unrealistic expectations of their children and, in fact, given the competitive nature of our culture, it is difficult not to have such expectations. "Show me the child and I'll show you the parent," is a cliché that is still lodged in the minds of many people, and often, without realizing it, our children become our most visible status symbols. Their mission in life seems to be to bring home to us evidence that they are the brightest, the most skilled, and the best-looking kids on the block.

But sadly, no matter how much parents want the prizes for their children, not every child can bring all—or even one—of them home.

After insuring that your parenting style is the one that will maximize your child's sense of security, it is very important to your shyness-reduction program to go farther and teach your child to be independent, learn to take risks, and develop skills that will give him or her self-confidence. Equally important is the role your *expectations* play in maintaining your child's shyness, and the role those expectations will play when applying the strategies we suggest in this chapter to help build your child's self-esteem and reduce shyness.

Whether or not a child's self-esteem suffers because of parental expectations depends pretty much on whether those expectations are *realistic*. If they are too *high*, a child may be set up for failure, and the parent may be set up for disappointment—disappointment that rarely goes unnoticed by the child.

If a parent's expectations are too *low*, it is likely that the child will perform *down* to satisfy the minimal goals with minimal effort. Although not failing under such conditions, the child's sense of success will be rather hollow and self-esteem will suffer.

When Parental Expectations Are Too High

A good example of the "my-child-should-be-perfect-or-at-least-the-best" syndrome can be seen in Betsy, a four-year-old we observed during the course of our study of nursery school children. Betsy first caught our eye when we noticed that she didn't play with the other children when they were all sent out of doors, but instead hung back on the fringes of the activity, watching as the others played ball or scampered around on the jungle gym and bars. Sometimes we noticed her hanging back in the classroom, wandering aimlessly around, or sitting in a corner reading a book. When we asked Betsy's teacher about this, she told us, "Betsy's very shy. Not only does she not play with the other children, she doesn't sing with the class or dance to records when the other children do. She spends most of her time sitting quietly and reading."

As it turns out, Betsy's parents seem to have internalized a cultural value not uncommon in a university community—the measurement of a child's worth based on intelligence and achievement—and they feel that reading at an *early* age is symbolic of that all too important brain power, so they have been pressuring Betsy to read since she was two years old. Betsy simply wasn't ready, but instead of letting her move at her own pace, her parents have met her "failures" by pushing harder, and increasingly, Betsy feels like a failure. The teacher told us that Betsy now stutters badly.

Because her parents' expectations were far too high, Betsy was programmed to failure from the start. Even now that she *can* read at four years old, rather than seeing this as an impressive accomplishment, Betsy quite likely knows that it isn't good enough because it's too little too late. It's our guess that she feels she will never be able to please her parents.

And there is little doubt that Betsy's confidence that she can accomplish *anything* has been undermined by her enormous failure to please her parents. We noticed this when she refused to play ball with the other children, crying out in a hysterical burst of stammering, that she "didn't know how" to throw a ball.

We have found a common attitude in shy people: taking the push from their parents who expect far too much, they internalize those expectations and impose them on themselves, and then they may not even try because if they can't do something perfectly, they won't do it at all.

It is important, therefore, for you first to recognize an individual child's readiness to master a specific task, and then for you to recognize, and to communicate to your child those kinds of performance—such as throwing a ball—that are largely a matter of practice, and which require analysis and learning to make the correct response. For example, Canadian children typically are skilled ice-hockey players by the time they reach their teens; their European peers do remarkable things with a soccer ball; Hawaiian youths ride the waves, precariously balanced on surfboards; while ghetto children often play basketball with an extraordinary competence. The key to a child's success is practice. They all start playing the local favorite sport at an early age, and do so hour after hour. It is not a matter of being born with special coordination or being "gifted," rather, for most of the youngsters, they learn to do through observation of others, trial-and-error, and working at playing the game.

But more to the point, in our children's eyes, we parents are authorities or experts, and when we convey to them the message that they ought to be able to accomplish thus and so, they believe it. Then when they can't do whatever is expected of them, rather than questioning whether the parent is correct, they assume that there's something wrong with *them*. Speaking to the misery children feel under such pressures, Eugene Kennedy, in his book, *If You Really Knew Me Would You Still Like Me?*, has this to say:

"Have you ever seen children striving to meet the demands of unrealistic parents? Such children desperately need and want to be loved. They struggle with all their might to find some way to get this response from their parents. And they sometimes bend themselves all out of shape in the process. They strain to match the ideal image their parents have for them, but this means that the truth about themselves is never good enough. Small wonder they never feel good about themselves. . . .

"They may be children, for example, who are only average, but whose parents have the idea that they should be getting A's and winning first prizes. Children who are viewed this way at home can never measure up in and of themselves. What they are can never be good enough for the parents who have decided beforehand how wonderful and famous their children must be. It is sad but not surprising that these children find it difficult to get in touch with who they really are, or that they can have lifelong problems of self-confidence and self-esteem."

We know a man who believed so strongly that being an accomplished ball player was an important measure of his son's worth that whenever the boy didn't play well in Little League, his father stopped speaking to him. In fact, on one occasion his son and another boy were playing on opposing teams. He drove both of them to the game and refused to speak to *either* of them on the way home—his son, because his team lost, the other boy because he hit the other team's winning home run. We do not know for a fact if the reason for this boy's shyness has anything to do with Little League, but it's a safe bet that the yardstick his father uses to measure his worth has a lot to do with the way the boy measures it too.

Unconditional Love Revisited

Returning to the example of Betsy, Betsy illustrates our belief that when children fail to satisfy parental expectations—or, as in her case, don't satisfy them on schedule—their feelings of failure combine with a sense that their parents' love for them is based on achievement. If they fail, they will lose their parents' love, and as a result the children question their own value as human beings.

From this point, the situation can only get worse. Betsy, for instance, "failed" to please her parents when she couldn't read. As they applied more pressure, she could only respond with greater failure, which ate away not only at her confidence in herself, but in her sense of security that her parents loved her. Now she stutters, which makes her feel self-conscious among her peers, and is also one more "inadequacy" to displease parents for whom verbal competence is so all-important (her mother is a speech therapist).

We can only wonder if Betsy will ever receive the parental reinforcement she so desperately needs. Our guess is that she will remain convinced that such will be forthcoming only if she meets the requirements her parents have set down for receiving their approval. So despite the fact that in their hearts they may truly love Betsy without reservation, because Betsy believes otherwise, these parents are *conditional love givers*.

When parents withhold affection and approval because their child doesn't perform according to the standards they have set, the child sees this as meaning that the parents' love is conditional. And parents who associate love with successful performance develop in their children the notions that: "I am only as good as my most recent performance," and "I perform, therefore I am." We have seen that one of the major problems for the shy is their conception of the world as a stage in which they are actors under constant scrutiny by critical reviewers. How can you relax, get "lost" in the task at hand, become totally absorbed in the process you are part of, if you are hypersensitive to the fact that what you are doing will be evaluated as a performance? The shys tell us they can't.

In reality, most parents love their children *unconditionally*, but they don't always convey that message to them. Even when we start out with feelings of abundant love, as our children grow sometimes it is easy to fall into a pattern whereby we *seem* to base our love and esteem for them on how they perform. When they are well behaved and acquire skills that make us proud, we give them strokes—affection and praise, the symbols of our love.

We may use the leverage of our love without awareness that a child can see this as a sign that our love is only present when he or she is living up to our expectations. So, we all need to examine the quality of our love—whether we show our children that it is a constant or send them another message when they let us down.

And, of course, we must maintain perspective regarding our expectations. Are they realistic? Are they too high? Do we view our children as "little adults," and expect performance that is beyond their developmental levels? Or, are our expectations too *low*? Do we assume that they are babies long after they aren't, and treat them accordingly?

When Parental Expectations Are Too Low

A two-and-a-half-year-old child of our acquaintance, distressed at being spoon-fed and excessively fussed over, boldly announced one day, "Grandma, don't treat me like a baby, I want to be like a grown-up!" A child's cry for independence must be acknowledged and encouraged within the boundaries of what is possible at each stage of maturity. But to feel independent, a child must perceive alternatives, be given meaningful options, and allowed to make choices. With such behavioral freedom comes the credit and sense of accomplishment for wise decisions as well as the responsibility for those that are not.

When parents begin with unrealistically *low* expectations of children, they may so undermine their children's confidence in themselves that the children may feel they cannot master simple tasks that are compatible with their levels of development. We know a mother, for example, whose habitual care-taking reflexes had her automatically cutting up the meat on her sixteen-year-old son's dinner plate while discussing with a houseguest the pros and cons of the Ivy League colleges to which the boy had applied. We know another mother who continued to dress her six-year-old "baby" until it was pointed out to her that her "baby" was perfectly capable of dressing herself, ought to be encouraged to do so, and would feel good about herself for being able to.

Remember, the parents are seen by the children as experts. So, if mother or father believes that a child can't dress herself, cut his meat, tie his shoes, or whatever, whether he or she can actually perform the task, the child may internalize the parent's view.

We know one parent who resisted her child's developing independence as an adolescent, and when her son started junior high school, panic set in. All of a sudden her once sweet boy "really had a mouth on him," and this mother became terribly upset over what she saw as her loss of control over her son. It is difficult to welcome a child's emerging independence when it surfaces in the form of diatribes against a parent that challenge parental authority, posing the threat that rebellious behavior is just around the corner.

However, recent medical evidence confirms our general observations concerning those who tend to be more submissive. Those patients, for example, who are the most likely to succeed in getting well the quickest are considered "bad" patients. It is the one who complains, stands up for his or her rights, demands explanations for what is or isn't being done to his or her body who has the best prognosis. Hospitals, like many other institutions, render patients (and clients) passive by doing for them what they could very well do for themselves. This imposed passivity depresses personality and homogenizes the variety of individuals in need of treatment for their medical problems into a common, undifferentiated mass of people playing patient.

From all we know about how readily shys cave in to the demands of authority, we'd have to predict they would be the "good" patients—those who would suffer in silence, not wanting to make trouble, "sir." And in return for their seemingly good behavior, they would be rewarded with a longer stay in the hospital. Another aspect of this issue is the reluctance of shy people to blame the situation they're in or to externalize justifiable anger, coupled with their readiness to redirect such negative feelings inward—to blame themselves. Such an orientation stimulates guilt feelings which, in turn, lay the foundation for depression and self-deprecation.

Beware of getting caught in, or being the one who casts the dependency trap that accompanies low expectations, and be aware of the need to imbue in your child feelings of independence and a sense of responsibility.

Expectations, Independence, and Responsibility

James, a college student who came to us for help with his shyness problem, is an extreme example of the dependence common in shy people. Before we realized it, we were doing many things for him—things he was perfectly capable of doing for himself—simply because he had transferred his dependence on his parents to our shoulders and wouldn't take responsibility for himself. Ironically, James had only himself and his concerns to think of while we were concerned with the very fulltime tasks of our jobs, our writing obligations, and the demands of our children with the various complications that were visiting their various ages. Yet one or the other of us, for instance, would call the transit company to request bus schedules that James needed, or drop whatever we were doing whenever he had an anxiety attack. If he was lonely, we invited him over to our houses to talk; we also invited him to our dinner parties, where he sat like a stone, letting everyone else take full responsibility for any conversation.

The more kindness we showed James, the more demanding and manipulative he became to avoid taking responsibility for himself. It suddenly dawned on us that instead of having a positive effect, our being so attentive and giving James the strokes he craved, was making him shyer by the day. The point is, the more you foster dependence in a child (or anyone else for that matter), the more you foster shyness, something *we* know all too well, but still, we wound up doing it—for a while. So, as parents, you need to guard against this and teach your child to be independent—to the extent of his or her capabilities, of course.

When shy children or shy adults leave a home where they have been taught to be dependent, they send out signals to others that they are not to be treated as equals. In our shyness clinic, for example, we commonly observe the telltale signs of "I'm fragile, don't challenge or I may decompose under the slightest pressure." Indeed, in trying to initiate conversations among a half dozen shy students, we felt as if we were walking blindfolded through a room strewn with eggshells: One wrong move and it's shattered shells everywhere. It is easy for others, then, if they don't reject the shy person outright, to adopt a protective role that shields their acquaintance from the harsh realities of social life.

This attitude by not-shy peers is *not* in the best interests of the shy person, however. In a study which compared the self-perceptions of shy students with those their roommates held of them, there were some traits of shyness that both agreed upon, some only the shy person thought were characteristic, and some only others felt were part of the makeup of the shy person.

As can be seen in the following list, the shared attributes tended to be those that were linked to observable behaviors (less talkative, unassertive, and so on). Since the shy person alone has access to his or her own thoughts and feelings, there are private attributes, such as "more readiness to feel guilt," "more likely to ruminate," "less likely to regard self as physically attractive" that exist only in the mind of the shy person. But most significant are those qualities which the shy people were not aware of that their roommates saw in them. These personality traits are quite negative. Some like "more self-pitying," "more self-defeating," "more likely to give up in the face of adversity" convey a portrait of their shy roommates as weak and unworthy of respect. Of course, the bases of these perceptions are rarely discussed openly because, as one of the

---

Perceptions of the Shy Person
(by shy students and their roommates)

A. As Seen By Both the Shy and Others
More submissive
More likely to keep people at a distance
More distrustful of people in general
More anxious
More likely to compare self to others
More emotionally bland
Less talkative
Less skilled in social techniques
Less likely to initiate humor
Less likely to behave assertively
Less gregarious
Less cheerful
Less socially poised

B. *As Seen Only by the Shy—Not by Others*
More sensitive to criticism
More introspective
More likely to feel lack of personal meaning in life
More generally fearful
More readiness to feel guilt
More concerned with own adequacy as a person
More likely to ruminate and have persistent, preoccupy-
　ing thoughts
More likely to have fluctuating moods
Less likely to arouse liking and acceptance in others
Less facially and/or gesturally expressive
Less interesting as a person
Less likely to feel satisfied with self
Less physically attractive
Less personally charming
Less verbally fluent

C. *As Seen Only by Others—Not by the Shy*
More self-defensive
More overcontrolled
More likely to give up in the face of adversity
More self-defeating
More self-pitying
Less likely to be turned to for advice or reassurance
Less interested in members of the opposite sex

not-shy roommates told us, "I don't think he could handle such
feedback, so I try to pretend I feel otherwise. But it gets in the
way of developing a close friendship."

The Importance of Solitude to Developing Independence

A paradox of shyness is that shy people, more than not-shy
people, dislike being alone and seem to be dependent on others for entertainment or to alleviate boredom. While we do not

want to encourage our shy children to isolate themselves, we *do* want to encourage them to enjoy the pleasure of their own company for two reasons: First, we want our children to be independent, and that requires that they be able, when the occasion warrants it, to entertain themselves. Second, we feel that if they are to be enjoyed and accepted by others, they must first be enjoyed and accepted by themselves. It has been said that to be liked by others, one must first like oneself. Thus, teach your children to enjoy the pleasure of their own company.

Another paradox of shyness is that *some* shy people are so dependent on others, and so yearn for the companionship of their peers that, however frightened they may be to reach out, they do—and come on too strong, which can, and often does, put other people off. We don't want their eagerness to scare off their potential friends, but instead want them to develop the strong egos that other people find attractive.

You can teach your children to be independent by encouraging them to do specific things alone, such as taking a walk down the street, going to the museum or the library, or when they are older, taking in a movie or going on a hike in the woods. These are just some suggestions to get you started thinking about some of the ways in which *you* might like to see your child be able to entertain himself or herself.

A recent study of Chicago high school students revealed that about a quarter of their waking time was spent alone. Solitude seemed to have the positive effect of heightening attention span and power of concentration. This study also found that learning how to value solitude frequently enabled teen-agers to *be more comfortable with others*.

Putting Independence and Responsibility to Work

You must be alert to those times when your children are ready to assume more responsibility for themselves, and then allow and encourage them to do so. How do you know when they are "ready"? Look, ask, provide opportunities, offer simple approximations of the desired behavior, make available small steps that will eventually lead to the big goal. For example, children of two years of age can learn to cook, by first assisting in small ways: adding premeasured herbs to sauces and cheeses to omelettes, breading fish, and similar simple tasks. They can also help with the cleanup, and take delight in doing so if it is not presented as a "work chore," and if a parent remembers that a child's standard for neatness may be a bit different than the parent's learned and practiced one.

The best place to begin, is to start by encouraging children to take care of themselves. You teach responsibility and independence simultaneously (fueling high self-esteem in the process) when you encourage and coax your children to:

• pick out the clothes they will wear and dress themselves. It fosters initiative and furthers the goal of independence if you let them make mistakes when matching up their clothes. You can, of course, explain that people don't normally wear one red sock and one blue sock at the same time, but if the child insists, the lesson will be more forcefully learned because the child has learned it through the experience of having done so. Your child should also be allowed to make the final choice among alternatives you select when buying clothes—and eventually select the alternatives as well. (Clarify value differences that often cause unnecessary clashes, such as: you want variety in the child's day-to-day appearance versus the child wants to wear a favorite pair of jeans again and again . . . and once more.)

• pick up their toys and put them away. It helps if you have a special place for toy storage in the child's room.

• make their beds. Depending on what the child is capable of, the bed may look worse after it's made. But we *do* learn by doing, not by having it done for us by a parent who is terribly concerned about unmade or sloppily made beds.

• comb their own hair, brush their own teeth, tie their own shoes—all, as soon as they show signs they are ready to do so.

• clean their bedrooms. But parents need to be vigilantly aware that parental standards are of a higher order than their children's are. When, for instance, you tell an eight- or nine-year-old child to clean his or her room, depending on your standards what you suggest may be as overwhelming as telling an inexperienced adult that he or she must build a house. And with small children, you need to remember that you have to show them how to do it, and often, work on it with them as part of a team. The important point here is to make the child feel responsible for policing his or her own territory.

• do their own laundry. From about eight on, you can show them which buttons to push and remind them to empty the lint trap on the dryer. Again, remember that their standards are not likely to be the same as yours, and they won't be preoccupied with whiter-than-white washes.

• make their own breakfasts in the morning; pack their own lunches.

• from about ten on, make their own medical, dental, and orthodontic appointments, and keep track of them.

• and when they are mature enough to do so, they should be old enough to get to their appointments, using either public transportation or their bikes, under their own steam.

• ditto for activities such as sports, or music and dancing lessons, and writing their own thank-you notes.

• practice using the telephone to check on show times, to ask for information, to call in their own regrets for not being able to attend some function to which they were invited.

Encourage children to be responsible for sharing the household load. Even young children can be made to feel that their contributions in this regard are important, that they are useful.

What are some of the things you normally do around the house that your children might well be able to do—feed the family pets? take out the garbage? load the dishwasher? get the aluminum cans ready for recycling? mow the lawn? vacuum a floor? put the sheets and towels into the washer and dryer?

Make a list of all of the household chores you can think of and then match them up with each child in the family, according to what he or she might be capable of doing. And be prepared to be open to negotiation when there is disagreement about some of the chores. When assigning household chores, it's a good idea to resist the temptation to limit delegating only those that are menial or unpleasant.

We also think it is easier to get children to do chores around the house and yard if they see both mothers and fathers doing them—and if *both* parents get involved in assigning the chores to the children. This is especially so when mother typically does most of the housework because children, not actually *seeing* their fathers working in the office, may get the impression, if he does little at home, he does nothing *at all* beyond watching football games on TV and reading the newspaper.

Finally, the key to getting children to do most anything is by doing it along with them. Share the activity at first, and then turn it over entirely to that responsible child.

Whatever chores you assign, and whatever method you devise for getting your children to do them, remember our basic rule: *Be realistic.* And remind yourself that it takes children longer to perform tasks than it does adults, and they need a lot of practice, so *patience* must be the second basic rule.

Beyond Chores: The Value of Teaching Your Children to Be Responsible for Others

Children can also learn to be more responsible and independent when they are taught to be responsible for other people. They can, for instance, take care of younger children in the family and help them with difficult chores and homework. A fringe benefit that is a hedge against shyness is that when children become involved in helping other people, it helps them to develop a pattern of focusing on *others* instead of self-consciously focusing on *themselves*.

For young children, the "generation gap" is typically that great gulf of time between one birthday and the next. Age is a very important aspect of choosing friends since there are often dramatic developmental changes at each year in the child's early growth. Same-age friendships are desirable because of their egalitarian nature, and because they provide the basis for making stable social comparisons (of one's abilities, opinions, emotional arousal). However, given that shy children often begin by downplaying their own attributes, there is much to be said for encouraging cross-age friendships.

Anthropologists who have studied cultures where children are expected to interact with siblings and peers of different ages report that these children come to be more concerned about the general welfare of the larger social community and are less ego-centered. Another benefit is that their greater independence and reliance upon age mates reduces the demands they put on their parents.

There is considerable psychological research that attests to the benefits of cross-age encounters for both the older child and the younger one, as well. For the older child, these contacts are nonthreatening, and they encourage both a leadership-assertiveness role along with being nurturant. There is abundant admiration forthcoming from the younger children (who often feel privileged that a big kid is playing with them) coupled with praise given by observing adults. While the "senior citizen child" is developing a sense of competence from such reinforcing contacts with the younger generation, the younger children are helped in several ways. Their conversational skills can be enhanced, they learn to follow directions and guidance, and they also get firsthand experience negotiating with role models more similar to themselves than adults are.

Since younger children typically can't resort to might to make things right, they have to rely on tact and diplomacy to get their way or their fair share some of the time. The subtle interpersonal skills involved in bargaining and maneuvering through situations of potential conflict are among the most valuable assets any person can possess. Research has shown that later-born children tend to be more popular and better-liked by more of their peers than are firstborns. Perhaps this occurs as a by-product of having had to learn how to use social skills and not physical domination to survive in a world populated with big sisters and brothers.

In the next chapter we shall review in some detail recent evidence from the University of Minnesota Child Development Laboratory that convincingly demonstrates the power of mixed-age pairings on reducing shyness. When older shy children are paired with younger children for brief play periods, they become less socially withdrawn later, in play groups of children their own age.

We recommend as a first step in helping a child overcome his or her shyness, the creation of opportunities for play (or help, as we suggested earlier) with one other child who is younger—and smaller. You might also want to try to monitor from a distance what the shy child does. Later, ask the younger playmate if he enjoyed the time they spent together (if so, why? if not, how come?). This information can provide constructive feedback that may help to shape the shy child's interpersonal skills and style.

Teaching Children to Stand Up for Themselves

One way parents can undermine—without meaning to—their children's confidence in themselves and in their ability to stand up for their own rights is to involve themselves in their children's battles. When a parent jumps in on the side of his or her child who is fighting with a peer, the child gets the message that he or she is not capable of handling the situation without the parent's help.

However, there's probably not a parent alive who hasn't run

interference when it looked like his or her child was getting the short end of the stick. Be alert to whether this is *really* the case, and unless the situation is one where a big kid is picking on a little one, it truly is better to let your children fight their own battles so they don't fall into a pattern of depending on you to do it for them, or a pattern of believing that they are inadequate to the task. We want our children to be appropriately assertive and want them to be independent whenever they can be.

Compensation, Risk Taking, and Parental Expectations

One important thing parents can do when their children are shy is find some compensating activity that will give a child an opportunity for building up his or her self-confidence through accomplishments, such as music lessons, dancing lessons, gymnastics, sewing, and artwork.

However, because a central process of shyness is an unwillingness to take risks, parents of shy children need to really encourage them to do so, but there are several points to remember:

• Try to determine whether the activity is something the child really wants. Ask why the *other* children are doing it, what *they* might be getting that is good from it. Used as a projective device, these questions will help to elicit your child's interpretation of what is to be gained from engaging in the activity.

• Assess what the child perceives are the costs, the hidden dangers, of participating. Why might a child not want to do a particular activity, even if that child knows how to?

• Determine what your child believes are the necessary skills or attributes one must possess in order to do well in a particular activity. Does your child have them?

• Having determined that a child has the motivation and the basic skills, you may then prime the pump of action. You do so by lowering tensions that are creating avoidance tendencies while boosting approach tendencies by describing both the pleasure of engaging in the process (of playing, hiking, and so forth) as well as the anticipated outcome benefits.

While parents need to provide the push, there is a fine line between encouraging and pressuring a child, and parents of shy children need to be especially careful not to cross that line while drawing their children out. For example, it would be just as big of a mistake to force Betsy to play ball with the kids as it was to force her to learn to read when she wasn't ready to. Betsy first needs to learn how to play ball, and then she needs to have confidence that she can do it, and she needs to understand that a necessary component in this process is that there is every likelihood that before she knows any measure of success, she will experience some failure along the way.

There is still another fine line between encouraging and pressuring a child that all parents need to be sensitive to—that is whether *what* you are encouraging is necessary or desirable to the child.

It *is* necessary, for instance, for children to do certain things at certain stages of their development: use the toilet, eat with utensils, dress themselves, tie their shoes, go to school. And parents must determine when their children are capable of doing these things and see that they do them. It is *not* necessary, however, for a child to be a dancer, a ball player, or a musician—or read at the age of two.

Put another way, if you have always had a secret desire to dance like Ginger Rogers and you've enrolled your daughter in a tap-dancing class and she doesn't like tap-dancing, you are pressuring her to fulfill one of your own personal dreams. On the other hand, if she *loves* tap-dancing, and wants to take lessons, you are providing her with an opportunity to do something she wants to do, something she will enjoy, and something that will probably result in building up her self-confidence.

Taking the First Step

Backing up for a moment and once again using the extreme example of Betsy, if she is to have a full life, she cannot be allowed to continue to do what shy people are real experts at—avoidance. Because in choosing not to try, she, like other shys, deprives herself of the very opportunity to build self-esteem, and her lack of courage inevitably contributes to her low self-image. To combat this, after determining that Betsy is perfectly capable of learning how to play ball, she must then be taught how, and given the opportunity to practice and master this new skill—*at her own pace*.

We can learn how to guide a child like Betsy by borrowing from the treatment that is used to help people overcome agoraphobia, an extreme form of shyness that can keep some people who suffer from it from taking even so much as one step out of the front door of their homes.

The therapists quite literally take agoraphobics one step at a time—and at the patients' own pace. First, it is one step out the door, and continued practice, until that's comfortable; then the second step is taken, and practiced, until ultimately the agoraphobic can make it to the mailbox, to the end of the street, and finally back into the world. The key is one step at a time, gradually to minimize the anxiety as the agoraphobic sees for himself or herself that nothing terrible happened at each stage of the struggle.

These are some points to keep in mind when trying to get your shy child to take risks—be it throwing a ball or learning to tap dance.

Often it is only the first step that is the difficult one, getting the child to raise his hand, say "Hello," voice an opinion, join in the game. Once that anxiety-filled action is taken, then the intrinsic pleasure of the activity will take over and it's clear sledding thereafter. Get the child to practice that first initiating action, role play the situation with the child and have him or her actually go through a dress rehearsal.

Reward the child's attempts in the desired direction, praise even the little approach steps, and be understanding of sources of fear—the child's eye view of the situation.

Preparing Your Child for Success and Failure

You've established that your child loves tap-dancing, she's taken her lessons, and there's a big recital coming up. You want her to perform and maybe try out for a part in a production that is being planned by the Community Center. But what if you encourage her to go public and she fails? Again, you must examine your motives. Do you want her to go public for *you*? Do you want it for her? If it is honestly for your daughter, the next thing you need to do is evaluate what her chances for success might be. You can ask the dance instructor whether or not your daughter is ready, you can observe her at practice, and you can *ask her if she feels that she is ready* for the big event. Then determine what chance she has for success. She doesn't have to be a shoo-in, but you don't want to send her in so unprepared that she will be a dismal failure.

Once you've decided that she's probably skilled enough to take the plunge, and she wants to do it, the next thing you need to do is advise her that failure to reach a desired goal is a distinct possibility. You don't want to suggest that there is every likelihood that failure will be the outcome, just that this is one possibility. A child can be made to understand that failure is a possibility and not all that dreadful by being taught that failure is likely at first when attempting anything new, whether it is swinging on the bars at preschool or trying out for the track team in junior high school. Parents can help a child to understand this by sharing their own "failures" in their own lives. Since you have survived, this offers living proof that your child will too.

A child needs to be told that there is no such thing as failure—that *genuine* failure is when someone plays it safe by never trying anything new or challenging. And not only should children be taught that it is better to have played the game and lost than not to have played at all, but they should be praised—by themselves and others—for having taken the risk.

You want to convey to your child that no matter what the outcome, taking a risk is, in itself, a measure of success. A healthy perspective that illustrates this point is what we learned from a psychologist who is also a senior army officer at West Point. He told us, for example, that one of the biggest problems the Academy faces in training leaders is the strong fear of failure in so many young people. They will seek "the approved solution," the old faithful, tried-and-true way rather than experiment, innovate, take a chance, gamble. And isn't that precisely what most distinguishes creative leaders from plodding followers? When we compared cadets who were shy with those who were not, sure enough the shys, on the average, had lower leadership effectiveness scores. Dependence, low self-esteem, avoidance of novel situations, and reluctance at initiating contacts are the shy person's handicaps in the quest to become a leader.

By taking many chances, the consequence of any one (or even a series) of failures is reduced in its magnitude as opposed to when it is the only failure of one's only attempt. If your child asks five children to play and three reject that offer, that is still two more playmates than if the child got turned down once on his or her only request. Door-to-door sales-people, Jehovah's Witnesses, and athletes all share the basic truth: Success comes from the times one "connects," regardless of the times one fails to score. The baseball world was all ex-cited by the phenomenal hitting prowess of George Brett who failed on about six of every ten batting opportunities—no other player has failed better since Ted Williams did so forty years ago by batting .406! So part of what constitutes failure is whether you look at the hits or whether you look at the misses in life. We believe shy children are inhibited by the fear of missing if they try, and they must be encouraged to overcome that fear.

Making Failure Work for Us

To get the most out of attempts that don't succeed in the ways we or our children had hoped they would, there are a series of steps to be followed.

• Define the failure. Be specific in describing the performance, the basis of its evaluation, and the standard or yardstick by which it is measured. Is the failure "absolute" (not making the team, flunking out of college) or more relative (not being chosen team captain or failing to get a "straight-A average")?

• Be sensitive to alternative interpretations of what constitutes failure for a given person in a particular setting at a certain stage in life.

• Make explicit the goals that were not attained. Who set them, were they what you or the child really wanted before or while trying to achieve them? Might the problem lie in the vagueness of the goals, the lack of more viable subgoals, changing motivation that altered the significance of the goals, or their unattainability at this time?

• Describe the kind of person who won, whose performance got the desired outcome. Would you (or the child) like to be that kind of person or do what he or she did to be successful (long hours of practice, the exclusion of other activities, friends, and so on)?

• Specify the extenuating circumstances that a good trial lawyer might invoke to account for the failure. Among the possible candidates:

> the level (or fairness) of the competition
> bias (or poor judgment) of the judges
> narrow sightedness, prejudice, or faulty evaluation by the other team members
> situational, context factors (home crowd advantage, distractions, the weather, etcetera)
> failure of those in charge to offer the appropriate information about expectations, opportunities to practice, building strengths.

• Determine (from observation of winners) what levels and kinds of skills are necessary to succeed; decide on how much practice will have to be invested and what types of sacrifices are called for.

• Define what needs to be done better the next time around.

What, on the Other Hand, to Do About Success

Let's assume that you have a child who is especially talented—or you think he or she is—in a particular endeavor, such as singing, dancing, or playing the piano.

The last thing in the world you want to do is to turn that accomplishment into a vehicle for generating feelings of shyness. Don't *force* your son or daughter to perform in front of relatives or friends when he or she obviously doesn't want to do it.

You can usually tell how a child feels by the dragging of the feet, the looking down at the ground, or the groaning when you make the suggestion in front of others. But rather than do this, you can find out *privately* how a child feels about performing by simply asking in advance. You can explain why you'd like him or her to perform. Ideally, it should not be to show off one of your possessions, but instead to share with others the talent or gift the child has—providing that the child wants to share it.

Sometimes children are suffering from stage fright, so let him or her think it over. Sometimes such anticipatory fears prove foolish after actually being with the other people, or when the setting is more conducive than could have been imagined in advance. So, ask again privately, or prearrange a "thumbs-up" or "-down" signal that gives the child the final decision. And abide by the child's wisdom, discussing afterward how a different outcome might be effected next time.

If the child does decide to perform, it is best neither to be an apologist nor run the advance P.R. barrage. You might simply announce that, "Adam would like to play a new composition for us that he's been working on"—or better, let the child make the introduction. In any case, don't let your child in for a letdown by your unrealistic buildup, with its inevitable, "Is that all there is?" from your audience. You might also invite friends and relatives to share their talents for group pleasure, not for personal pride.

Incidentally, visitors to the People's Republic of China, as well as our colleagues, who have studied the children of China, remark at how outgoing and "unshy" the children appear. They are eager to be guides, to show their school, sing songs, recite poetry—even for total strangers. This social responsiveness stems, in part, from the orientation their parents and teachers have instilled in them—what they know and what they can do artistically is not to be used as a measure of their individual self-worth, but rather as a means for bringing happiness to others and praise to their culture. Consider how very different our typical orientation is toward public performances, and you have part of the explanation for why "giving a public speech" is the number one phobia among Americans.

Keeping Parental Expectations in Line

Isolated incidents that reflect unrealistic parental expectations don't do much harm and are even laughable. But when the incidents are frequent, and part of a pattern reflecting either too much of a need for parents to bask in the glow of their children's high performance, or reflecting a parent's conviction that a child is helpless and incompetent, the accumulated effect will be damaging to a child's self-image. And it will probably only serve to make the shy child more shy.

In the instance of the mother who cut up the meat on her teen-age son's dinner plate, it is apparent that although she loves her son and means well, this has been her pattern all of her son's life. She has hovered anxiously about him, always dressing him, insisting he wear earmuffs, eat everything on his plate lest he die of starvation, while advising him of every conceivable danger in the world. Not surprisingly, her son, who has grown to feel like some sort of defective who can't even tie his own shoes, is quite shy when he feels he *must* perform in any social setting.

When parental expectations are too high, one thing parents may not be actively aware of is *why* we sometimes expect our children to be exemplary. In trying to get them to perform in ways that meet our approval, we too, sometimes, may be seeking approval for ourselves. There's probably not a parent in the whole world who hasn't, on occasion, fallen into the what-will-other-people-think trap to such a degree that he or she has either made demands on a child or been embarrassed when a child's performance or behavior was not the best, simply because of worry over what others might think of them as parents. Sometimes we parents feel that the whole world is watching as we struggle to do the right thing, and then when our children don't quite measure up, we fear we will be graded for their failures, large and small.

Probably at no time is this more true than when our children are in school. Starting with the first grade, and often throughout a child's entire career in school, the child is rather like a mirror of the parent, reflecting what sort of parents we are in how well he or she does.

"Partly this is because they are always told by teachers that their children could do better," Dr. Louise Bates Ames of the Gessell Institute told us. "Most parents worry that their children aren't doing better in school. Well, usually, unless the child is failing, he is actually doing as well as he can at the time. But many parents worry excessively if their children aren't getting all A's or B's."

Working vigorously to resist falling into the what-will-other-people-think trap is one way to keep our parental expectations of our children in line. As one wise mother told us, "I tell my kids if a C is the best they can do, it's an A to me." This is certainly a parental perspective that can be applied to all facets of a child's life.

The following is a checklist that will help you to develop that sort of perspective and keep your parental expectations in line:

• Has early accomplishment nearly always been important to me? Have I expected my child to be potty-trained at eighteen months, able to read at two, tie his or her shoes at four, and ride a two-wheeler at six—and been disappointed when he or she didn't?

• Have I fretted when a child couldn't accomplish some particular task, fearing that there was something wrong with him or her?

• How do I determine when my child is ready to master a new skill—by the child's age? size? by what my friends' children are, or have been capable of? Have I been indifferent to the signals of readiness, or nonreadiness, that he or she sends out?

• Do I sometimes withhold love and affection when my child misbehaves or doesn't perform well, sending out the message that my love is conditional rather than constant?

• Am I so in the habit of doing things for my child that I continue to do them long after he or she is perfectly capable of doing them for himself/herself?

• Do I hover about, doing such things as helping a child on with a sweater or forcing food down his or her mouth? Am I a meat cutter?

• Do I have ambivalent feelings about my child needing me less? Do I sometimes wish he or she wouldn't grow up so fast and be so independent of me?

• Am I still making dental appointments for my twelve-year-old? (Note: The most extreme example we have run across is the mother who makes them for her twenty-one-year-old son whose wife, if he marries, will most likely assume this caretaker role).

• Am I still the chauffeur on call when the children are perfectly capable of getting to all their own appointments under their own steam?

• Do I fight my children's battles—even when there is no genuine need for my intervention?

• Do I really encourage the children to do household tasks, to be helpful to others, and be generally independent and responsible?

• Do I provide my child with the opportunities and the tools to try new things, and then encourage him or her to take risks—and then remember to always have realistic expectations regarding the outcome?

• Do I pressure my child to do those things and be those things that were important to me, but I never was able to attain?

• Am I a good loser, and do I teach my child to be one too? Or, do I become upset when he or she loses the game or doesn't bring home the prizes? And, for *whom* do I get upset?

• Do I, on such occasions, convey my disappointment *in my child*?

• Do I make it a practice to force my child to show off his or her accomplishments to friends and relatives even though I know that he or she doesn't want to perform?

• Am I as sympathetic as I should be when my child doesn't do well in school?

• Do I ask the child's permission before retelling a story about the child or displaying something that he or she has made? (Doing so tells the child he or she is respected and treated as an individual with rights, not merely an extension of parental ambitions.)

For some parents, knowing what can be realistically expected of each child at each stage of development and what goals they ought to set, is very difficult. Some knowledge of child development is important to help you know when a child's behavior and performance is usual, and when you can expect more maturity.

Child-development guides are helpful, as long as you understand that they are based on a wide range of behavior—that, for example, when we are told that a child usually takes his or her first steps at one year of age, this is based on an *average* of children who start walking at anywhere between ten and sixteen months.

Intellectual and motor development occurs in rather fixed stages that all children go through in the same sequence at approximately the same range of age. But social development, while dependent upon verbal skills, memory, and the development of role-taking abilities, shows much greater variation from child to child, across social-economic classes, and from culture to culture. There is no objective yardstick against which to assess your child's social development. Instead, the issue is whether the child enjoys being with others, acts in ways that attract—not repel—others, derives pleasures from and gives pleasure to other people. In addition, social life should be part of a total set of balanced involvements which include solitary activities (reading, writing, hobbies) and the enjoyment of being alone in the company of one's own thoughts, feelings, and visions.

It is essential that as a parent you do all you can to encourage your child to share with you his or her *intepretation* of why he behaved in a particular way. That knowledge is often more important than the fact of having done or not done something.

For the parent who remains confused in tailoring his or her expectations of a child's motor and intellectual development and social skills, consultation with a perceptive pediatrician can be most helpful.

However, more important, if your child is a little slow and doesn't reach every developmental milestone on time, accept him or her for what he or she basically is. Acceptance is love. But, don't be too quick to judge a child as slow—remember, Albert Einstein didn't talk until he was three years old, but when he was ready to say something it was really something!

CHAPTER FOUR

Teaching Your Child to Be
a Social Being

Ken Margerum is an All-American football player who recently set a collegiate record for catching the most touchdown passes. During a postgame interview, he surprised reporters by remarking that once a game was over, he rarely talked about it, nor did he save newspaper clippings of his exploits.

"I take what I *do* very seriously," he said, "but I don't take *myself* seriously."

Here we have the antithesis of our typical shy person who proclaims—in sotto voce—"I can't take what I do too seriously because I'm always taking myself so seriously." It is difficult for shys to get absorbed in any task more than they are in themselves. Thus, most are unable to let the natural intrinsic joy of a game, a dance, a play, a social event take over. Whenever other people are involved as participants or spectators, the shy person is usually excessively concerned about *impression management.*

We all work at trying to manage the impressions that other people will form of us. We do so by making conscious and even subconscious decisions that direct our appearance and conduct. Most people want to convey a positive image of themselves to others so as to gain recognition and social approval from them. A good way to do so is by engaging in activities that others value, or enjoy. Or, we might make a positive impression when we do things that lead others to think of us as "interesting," "attractive," possessing some attribute or skill that is special, or from which they can benefit. Sharing resources such as toys, games, sports equipment, and so forth helps to create a positive image. So does being supportive, encouraging, helpful, nurturant, and complimentary. Think of the kind of person you are when you're around people you want to like you. And consider what others do to encourage your positive appraisal of them. The features of the situation are important, whether it is an intimate one-to-one setting, a small group activity, a formal dinner, or a chance meeting. Also important are the age, sex and background of your "target."

Our shy youngster adopts a different impression management strategy, one that reflects a *protective self-presentation style.* Rather than acting so as to gain approval, the shy person acts so as to minimize disapproval. This chronic style of approaching the world arises, as we've discussed before, in part because the shy person anticipates negative evaluations from others. This orientation may stem from the shy person's low self-esteem. Or it may result from having a high level of social anxiety. Research has shown that people high in social anxiety are particularly sensitive to public scrutiny of their behavior. As a consequence, they become more *modest* about their abilities and attributes when they come across a public challenge that might prove embarrassing. Not only do they present a public, "unflattering, modest" self to the world, they usually come to accept it.

Moreover, research has shown that while college students who were *not* socially anxious were actively "reward oriented" in dealing with others who were evaluating them, their high-social-anxiety peers assumed more responsibility for failure than success. There is other research evidence which indicates that such people become so overly self-preoccupied when confronted with the "threat" of being evaluated that they don't devote sufficient attention to the task at hand. In fact, they do more poorly than those low in social anxiety who aren't so debilitated by the prospect of being evaluated.

Understanding shyness in this way, as a protective style, helps direct our strategy for overcoming shyness in children. We can better understand the conservative, innocuous image of the shy person that is characteristic of the "reticent syndrome" (as described by speech researcher Gerald Phillips). The shy child is reluctant to interact with others, because he or she has decided that what might be gained is outweighed by what is more likely to be lost by getting involved and letting The Other get close enough to discover all the flaws that are there (hiding like horrible acne under flesh-toned ointment). Novel, unfamiliar, unstructured, evaluative situations are shyness elicitors because they pose a greater risk for acting inappropriately and getting rejected. By assuming a modest or even self-deprecating manner, the shy person takes the wind out of the sails of potential critics even before the judging can begin. After all, how much can a shy person be hurt by throwing himself out of the basement window where his ego lives?

This excessive fear of being evaluated negatively may be handled in a quite different manner yet achieve a comparable goal. Instead of adopting the wallflower, timid-soul image, we have seen shy people keep others at bay by being "bullies," compulsive talkers, or weird in dress or manner. Rather than wait for the negative verdict to come in whenever it may, the obnoxious or rebellious shy person reduces the uncertainty by taking charge, *causing* the negative evaluation and driving others away: "See, I told you so, they're not worth the effort; they're sissies, have nothing to say, nothing in common with me, and are too hung up on superficials like how a person looks." End result: one isolated, soft-centered shy person hiding under a tough shell.

The confusion and conflict between the public self-image and what the shy person believes is the "real private self" is powerfully expressed by Sheryl (writing for advice from Dr. Schlessinger, whose column appears in the *San Francisco Chronicle*):

My insides are definitely different from my outsides. On the outside I am rebellious, gregarious, outgoing, glamorous. On the inside, I am shy, remote, prim, frightened—sort of a little girl with dirty feet.

I have always felt that this is unacceptable to everyone around me. People need me to be a certain way; it is my responsibility to be the way people want. I feel that people use me to fulfill their fantasies!

"Used," "abused," "ignored," or "refused" are central themes in the vocabulary of the shy for describing how they passively allow the world to treat them. We must help the shy child to see people as a precious resource to be actively sought out and prized but not bought at the cost of one's integrity or independence. We must do all we can to help a child to like himself or herself and be liked by others. We must work to forge each of our children as a vital link in the great chain of social being that is the human connection.

Children as Winners

In this chapter we outline our general game plan strategy as well as develop some specific tactics for making children feel and act like winners. In the process of fashioning a new future for the once-shy child, we will show how to minimize negative home and school practices and how to build up areas of a child's strengths and competence.

A Child for All Seasons

"I am good!" "I am loved!" "I can do it!" This is the positive image we want our shy children to have. We can accomplish this by sending more flattering, reassuring statements his or her way rather than negative, detracting comments such as: "You are a booby," "Not even your grandmother could love you," "Don't even try, you're hopeless."

Begin by monitoring how often your child says good and bad things about himself or herself. Also notice the frequency with which you and others send out each of these types of messages to the child. If, as we suspect, the negatives outweigh the positives, a change is in order.

Reinforce all self-statements that portray the child in a favorable light, as well as constructively critical ones that indicate what can be done better next time. "I'll be able to answer the teacher's question better if I review the class notes while waiting for the class to start," instead of "What a fool I made of myself not being able to answer such a simple question."

Negatives: "Stop!"

Put-downs: "No good!"

Bad mouth labels: "Not around here!"

Can't do's: "With practice, you can tomorrow."

Getting the child to say and think good things about him or herself is part of the process of covert conditioning. Psychological research has demonstrated that such "silent" learning can exert powerful effects on changing behavior in desired directions.

But you may need more. The world view of the shy child needs shaking up by means of "cognitive restructuring." The child needs to be told and shown that the world is not filled with an audience of critics waiting in the silent depths, like sharks, ready to devour incompetents who get in the swim over their heads. Rather, we have around us millions of people who would love to know us and who want to share the joys of living if we but give them the chance. Imagine not swimming in a lake because there are sharks far out in the ocean!

It is imperative that children look for the silver lining and not the dark clouds. Adopting a positive orientation in which reward and approval is always possible enables the child to act in ways likely to create a self-fulfilling behavioral prophecy (as demonstrated in the research of Mark Snyder). The optimist who smiles and sends out greetings will discover that at least six of every dozen people are happy, while the shy pessimist notices the six frowning back.

Children can be taught that we learn from our mistakes, that constructive feedback is more valuable than uninformative approval. So we want to have people around us who will tell us when we are "out of line" in order for us to engage in our own self-analysis and decide on means of improvement. However, it is important to recognize that at times criticism comes from personal motives of the critic, motives such as to show off, to exact revenge, or to arouse guilt so as to gain a power advantage. Try to use concrete examples of this "hostile criticism" to enable the child to discriminate it from acceptable criticism.

Other messages that are an integral part of this network of ideas to be conveyed to your shy child include:

• Take intelligent, calculated risks; there is nothing to lose.

• What you are as a person is not always the same as how you behave in public as an actor.

• Ego is not diminished by poor performance, but educated to do things differently next time.

• You never fail by trying since the process is exciting and the experience informative.

• You always fail by refusing to try when you have the ability and the motivation to do so.

• Though we must plan for the future in order to coordinate our means with our goals, once the task begins, let it be all consuming. Approach every social task as a child in play. It does not matter so much what the outcome will be to the game, but that by being absorbed in it fully for a time we are enriched.

• We often carry around irrational thoughts that block effective action and make us think poorly about ourselves. Noted psychologist Albert Ellis has shown how these irrational thoughts can hurt us emotionally. Here is a sample of ten such common irrational thoughts:

Irrational Attitudes and Beliefs

1. In order to be happy and worthwhile it is necessary to be approved of, and loved by, almost everyone for virtually all that one does; that if one is criticized or rejected this represents

a catastrophic personal failure for which one should be punished and/or feel totally miserable.

2. In order to be worthwhile as a person it is essential to be thoroughly competent, adequate and achieving in all possible respects.

3. Certain people are bad, wicked or villainous, and should be severely blamed for their wrongdoings. One should be blamed (as opposed to being held responsible) for mistakes. One should never act badly, and one should feel totally worthless if one does something wrong.

4. In order to be happy one must never be frustrated for long: it is unnatural and catastrophic when things do not go the way one would like them to; and one should react to frustration with indignation.

5. Happiness is largely externally determined and one has little or no ability to rid oneself of anxiety and other negative feelings.

6. If something is, or may be fearsome and dangerous, one should be completely concerned and occupied with it, i.e., keep thinking about the possibility of its occurring.

7. One should try to avoid most of life's difficulties and responsibilities and always insist on immediate gratification. One should not make long range plans for one's pleasure and enjoyment.

8. One's past is all important in determining one's happiness: because certain events once strongly affected one's life, they must inevitably continue to do so.

9. People and things should be better than they are, and it is catastrophic if perfect solutions to the grim realities of life are not immediately found.

10. Maximum human happiness can be achieved by inertia, and by passively and uncommittedly "enjoying oneself."

And here is an exercise for a shy child of junior high age or older:

(a) The child writes down several statements that describe

his or her mental attitude when approaching an adult in authority from whom help or advice is needed, and also when approaching someone of the opposite sex to request a date. For example, "I feel that he'll think I'm a dummy for asking for help."

(b) The parent reads over the list of the ten irrational thoughts and decides which ones fit the child's personal mental attitude statements in the situations described.

(c) The parent and child discuss how those self-statements could be changed to make them more rational and better for the child's emotional well-being.

The essence of this image building is developing a style that is not conservative, constrained, and protective, but venturesome, flexible, and open to new people and ideas.

Remember the difference between the Israeli and Japanese patterns of child rearing in which the Jewish child is primed to get the good things that life has to offer while the Japanese youth is taught to avoid failure and shame. In the same way, by diminishing the shy child's concern for negative evaluation, failure, shame, and rejection and encouraging the child to seek rewards for trying and achieving what is possible, a new child is born. This child will be able to accept success and have the strength to cope with adversity regardless of the reason.

Down with Social Anxiety

To relate effectively to other people requires wanting to make contact, having the basic social skills and a good sense of self-esteem, and not being so anxious that it interferes with one's performance.

The high level of social anxiety shy children experience in social settings has an arousing, physical component as well as a thought and feeling component. Both can be brought under control by a practice termed *systematic desensitization* developed by Joseph Wolpe. This approach to reducing any kind of anxiety involves four steps: relaxation training, construction of a specific anxiety hierarchy, visualized behavioral rehearsal, and practicing the desensitization in the actual anxiety-provoking situation.

Relaxation Training. Relaxation training is usually carried out by using tape recorded instructions that describe how one's muscles are relaxing, starting with those in the head and face and progressively moving to each muscle set in the body. There are ads for such cassettes in any issue of *Psychology Today*, which might be useful as a general guide for parents. But it is enough to have the shy child comfortably seated, eyes closed while a parent talks in a calm, quiet, soothing tone about a gentle wave of relaxation flowing over the child and relaxing all tense muscles. The child might also imagine some situation that is associated with good feelings and a relaxed state of mind, such as sunning on a beach, floating, taking a warm bath, or watching a fire. When the child reports feeling relaxed and calm and ready to try the next part of this game, then the parent continues.

Anxiety Situation Hierarchy. Any social situation that makes a shy child anxious can be broken down into discrete units. They are separate steps (in time and distance) arranged from least anxiety arousing (most remote) to increasingly close, finally to the most provoking aspect of that situation.

For example, a model of such a hierarchy given by F. Orr and his associates, describes a situation in which the shy youngster is invited to a party where a member of the opposite sex that he or she is attracted to will also be. The decision to speak to that person is highly anxiety provoking, while accepting the invitation five weeks earlier has the least anxiety associated with it.

Visualized Behavioral Rehearsal and Desensitization. While still relaxed, the shy youngster is encouraged to visualize (using all senses) each of the steps of the anxiety hierarchy starting with the most remote item. "Imagine you are there, it *is* happening, you are experiencing it, but you are relaxed and comfortable as you are now. Rehearse what you say and do to get the result you want."

At any step where the anxiety becomes too great, the shy person goes back down to a previous step, is relaxed deeper, and proceeds on again. The parent (or teacher) may offer advice on specific wording or approach tactics to help build up the child's deficient social skills. After some social skills training, to be described, then the shy person is encouraged to systematically go through the series of steps in the real life situation. With practice, this systematic desensitization procedure will enable the shy person to take even the most previously feared action. Once having done so successfully is a powerful boost to feelings of mastery and self-worth.

Teaching Basic Social Skills

Why does a child need to be with others? Arnold Buss, the University of Texas researcher specializing in the study of self-consciousness, offered seven good answers to that question in a speech before the American Psychological Association. People need people for:

1. soothing (hurt, pain, disappointment)
2. stimulation (competition, social facilitation, excitement)
3. attention (recognition of their identity)
4. praise (rewards for successful activities)
5. sharing activities (that can't be done individually, as playing in a quartet)
6. affection (giving and receiving love and tender sentiments)
7. social comparison (assessing the quality of our opinions, abilities and emotions in comparison to those of comparable others).

To the extent that a shy child feels awkward or tense in the presence of others, he or she will reduce the chances of receiving these lifetime benefits that all sociable human beings should have in their "trust fund."

With younger children, shyness seems more related to a lack of appropriate social skills than to the overwhelming social anxiety that gets built up in older shy people over years of excessive self-preoccupation and obsession with negative evaluation. In many instances, shyness would stop being a problem if the child just had a few friends, or when older, could feel at ease in heterosexual situations.

"If I was shy and didn't want to be shy anymore," advised four-year-old Timmy, "I would just talk more." That's clearly a start in the right direction. But what to say, and how, and when, and what to refrain from saying? A child must learn a complex set of tactics for getting in touch with other children, singly or in groups, along with the unwritten rules about social timing.

The use of "access strategies" by nursery school children has been studied by William Corsaro who describes for us the following ritual:

"Two girls, Jenny and Betty, are playing around a sandbox in the outside courtyard of the school. I am sitting on the ground near the sandbox watching. The girls are putting sand in pots, cupcake pans, bottles and teapots. . . . Another girl, Debbie, approaches and stands near me observing the other two girls. Neither Jenny nor Betty acknowledges her presence. Debbie does not speak to me or the other girls, and no one speaks to her. After watching for some time (five minutes or so) she circles the sandbox three times and stops again and stands near me. After a few more minutes of watching, Debbie moves to the sandbox and reaches for a teapot in the sand. Jenny takes the pot away from Debbie and mumbles. 'No.' Debbie backs away and again stands near me observing the activity of Jenny and Betty. Then she walks over next to Betty, who is filling the cupcake pan with sand. Debbie watches Betty for just a few seconds, then says: 'We're friends, right? We're friends, right, Betty?'

"Betty, not looking up at Debbie and while continuing to place sand in the pan, says, 'Right.'

" 'I'm making coffee,' Debbie says to Betty.

" 'I'm making cupcakes,' Betty replies.

"Betty turns to Jenny and says, 'We're mothers, right, Jenny?'

"Jenny replies, 'Right.'

"The three 'mothers' continue to play together for 20 more minutes, until the teachers announce cleanup time."

Debbie's "nonverbal entry" is typical of nursery school children who don't often use direct verbal strategies that convey in some form, "Hello, may I play with you?" Perhaps they have learned that other children get so absorbed in their play (or TV watching) they don't hear and respond to "intrusive" openers. When Debbie's next strategy of encircling the area gets ignored, she takes action. In picking up the teapot she signals loud and clear that she wants access. When rebuffed, as often happens to outsiders trying to establish a beachhead in a protected activity shared by two or more children, Debbie demonstrates an access skill that saves the play. "We're friends, right, Betty?"

This explicit reference to affiliation accomplishes several things at once. It singles out Betty as special; she can continue to play with Jenny as well as continue her friendship with Debbie by including her in this game. Of course, there is a risk that Betty will reply in the negative, "No, we're not friends!", but that is unlikely since it is such an extremely assertive and hostile action. Moreover, the direct approach to Betty allows her to take unilateral action of admitting Debby without consulting Jenny. Since Jenny already rejected Debbie's earlier advance, Debbie wouldn't want to allow her to have an equal vote on the admission issue. Finally, Debbie conforms to the ongoing pattern of behavior and makes sure the others realize this by explicitly describing her coffee-making activity. Betty, now lost in the decision-maker's role by Debbie's access strategy, brings Jenny into the fold by having her agree that they are all mothers, "right?"

In his superb book, *Children's Friendships,* Brandeis University psychologist Zick Rubin underscores the important roles that parents and teachers must play in regard to helping children learn how to develop friendships. These roles include: "providing opportunities for toddlers and preschoolers to interact with peers, helping children to develop social skills, and providing understanding and support when friendships fail or end. Especially with younger children, adults can make an effort to encourage cross-sex and cross-age interaction. Finally, there are times when adults must step in and remove a child from a friendship or clique that is doing him [or her] harm."

And of course we think it is important for parents to be supportive of their children—to "stick up" for them, be loyal, and to give their children the benefit of the doubt when they report that they've been treated unfairly—this helps them to know that you love and trust them and that they can count on you. However, of equal importance is how and when you give them your unqualified support. You do your child no favors when you always assume that he or she was the wronged party, and sometimes you can reinforce the sort of antisocial behavior that may ultimately spell rejection of your child by his or her peers.

An example that makes the point is a mother who, when her daughter would complain that one child or another had been mean or unfair "for no reason at all," would become angry at the other child and say such things as, "Patty's just mean and hateful, and you shouldn't have anything to do with her," or, "I'm just going to call up her mother and tell her off." Sometimes this mother would even tell off the other child.

Over the years, it was always assumed that the daughter was always right and the rest of the world wrong. Now the odds are against *anyone* always being right. And because in this case there were so very many instances, involving playmates and, later on, classmates, teachers, and other adults, somewhere along the line this mother ought to have realized that her daughter's indignation over various slights couldn't always have been justified. Most telling of all should have been that although the girl is physically beautiful and quite intelligent, when she was in high school boys never asked her for a second date and she had only one girl friend—and that was on an on-and-off basis. Now a young woman in her twenties, she epitomizes the lonely and shy person who yearns for companionship and who not only fears people, but doesn't like them—and she herself is not likable.

Parents need to be alert to those times when they may be reinforcing antisocial attitudes in their children. Instead of always rushing to the defense of a child, explore with him or her the possibility that the situation in question isn't always as it appears to be and suggest ways to establish relationships on a give-and-take basis.

Another way parents can use a child's conflict with someone else to advantage is to use it as an opportunity to teach him or her how to get along with other people. For example, one mother overheard her twelve-year-old son and another boy quarreling and realized that her child was being very insulting to his friend. She called him into the house while the other boy waited outside and told him, "Honey, I know you like this new friend and I don't want to see you lose his friendship. But you have to let him know you like him. I couldn't help but hear what you were saying to him and I'm afraid that if you keep that up he won't come back."

"But, Mom," said the boy, "I've had a bad day at school and I'm in a bad mood."

"I understand," said his mother, "and let's talk about what's bothering you later, after your friend leaves. But for now, just remember that to keep a friend means that you don't take your problems out on him—you treat him like you *like* him."

The boy then went out and apologized to his friend and the two of them resumed the work they had been doing on their bikes when the argument broke out. Without spying on your children or eavesdropping, you can be open to such opportunities to illustrate to your children the importance of being nice to other people.

Our research with parents of preschool and junior high school students reveals a tendency for shy parents to be more likely than not-shy parents to have one or more shy offspring. For them the task of teaching their children social skills is greater than for most and poses more of a personal challenge. This may well signal a time for self-examination and change for such parents, since children learn social skills by observing how significant models (starting with parents) behave. They are also learned via direct instruction: "Say 'good-bye' when you must leave a friend you've been playing or visiting with, don't just walk away." But the lessons learned must be put to practice and followed by specific, immediate feedback that rewards an appropriate response and redirects undesirable actions. Thus, parents (and especially shy ones) must reexamine their own social skills and make explicit what they believe is correct as well as inappropriate behavior—and explain why. You cannot teach a child a foreign language without speaking the language. Similarly, you cannot teach a child the language of friendship without practicing it daily in the home.

• Discover your child's knowledge of tactics for making friends by having him or her role play the following situations:

> making friends with a new child in the class (of the same sex, and of the opposite sex)
> making friends with a very popular child
> making friends with a handicapped child
> making friends with a younger, and also an older child.

Researchers have found that children judged as popular by their classmates had more knowledge about how to make friends than unpopular children did. Where the knowledge is lacking or wrong, provide the correct information or arrange for a popular, "knowledgeable" child to join in this role-playing session.

• Practice "private speaking" to develop conversational skills in your child. Usually communication apprehension comes from lack of practice and unrealistic expectations about the need to sound like Richard Burton or be as verbally skillful as Barbara Walters.

Richard Garner, author of *Conversationally Speaking*, reminds us that although public speaking is taught (poorly) in schools, private speaking is neither taught nor even encouraged. "Schools exist," Garner says, "to tell you to shut up. They are places of silence." Is that true of your home as well?

• Teach how to ask open-ended questions rather than close-ended ones which require only a one or two word answer. Observe how masters of the art, like Johnny Carson, draw their guests out and make them feel special by asking open-ended questions. "How?"; "Why?"; "Tell me about the time . . ." are openers that encourage talk.

• On first encounters name exchanges are important; the child should state his or hers loud and clear (and correct mispronunciations of it). Likewise, the name of the other child, children, or adults should be solicited and repeated, to be sure it's right as well as to help remember it by repetition. On making telephone requests or answering the phone, the child should always identify himself or herself. Upon meeting again, people are impressed when their names are remembered, thus the child should work at improving memory for names and faces.

• Teach the child a variety of standard openers and closers, "Hello—Good-bye"; "Hi—So long"; "Good to see you again. It's been good talking to you"; "How are you—I hope we can get together again soon"; and for variety, try foreign greetings "*Bonjour*," "*Buon giorno*," "*Ciao*."

• Pose the following problem to your child, changing the sex and age of the protagonist to those of your child. Discuss openers and where to go from there:

"A cute boy my age—14—just moved in next door. He's as shy as I am, and I think—like me—he hasn't dated. Every time I see him I wait for him to say something, and he is probably waiting for me to say something to him. He smiles, and darts his eyes away. We could go on forever not saying anything."

• Practice fast replies by playing rhyming games alternating questioner and responding as quickly as possible.

> YOU: What rhymes with two?
> CHILD: It's a canal, and you?
> YOU: I'm blue.
> CHILD: What rhymes with machine?
> etcetera

You can also do so by inviting the child to list a distinguishing characteristic for each of ten people you mention—as quickly as possible.

• Practice telling jokes and understanding what is funny about a joke.

• Encourage the child to have a sense of humor about himself or herself as well as to occasionally exercise *tact* by acknowledging a problem or deficit the child's friend is facing that is similar to one of the child's.

• Interruptions of another person's talking should be preceded by recognizing this infringement upon the speaker's right to the floor: "Excuse me, but . . ."; "Pardon me, but are you saying that . . ."; "I'd like a chance to say how I feel about . . ."

• Friendship skills also involve being a *friend who makes others feel special about themselves*. The child conveys this feeling in several ways, by:

being an attentive listener, and at times an approving audience, yet a discriminating reviewer ("I like how you did that, but I might have done that last part a little differently. . . .")

sharing resources

self-disclosures; secrets that are entrusted with the other person (small ones at first, more "private" ones as the trust is reciprocated)

giving praise and compliments for specific acts as well as general behavior, "Your hair looks so good in that style"; "I really enjoy being with you"

negotiating disagreements through bargaining and compromise, rather than ultimatums or silent anger

having some area of expertise or strength to contribute to the relationship.

• Help your child to be a more interesting person. Encourage areas of expertise through hobbies, reading, discussions, travel. Enroll the child in a class that will build body appreciation and coordination, such as dance, gym, drama, martial arts or body building. Children can learn to do tricks with a gift of a magic set and some guidance. Playing a musical instrument for social and personal entertainment is an invaluable asset for making contact with others.

• Teach the child to take the perspective of others in the situation, to see the events from their view. This training promotes empathy and tolerance. In addition, it also allows the child to propose alternative explanations for why someone was mean or rejecting. The resilient child does not blame himself or herself for such adverse reactions of others but can understand that others have bad moods, or can grasp concepts such as, "He may have been upset at me because the teacher punished him."

• Provide opportunities at home for your child to play with a younger child to gain friendship.

• Arrange "jigsawing" games in which each child in the group has a part of the information the whole group needs to complete a project. Elliot Aronson's research using this technique with Texas schoolchildren has demonstrated that they become more cooperative, friendly, and tolerant than in traditional competitive arrangements where those with the most win out over those with less.

• Shy children are slow to respond, give them enough time to do so. That means learning to wait, be patient, accepting silence, and not overcontrolling.

• Being the focus of attention elicits shyness, so give your child practice in being the center of attention in a safe, supportive environment—all should stop and listen to the performance. "Bravo," then applause should follow the attempt and the willingness to step into the spotlight. Watch how babies of eighteen months learn with delight at such treatment.

• Teach the child the difficult skill of alternating between being absorbed in the game, making conversation, attending to the task at hand, and momentarily detaching enough to monitor global aspects of the process (such as, is everyone participating, does someone need special efforts to be drawn in, am I being too dominant?).

Two Games to Teach Social Truths

THE LABEL GAME

Demonstrate to older children how our behavior is controlled by how others react toward us. Play the label game with a small group of five or so children. They are to discuss some "hot" topic on which there are differing opinions ("Should women be drafted into the military?"; "How should criminals be treated after they are found guilty?"). Before they start, a label is stuck on each child's forehead that the child can't see and the others must honor but can't reveal. The most talkative, outgoing child gets the label "Ignore me and what I say." The others are labeled, "Disagree with me," "Agree with me," and "Be uncertain of my position." Let the discussion go for twenty to thirty minutes, observing how the participants react. Then ask each one how he or she felt during the game and explain why. Reveal the labels, and open a discussion around the issue of "we are what others make of us" (a theme interestingly explored in the novel, *Cards of Identity* by Nigel Dennis).

THE HOT SEAT GAME

This game will give youngsters an appreciation of the impact of rejection as well as the power they have to help others who are not being socially accepted. It works from junior high through college. Again, in a group of five to a dozen members there will be an interesting discussion (which the parent or teacher may join in). One youngster is arbitrarily chosen to sit on the "hot seat," a seat about ten feet away from the circle of friends. An invisible wall around the hot seat prevents communication to or from it. The displaced person partially hears what is being said but can't participate. After about two minutes any child may change places by asking permission to leave the circle of friends; walking over to the hot seat, saying "I'll take your place now"; and be willing to remain there in isolation until someone else elects to make a similar sacrifice.

The game is played for about twenty minutes, after which each person describes how it felt to be on the hot seat, not to be on the hot seat, to be in conflict about whether to exchange places, how it felt when someone did come to the rescue. In a very real sense the hot seat game sensitizes not-shy and shy youngsters to the emotionally draining experience of feeling rejected and to the social responsibility we all bear for making others feel accepted.

Body Language of Friendship. Often shy children are not aware of how much they talk with their bodies even when their speech is silent. "I am not accessible" one's body tells others when one's arms are folded across the chest; one's head is down, gaze averted; a frown is on one's face; legs are crossed; laughter, if any, is nervous or forced.

The shy child who wants to make friends needs to be shown how to convey a quite different impression by means of body semantics. To begin to replace the protective self-presentational style with an open, adventurous one, the child needs to practice smiling, making eye contact, standing or sitting in a comfortable position (not fidgeting) with legs astride and hands gesturing appropriately to visually carry along the verbal message. The accessible child sits or stands reasonably close to the other child and responds when appropriate by touching the other child; or accepting friendly physical contact such as pats on the back, hand holding, hand shakes, or friendly taps on the arm or shoulder.

In addition, the shy person should be instructed in ways the physical environment may intrude upon the nature of the social contact, and then be encouraged to restructure the environment to make it serve social needs rather than passively allow social behavior to be structured by the physical setting. For example, on the "Phil Donahue" show, Phil arranged for two shy strangers to enact a first meeting. They were seated in chairs side by side, facing the audience. They talked awkwardly for several minutes, exchanging sideways glances as they groped for things to say while looking out at the sea of faces in the audience. All they had to do to dramatically alter their situation was to turn each of the chairs slightly so they would be facing each other. In such a setting they'd be more likely to make eye contact with one another and not with the anonymous audience. It would have helped to make an admittedly stressful situation more comfortable. But as a general rule shy people are likely to accept the status quo, take what is given without questioning, challenging, or trying to alter it to better fit their needs or the purpose the environment should be promoting.

Friends as Dates.   Much sex-role training in our society and others is designed to erect barriers of "differentness" between the pink- and the blue-hued people from their baby bunting to their casket lining. Without delving into the reasons for such practices, the consequences are all too apparent. The segregation of people by sex has been—and still poses—one of the strongest prohibitions against getting to know, feel comfortable with, and have as friends "those other kind of people."

Anxiety often accompanies the uncertainty of having to cope with unfamiliar situations where the reactions of others are not seen as predictable or as controllable as one would desire. Little wonder then that surveys of young people reveal a high frequency of concern about their heterosexual relations. About a third of a large sample of 3,800 American college students rated themselves as "somewhat" to "very" anxious about dating in one recent study. Another American study reported more than half of all social situations in which undergraduate males had difficulty were those concerned with dating. A number of Australian studies similarly report a high level of concern among their youth for "getting on" with members of the opposite sex. Our own surveys of young people from eight different cultures further implicate one-to-one heterosexual interactions as a major trigger for releasing shyness. There is also evidence of the importance of satisfactory interpersonal relations with the opposite sex in marriage and later emotional well-being. Three important points for parents to work on with their children, shy and not, are:

• Children need to be encouraged at all age levels to have friends from both sexes and to learn the rules that govern appropriate conduct with each.

• Children need to learn by observation and practice how to approach and when to reinforce someone of the opposite sex. Research shows that socially competent individuals develop a good sense of timing for making reinforcing responses to another person during a conversation. In contrast, those who are generally incompetent socially make as many responses but they are often "wasted" because they come too soon before or too late after the time they would be most appreciated by the other persons.

• Making a date involves the courage to initiate a sequence of actions, knowing the rules for appropriate conduct (dating etiquette), exercising some basic social skills, and planning. The shy teen-ager needs to be taught how. In chapter 9, "The Student's Shyness Handbook," we give specific instructions directly to students. Parents can either refer their sons and daughters to this material, or review it so that they can instruct them in the fine art of dating. For shy young people interested in more comprehensive material on shyness, we recommend our earlier books, *Shyness: What It Is, What to Do About It*, (Addison-Wesley, Jove Books), and *The Shyness Workbook*, (A&W Publishers).

Neutralizing the Differences

There is nothing parents can do about those qualities, such as the way a child looks, that are fixed and may be the basis for prejudice or nonacceptance. But parents *can* keep from making matters worse. While on the one hand, we want to teach our children to value uniqueness—their own and that of others— the fact is, once they are part of a group, they turn into the world's greatest conformists. You can tell a child, "Be original," or, "Be yourself," or "Beauty is only skin deep," until you're blue in the face, but it won't mean anything if they see themselves as very different from their peers—and if the peers see them that way too, and treat them accordingly.

So whether your child is a raving beauty or has a face only a mother would love, you'll want to avoid doing, or forcing them to do, things that set them apart. Here are a few suggestions for doing just that:

• Do not force your child to dress dramatically different from other children. If all of the girls in preschool or the play group wear corduroy coveralls and sneakers, for example, don't insist that your daughter wear frilly dresses and patent-leather Mary Janes. Or, if all of the boys wear blue jeans, don't make your son wear Little Lord Fauntleroy suits. And this tolerance and cooperation should continue as your children grow.

• If Holly Hobbie and Star Wars lunch boxes are "in" then don't force your child to carry one just like the one you carried thirty or so years ago.

• If your child has a habit that is cause for teasing or rejection, such as thumb sucking; hair chewing; or, God forbid, nose picking, do what you can to break the habit (without breaking the child). Consult with your pediatrician for guidance; institute a system of rewards; or, in the instance of thumb sucking, consult a speech therapist, as there is a new technique for breaking this habit.

Providing Social Opportunities

Not surprisingly, a number of the parents of the nursery school children we studied indicated that they felt their children were shy because they had little exposure to people other than their parents or immediate family members. Mothers of shy children, for example, said that their children were rarely left with sitters and spent virtually all of their time at home before starting preschool.

Many well-intentioned parents make the mistake of acting on the belief that "good" parents never (or rarely) leave their children in the care of others. A number of mothers of preschoolers in our survey reflected this view, and then regretted it because their children's lack of exposure to other people, they now believe, contributed to their shyness.

We believe that it is better for children to have as much exposure as possible to many different people, and the younger they are when they have it, the better. And that includes being left in the care of others (it is much less traumatic for a child to be left when there is no choice if he or she is used to it, and has been eased into this pattern). In any event, we recommend having many visitors to the home and taking children out visiting whenever possible. You can prepare a young child for a visitor by telling him or her in advance of the event what the person looks like and something about him or her. When you make children feel that they are part of a particular social event, they most likely will look forward to it.

But more important, parents should provide a growing child with opportunities to interact with the child's peers.

If you have young children and live in a neighborhood where there are many young families, you are way ahead. Children have a way of finding each other, but it never hurts for their parents to get to know the neighbors, and for all of the parents to provide opportunities for the children to play together.

If there are no young children in your neighborhood, you can take your children to the park and let them play with others there. A rule you should follow is to allow them to respond to or approach other children at their own pace instead of pushing them into playing with others. If the park isn't an answer for you, look into play groups that are established by community organizations such as the YWCA, young parents organizations, and childbirth groups.

If your child is already so shy that he or she is terrified of the idea of playing with children or getting into a play group, you might consider starting a play group in your home. Everyone, and certainly children are no exception, is always more comfortable on home turf. You can ease your child into a one-to-one situation by having a friend bring his or her child to your house to visit. Gradually, you can increase the number in the group by including children of friends and relatives. (It is unwise, by the way, to have a group of three, because when young children get together, often two of them will pair up and leave a third one out. That doesn't do much for that child's self-esteem or desire to be sociable.)

Some points to remember when entertaining children in your home are:

• If your home is a comfortable and inviting place for children to be, the chances are that your child will be well ahead of the game socially.

• Get into the habit of being prepared for children's visits. Have a room or a corner of a room where children can play without being under constant surveillance (safe, and not loaded with your treasures).

• Keep on hand games, puzzles, and noncompetitive toys; crackers, cookies, juice.

• If you have an out-of-doors area that will accommodate them, a sandbox, swings, and other play equipment tailored to the ages of the children help to make your home the place where children like to be.

When both parents work outside the home, obviously, it's not possible to take children to the park frequently, to a play group, or have children come over to play. Thus, a child's social life will pretty well depend on the child-care arrangements. The ideal arrangement for young children who aren't in preschool beyond a few hours each week is being cared for by someone who takes care of several children at the same time. Thus, working parents need not just look for quality child care, but also for child care that will provide their children with the opportunities to meet other children and form friendships— especially when a child is shy.

Some parents of older children don't want their children's friends and classmates around the house because they say they eat them out of house and home, and are even noisier than the younger ones, hard to control, and make big messes. This is understandable, but when weighed against the importance of friendships to the growing child, it seems to us a small price to pay—and it doesn't, after all, go on for the rest of your life. And one fringe benefit of having your home the place where kids want to be is that you know where your own children are and

what they are doing—something that will be especially important to you when they are in the adolescent years.

So, we recommend that in addition to adopting an attitude
of grin and bear it, parents go a step further and have a few
attractions—such as stereo equipment, Ping-Pong tables, and
other things that interest older children, around the house, if at
all possible.

And to cut down on the number of things that irritate you,
establish some rules of conduct concerning eating, noise, and
making messes.

Giving a Child Time for a Social Life

While it is important to provide a child with opportunities and
tools to neutralize differences and build self-esteem, too many
activities that are designed to do that may turn out to be barriers to his or her developing social skills and friendships. For
example, one mother who told us her son was shy, also described the boy's schedule. It was enough to exhaust an
energetic adult. During the school year, afterschool hours were
consumed with homework, music lessons, private swimming
lessons, and special tutoring in math. Weekends were family
times: camping, skiing, outings to museums, fairs, concerts,
and all manner of enriching experiences, and all to the good—
except that they allowed little time for the boy to be with his
friends. Summers were not much different, as the boy went to
summer school and then to camp, with all of the other activities
sandwiched in wherever there was a slot of free time.

By the time this boy was old enough for group activities,
such as scouting or soccer, he was already shy. It is thus vital to
his or her well-being to include time for friends in your game
plan of activities for developing the body, mind, and social
responsiveness of your child.

CHAPTER FIVE

The Preschool Years
(from 2–6)

"When my wife decided to return to her teaching job" (writes the father of little Maria), "and our baby-sitter took another job, in desperation I called several preschool programs hoping to enroll our two-year-old daughter part time. Fortunately, she had just been toilet trained (following the expert program outlined in the book, *Toilet Training in Less than a Day*), since that is the minimal condition in virtually every preschool. A local Montessori school was the only one that did accept children younger than three years old, and off we all went for 'our interview.' The principal said he would accept her on a trial basis, but only for a full day's program from 9 to 3, every day. My baby going to school all day long! Unimaginable! Of course, there would be rest periods and naps, and she would get special attention as the youngest child in a mixed-age class of mostly three- and four-year-olds with a sprinkling of older children of the advanced age of five.

"To ease her into this new situation, after class was out, the teacher invited her to explore the attractive classroom with its many treasures and activities awaiting her. On the next day, we came to observe the children during a play period and our daughter was invited by one of the older girls to play (at the teacher's tactful suggestion). Then came the Big Day. Despite our buildup of the joys of this new school, the apparent fun her prospective classmates were having, and the sensitive support of the teacher (and assistant teacher, as well), our little girl clung tightly to Mommy's skirt, tears welling up in those baby blue eyes as she begged, 'Please don't leave me.'

"Just as we were about to give in and give up hopes of this promising solution to our two-career marriage dilemma, the teacher came to the rescue. 'It's time for parents to go to work and children to go to school now.' She continued in a compassionate, though firm tone, 'I will take care of you and you will have a lot of fun things to tell your mommy and daddy that you did today in our class when they pick you up when school is over.'

"Our feelings of guilt lasted for the next few days as the scenario was replayed, though with less intensity each morning. By the end of the week our baby took the teacher's hand when the school bell rang, waved bye-bye, and gave us a reassuring smile designed to tell us that we had not betrayed her trust and abandoned her to 'strangers.'

"Little Maria had entered the ranks of the Preschool Generation. It turned out to be the very best gift we could have given her; not only did it stimulate her intellectual curiosity at this time of optimal openness to new learning experiences, but even more so, it gave her the opportunity for a rich social life with peers that we never could have provided in a home where she was the only child and in a neighborhood with few children her age."

Little Maria's report card reveals how successful this preschool experience has been in developing her self-confidence and social development. The comments of Maria's teacher reflected the change:

Two months after she started: "She seems to be a very happy child and well liked in the classroom. She can be very assertive with the other children."

One year later: "Seems very comfortable with her environment and participates in large and small groups. Will get tired around lunchtime and then is easily upset, but not to the point beyond control. She is very fair and presents herself to her friends as a warm, nonthreatening, and imaginative person."

One-and-a-half years later: "She is considerate and fair with the other children. She initiates new games, helps those younger, and is sought out by many as a comfortable person to be with."

Two years later: "She is a sought-after person by all the other children—she is gentle and fair. Has pretty much stopped taking naps now; as always, Maria has helped make our class a pleasure to work with."

And most recently, after *two-and-a-half years,* her teacher writes, "Maria has a rare quality that allows all the children to seek her friendship and companionship with respect and enthusiasm. She is able to express her likes and dislikes to all in a manner that is nonthreatening, clear, and imaginative. She is an inspiration to all of us, and a pleasure to know."

In this chapter we shall encourage parents to take advantage of available preschool opportunities for their two- to five-year-olds. In addition to suggesting what to look for in selecting the right school for your child, we will outline ideas for encouraging sociability during these sensitive years of early development. We assume that most parents would like to get a report card of their son's or daughter's social life similar to that which Maria received from her teacher. Some of our suggested strategies are geared to preventing shyness from ever getting a stronghold, others to undoing it before it begins to be a "problem personality trait."

We shall examine the kinds of things Maria's parents did to lay such a solid foundation upon which she was able to develop into a desirable, sought-after playmate. In addition, we will draw upon our personal observations of preschool classrooms, as well as teacher and parent reports of shyness in their children. And we will also hear from four-year-olds, some of whom have definite ideas about what shyness is and how it should be treated when it shows up in another student in their class.

Inoculations Against Shyness

Children can easily appreciate the moral of the tale of "The Three Little Pigs," that taking the time and investing the effort to build a solid structure is the best security when the Big Bad Wolf starts huffin' and puffin'. But those precautions must begin long before any potential menace is at our doorstep.

For parents, this means an early awareness of the dangers shyness poses for their children. Shyness functions like a contagious disease: it's a widespread debilitating condition that afflicts over 30 percent of the children (according to our survey of parents and preschool teachers). As these children get older and head out into the world beyond the home, the problem gets worse, especially during the years of adolescence.

Caring, Sharing, Daring, and Swearing

Let's examine some of the ways in which Maria's parents put into practice their program to prevent her from becoming shy. Having seen the often painful consequences of shyness in their nephew, they were determined to try their best to prevent its reoccurrence in Maria.

The four main areas around which they developed specific exercises and games can be called: caring, sharing, daring, and swearing. *Caring* is the general term for open displays of love and affection. Under *sharing* comes all behavior that involves giving of one's self and possessions to others, and likewise being open to accepting what others are offering. *Daring* represents risk-taking, encouragement for activities that have desirable goals which can only be attained by taking some chances. Finally, *swearing* means providing opportunities for the child to express openly strongly felt negative emotions, such as anger over frustrations and injustice.

Aware of Maria's tremendous learning potential, her parents started their shyness program during the first months of her life. According to Dr. Burton White, director of the Preschool Project of Harvard's Graduate School of Education, it is important to help children develop effective patterns of responding to others during their first two years because by the age of two

They are crystallized into their basic social patterns; and we see those social patterns applied to all social encounters in the next year or two to other children who come into the home, to older siblings, and to other adults. A human personality is being formed during those first two years, and there is no job more important than doing that well.

Caring. "I love you" was said and expressed physically with hugs and kisses every day from birth on, so that it became a natural part of the greeting between parent and child. Maria was taught to blow kisses at about the time she was taught to point out her nose, eyes, and mouth. Before the age of two she had learned a game of secret communication played in public places with symbolic gestures. When her father touched his chest, made a double circle around his heart and pointed to her, it meant "I love you," or "Daddy loves Maria." Soon she would reciprocate and extend the circle of love to Mommy, and at times to her dress or the dessert.

"Kissing sandwiches" were delicious treats with the child in the middle, as both parents simultaneously kiss her cheeks. Later on, they each got a turn to be "inside" the sandwich.

"Before you were born I was often sad because something important was missing from my life," Maria's mother would tell her, "then you came along and my heart danced with joy, I became happy all over and what comes over my face whenever I think about how lucky I am to have such a wonderful daughter?"

"A big smile, Mommy!"

"Yes, and when other people get to know what a lovely girl you are, they will be happy too, and what will be on their faces?"

"Another smile."

Such simple acts of caring communicate in a very direct way that the child is wanted and loved. They are backed up with questions about the child's daily activities, especially when the parent first comes home. Children live in an "expanded present" time zone in which *now* is the only reality. They must learn to add future and past time frames in order to form a temporal perspective—one of the major accomplishments of our system of education. Until a child learns about these time frames, we must deal with them in the present. So when a parent, tired from a hard day's work, says essentially, "Later for you," to a child who has waited ages for the return home of the king or queen, it is the same as saying *no*.

Maria's parents, who both worked as teachers, recognized that a little immediate attention to the child's needs for "show and tell" would satisfy her sufficiently so that she could later accept being told "I'm too tired now to read another story or play 'all fall down.' "

They were especially ready to express love whenever disasters struck—when the inevitable glass of milk got spilled, or the best beloved toy mysteriously "got broked"—the perfect time to convey the unconditional love they felt for their child. In addition, the "goof burden" was lessened by reciting who it was who knocked over the wine in the restaurant:

"Daddy did it!"

"And who was it who lost the keys to the car?"

"Mommy did that!"

No one is perfect, but we are all loved nevertheless.

Sharing. Sharing with others is an antidote for the self-centeredness of shyness. The ability to imagine what the world is like from any but one's own perspective, to role play someone else's position, to empathize with another person's situation, is a complex cognitive skill that develops slowly during the preschool years.

By making a virtue of sharing and allowing the child to witness the joy that others derive from receiving a shared offering, Maria's parents helped bridge the awful "we-them" gulf. First, things were shared—chocolate chip cookies, potato chips, toys, and so forth. Then less tangible commodities were shared, starting with TV viewing (even where the family had two TV sets): "Now it's Maria's turn to watch a children's program, then it's Daddy's turn to watch his Monday night football game." Sharing also is extended to conversations where taking turns is critical for keeping discussions flowing and all parties involved. Children must learn a variety of subtle rules that govern who talks when and for how long during a discussion. It is often painful for a child who is bursting with something to say and just can't wait to say it, to wait patiently while another speaker finishes what he or she has to say. Until they learn how to converse, preschoolers are like little public lecturers, they launch into their topic of the moment with a gusto that deafens them to what anyone else is saying.

Maria's task was to get a playmate who was also loudly professing on some subject, to stop and listen attentively to what she had to say.

"Be quiet and listen to *me*!!" is what she would have liked to proclaim. Instead, she learned to say, "That's nice, do you know what happened to me?"; "Excuse me"; "I have a good idea," or, of her own making, "Do you know what?" She was also encouraged to say phrases like, "What do you think about that?" to give her playmates a further chance to comment. Little wonder then that Maria was judged to be fair, considerate, and interesting by her peers.

Praise and compliments likewise are valuable commodities to be traded liberally. Sharing praise you have gotten with others who've helped you adds to the number of those who feel good about the success. Similarly, sharing with others the positive opinion you hold of their appearance or performance is very rewarding. Maria's parents directed her attention to the positive qualities of others and to how one shares with them the good feelings they bring out in you.

"Doesn't Uncle Charlie make everyone laugh with his funny jokes? We should tell him how much fun he is."

"See how Grandma makes Daddy feel special when she cooks his favorite food, and look at how happy she gets when he tells her how much he loves her cooking."

"How well you dance, Maria. When you were a little girl you couldn't dance at all, now you're like a ballerina. I'm so proud of you."

Shared too by Maria's parents were smiles, eye contact and, those magical "open sesame" words, "thank you," "please," "hello," and "good-bye."

A sense of effectiveness develops from being able to successfully complete tasks of some difficulty. Maria's parents tried hard to restrain the urge to supervise, to do it themselves faster and better than their child could; they'd take over only when asked to, but not until the child tried to carry out the task on her own. When Maria would say, "I can't do it, you do it for me," her parents countered with:

"I think you can if you try. It takes a little practice until you can get it right, let me show you how to start. When I was a child of your age I couldn't do what you can do now. That's how you become a grown-up, by being able to do many things by yourself without always asking your mommy and daddy to do it. But whenever you need help to start something that you don't know how to do, you can always ask for help."

Daring. Shyness is a psychological state that often shows up in the company of physical timidity and fear of taking risks. "Being scared of a new person," a typical preschooler's definition of shyness, becomes associated with the more general condition of being scared to take chances.

Children need to have confidence in their bodies, to feel coordinated, strong, and able to play physically demanding games. In places where young children help with farming, or learn to hunt for food, or are responsible for strenuous household tasks, their early physical development is encouraged through practice, games, and exercise. Urban, middle-class children are more sedentary, they sit and read, get driven to and from, sit and watch TV, sit in class listening to the teacher. Their minds are stimulated often while their bodies are allowed to stagnate. Physical fitness expert Bonnie Pruden has reported that the vast majority of American children fail basic tests of fitness. Their muscle tone is poorly developed and their movements are not well coordinated. The fit child, she has found, does better in school, is not a sick child, has fewer emotional problems, and is able to enjoy more and be more enjoyable.

Maria's parents took her to a kindergym at a local "Y" when she was a year old. Later on, she went to a weekly ballet class and took swimming lessons when she was four. In between, they played physical games with her; had her jog along with them for longer and longer distances; practiced catching, throwing, and hitting—first balloons then progressively smaller balls.

• Help your child develop a sense of physical competence through regular exercise, physical games, and sports. Preschoolers love the sense of pride that comes from weight lifting—try three-pound rubber weights (sold in sporting goods stores for women).

• From infancy on, practice physical risk taking with your child—let the child jump off a table into your outstretched arms only a few inches away at first, then farther and farther away.

• Hang a rope ladder in the child's room (the kind used for fire escapes). It can be used as a swing with the child seated across a rung while the parent pulls the doubled-up bottom part of the ladder to and fro. But greater value comes from the child's learning how to climb up and down this free-hanging ladder and later on to hang upside down and do simple acrobatic tricks on it.

Risk taking does not mean taking foolish, impulsive actions that could hurt the child. The child who is aware of his or her physical capabilities is better able to judge what he or she can do and be less likely to try something unsafe. We believe a child should have a positive attitude toward accepting a certain amount of risk. Risk is the challenge of uncertainty and novelty. A risk that is successfully attempted not only is rewarding in itself, but stimulates a general willingness to take the initiative in situations when others are holding back. It is the characteristic of leaders and people who are successful in business and career.

A child who is challenged rather than frightened by risks, will be less shy, but even more crucial, will be able to cope with the complexities of modern life. Walter Lippman reminds us of the difficult voyage that faces a child of these times: "No mariner enters upon a more unchartered sea than does the average human being born in the 20th Century. Our ancestors knew their way from birth to eternity; we are puzzled about the day after tomorrow."

Swearing. Children need to express strongly felt emotions. They must be able to acknowledge tender feelings of love and sorrow as well as tougher feelings of anger. Often their anger is associated with experiences quite different from those that provoke anger in adults. They may respond with anger when sadness is the appropriate adult reaction. Failure, rejection, and frustration can also trigger angry outbursts. At times the child may be unaware of the true cause of the anger, such as when it comes from anxiety about loss of control over a given situation or feelings of dependency. But when a child has good reason to feel the temporary emotional state of anger and is made to feel guilty for expressing it, then trouble can start.

If a child is not free to express anger outwardly towards its rightful target, the anger may get misdirected and turned in on the child in the form of lowered self-esteem, or even masochistic behaviors. The child doesn't have to use swear words, but should be able to say, "That makes me angry," or "I feel angry when you always say my sister is right before you hear my side of the story." And when the cause is not obvious but the strong feelings are still there, the child may need the catharsis that comes from yelling or crying.

Parents and teachers can help the child explore the basis of the anger, direct it into nonhostile channels while trying to change the conditions that provoked the anger. But they do well to begin by respecting the legitimacy of the emotion and encouraging its open expression.

The connection between anger, its suppression, and shyness can be seen in many of the clients in the Stanford Shyness Clinic. One of them was a beautiful woman with a very poor sense of her abilities and attractiveness. She was too shy to join in dinner conversations with her husband's colleagues. When we probed beyond her self-deprecating façade of "I didn't have anything worthwhile to offer," anger burst forth: "They think of me as a dumb blond when in fact, I've read more than they have about the political situations they are discussing without any solid information to go on. I'm angry at them for putting me down, and I'm angry at my husband for imposing those show-offs on me, but most of all, I'm angry at myself for not being able to say what I know or even tell them what I feel."

Another client, a middle-aged woman raised in a traditional Chinese family, was never permitted to express the slightest bit of anger even in silent facial gestures. She would rustle the garbage bag as an outlet for her anger, but even that her father prohibited. She grew up as an obedient, good little girl, one who feared and hated authority, but could not respect the value of her own feelings and opinions.

In suggesting that children be given outlets for anger, we do so aware of the lethal consequences that can occur when the shy child who never says "no" grows up to be a shy adult unable to express his anger in acceptable ways.

While observing a second-grade class, we noticed that two children were leaning against the desk of a very shy young girl. Without realizing it, they were sitting on part of the drawing she was making and she couldn't pull it out from under them. She tugged and pried and finally, the drawing ripped in two. Tears rolled down her cheeks, the boys walked off, insensitive to the conflict they had created. The teacher, seeing her torn drawing, scolded her for being sloppy and irresponsible. She cried. "Tina is a cry baby" whispered the boy in the next seat. A disaster day at school for Tina, one that will be repeated with variations as she grows older, unable to state her rights, express feelings, or be angry at life's injustices. If she could "swear with clean words" at school and at home, then at least she wouldn't turn the anger in on herself and feel guilty, worthless, and confused.

To make matters worse, shy children tend to be evaluated by their teachers as "well behaved" more often than do not-shy children who "misbehave" more. Thus it is likely that teachers will reinforce the passive, quiet, nonassertive behavior of shy children because that makes them "good pupils" (i.e., easier to manage). It is only when they are "too shy" that this virtuous aspect of shyness becomes a matter of teacher's concern, but then it is often a little too late to change the child by simply saying "Don't be so shy!"

Detecting Shyness

The best way to discover whether an adult is shy is to pose the simple, straightforward question, "Do you consider yourself to be a shy person?" Many young children will also be able to give a valid answer to that question. But we want to use the shyness label as little as possible with preschoolers. So instead, observe their social behavior, talk to their teachers, and listen to what the other children in the neighborhood or school say about your child. It often happens that parents are surprised to discover that their child is shy when away from home. The sooner a parent knows that, the sooner remedies can be put into practice.

One five-year-old we observed (along with her classmates) for four months is typical of a truly shy child. She virtually never smiled, she did not have a happy or lively look, and she seemed to be totally uninterested in many of the class activities. She preferred to roam around, touching windowsills and doorknobs during those times when the other children were singing, listening to a story, or dancing. On one occasion, while doing crafts, she needed to use the stapler to finish her work. The boy sitting next to her was using it and setting it down every few minutes. Not only did this little girl not reach for the stapler when it wasn't in use, but she didn't ask to use it. She simply stared at it intently, and quietly waited until the boy finished his work and left to move on to something else. On another occasion, when the class was singing and the teacher would make the song be about each individual child, when the teacher started to sing about her she asked the teacher not to.

All in all, we were left with the impression of a sad, lonely child who took absolutely no pleasure in those things that are, for other children, wonderful experiences.

Our teacher ratings of their three-, four-, and five-year-old preschoolers indicate that the shy children can be identified in comparison to their non-shy peers as being less friendly (have fewer friends); actively avoiding others; being less active (sit and watch rather than play or act vigorously); being less assertive (let things happen, don't voice opinions); being less self-directed or independent (fail to initiate, to persevere without teacher's help); not being leaders (chosen or self-appointed); being more sad (smile less, not enthusiastic); and being more well behaved (follows orders, doesn't get into trouble).

Less frequently reported by teachers were reactions that also occur in only a minority of shy adults: blushes, stutters, and sucks thumb (which shy adults have learned not to do in public).

The shy children we observed gave off all these clues to their shyness and more. They don't make eye contact, they hang back, and they rarely volunteer. The shy child doesn't ask for help (or tools or materials) when needed, especially not from other children. It seemed to us that they played near but not with other children. Some wandered about aimlessly, while others stayed close to the protective shield of the benevolent teacher—which helped keep the other children away.

When we asked the children themselves to tell us how we could know if a child was shy, the psychological wisdom of these four-year-olds was remarkable:

"They're scared a lot of other children. You don't play with somebody. You play alone."

"He doesn't want to have to talk to other people."

"He goes to the teacher all the time."

"Helene is shy of me because every time that I look at her she makes a face—a sad face—and hugs her dolly."

Regardless of whether or not they were shy, according to teachers' evaluations, the thirty children who played our "Which puppet is shy?" game were in agreement that the shy puppet is the one who plays alone the most; has fewer friends; laughs less; doesn't raise his or her hand to answer the teacher's question; doesn't perform at show-and-tell time; doesn't like to talk to other people.

When asked which of the puppets were most like them, the majority of the shy *and* the not-shy children pointed to the not-shy puppet! This may be wish fulfillment for the shys (whose verbal output actually differed from the not shys in giving significantly fewer reasons when explaining any of their answers).

Shyness Eliciting Situations

Teachers and parents rated the kinds of situations that triggered shyness reactions in each of the seventy-eight preschool children we studied intensively. Their ratings on a scale where 0 = not at all shy, 3 = moderately shy, and 6 = extremely shy, are given in the chart.

Shyness Elicitors for Preschoolers

TEACHERS' RATINGS		PARENTS' RATINGS	
1. Strangers	4.2	1. Strangers	2.9
2. Focus of attention	3.8	2. New situations	2.7
3. With peers	3.4	3. Focus of attention	2.2
4. With opposite sex	3.1	4. With adults	2.2
5. With teachers	2.7	5. In class	1.8
6. In small groups	2.2	6. In stores	1.5
7. At playtime outside	2.1	7. With parents' friends	1.5
8. In singing group	2.0	8. With peers	1.4

Parents rate their child's shyness as less extreme than teachers do. This might reflect that the child shows more shyness in school because of the greater variety of children and new activities there. Or, teachers may be more sensitive than parents to relative differences between shyness in children since they see so many of them behaving in similar situations. Nevertheless, these data indicate that parents and teachers must talk to each other about the social-emotional development of children whose level of shyness in any situation is inhibiting. The view each holds of the child is not always shared—and should be.

It is very important to remember that a child may behave shyly only at home or at school, so parents and teachers may be surprised to learn the child is shy in the other setting. Shirley, for example, was totally unaware her six-year-old daughter felt shy at school because she was gregarious at home and had lots of neighborhood friends. It wasn't until her daughter told her she felt shy at school that she knew the extent of it. Teacher-parent communication is important.

Remember how slapping the "shy" label on a child may turn his or her normally quiet, reserved manner into a true case of shyness. A study (by A. Thomas and associates at New York

University Medical Center) of 136 people from birth through adulthood found that the nursery school child who stands at the periphery of a group instead of participating actively may have that normal temperamental tendency to warm up slowly.

Children who tend to stand back quietly should be allowed a longer time to get into ongoing activities. That means more patience on the part of parents and teachers. It also means that they should be gently encouraged to participate more. Other, more outgoing children can be enlisted as their "big brother or big sister" social facilitators. But the young child should never be made to feel that *shyness* is the *cause* of not being more of a social butterfly. When that happens, as it did with one of our best Stanford college students, the child may come to use that label as the excuse or justification for not participating—"I can't talk in class *because* I am shy."

John remembers being quiet all his life, enjoying people and activities without talking a great deal. He liked to observe, think, and get involved, but not to initiate conversation. Moreover, he was friendly and well liked. John came to think of himself as shy in preschool when the first of a long line of report cards told his parents that something was wrong with him. It is instructive to look at some of the teachers' comments on John's report cards (all of which he has saved but not savored).

Nursery school: "John is a friendly youngster who enjoys being a part of the four-year-old group. Because of his shy and quiet manner, John prefers mostly small group play; however, more and more he is tending to enter larger, more vigorous activity. He can enter a group easily when he feels the need, but his real wants often have to be sought out by a teacher. He still does not feel free to come to us, but when approached, he is able to converse easily."

First grade: "He is still very dependent on his teachers."
Second grade: "He is quiet, but very well liked."

Third grade: "John's shyness has prevented him from participating as much as he should."

Seventh grade: "John has been quietly going about his business. I have heard little from him and suspect that he would benefit from asking a few more questions. . . . If John is puzzled, I encourage him to ask more questions."

"Although a bit on the reticent side in class discussions, John seems quite attentive. . . ."

"John is quiet and competent. . . . If John is enjoying Lakeside, he doesn't let on in gross, outward display; but I suspect that he is."

"I do wish we'd hear from him a bit more often, voluntarily, in class discussions."

"John seldom comes for extra help, even when he has difficulty."

"It is very rewarding to hear from John without feeling that his response is prompted by something which 'Excedrin' would alleviate as easily as 'speech.' "

Eighth grade camp: "John was one of the most quiet members of our group but he was just as involved in all our activities as our noisy ones were."

Ninth grade: "John continues to produce work of high quality although at times I think he could be more aggressive about making known his questions and problems."

"John is one of the quiet ones who does competent work but volunteers little in class. Both he and the class would profit if John would be more aggressive in stating his opinions."

"John's only shortcoming would seem to be a lack of flamboyance, if that can be termed an attribute. In his own view, he is quite verbal enough in class, but I know from my acquaintance with him that he is unobtrusive and well mannered, and that he hardly ever communicates strong feelings. . . . We have not seriously explored academic weaknesses. I have let his usual quiet and self-contained manner lull me to inattention."

Tenth grade: "John is quiet in class, but is generally able to contribute to class discussions if I call on him. . . . He is quiet and conscientious and seems to be making progress smoothly."

"John does his job quietly but powerfully."

"John is very quiet in class, but he demonstrates a concern for the material and a fair amount of writing ability. I hope I can encourage him to project more of his own ideas into papers and class discussions. . . . John has made more of an effort to speak out this term. . . . With a new class and a new teacher, John is still lying low. His writing is competent, but I get very little response to the ideas we raise in class. . . . He's smart and informed. *Why* so quiet in class?"

In reviewing John's report card his tenth-grade advisor gave him some very valuable advice which needs no further comment. "I've told John to be tolerant of teachers who keep commenting on his 'quietness.' It is o.k. to be quiet—the world is too full of people who talk too much! We do appreciate his remarks when he feels like speaking, for his comments are thoughtful."

A four-year-old child told us that her friend Leah was not shy (as the teacher had said): "She only has a quiet voice!" Sometimes it is more important to accept what the child is and find ways to build the child's strengths around his or her personality style than to try to change the child to fit an image of the super extrovert, "All-American Preschooler."

Two Methods of Boosting Sociability

When your child would like to have more friends, be able to play more spontaneously with other children, and not be fearful of "people situations," we recommend you try two very different approaches. One of them changes the child's self-image through mental rehearsal of scenarios in which he or she plays the dominant role. The other changes the child's play behavior by being paired for short periods of play with a younger child.

From the earliest age, bedtime stories should occasionally include tales that combine fantasy with elements of reality in which the child is the hero or heroine. The scene may be set in your family's country of origin: "Over mountains too tall for an eagle to fly above, beyond seas filled with great white sharks that play gently with beautiful mermaids lies the island of Sicily." The main characters are family members, sometimes with slightly altered names and often royal stature (King Fillipo), with the child as prince or princess. There may be an alter-ego brother and/or sister, like Brünhilde or Clotilda who gets into trouble or does bad things that the good child must remedy. The child is described in the most extravagant terms: "Eyes as blue as the water of the Blue Grotto in Capri"; "skin as smooth as the finest silks from China"; "muscles as powerful as those of the Green Hulk"; "runs as swiftly as the fastest of animals, the cheetah," and so forth.

The core of the story is a problem to be solved by the child (with the imaginative assistance of the storyteller). As the problem is revealed, the adults are unable to come up with a solution, or have no volunteer for their plan of action: ". . .When from the back of the hall in the great castle a small hand was raised and a small voice said, 'Daddy, I will do it, I know what to do.' All eyes turned to see who was so brave to volunteer for this dangerous mission. It was little Zara! You are too young, my child, said the king. 'No, I can do it. Yes, I will do it,' said the child."

The plan was discussed, a course of action developed, and then it was successfully executed and praised. Over time, the child—initially listening passively—will often speak out and enter a dialogue with the storyteller. The child will say, "Daddy, I'll do it," or even alter the previously formulated game plan.

Some of the solutions to the problems require feats of daring as when the bad sisters Brünhilde and Clotilda cover Michelangelo's statue of David with mud. The princess must drive a crane, climb out on a railing, and clean the statue with an enormous toothbrush. Other problems arise when a real sibling's birthday presents are stolen and hidden at the bottom of the sea. The child must then swim far out to sea, call her friend the porpoise with a purpose to ask the starring starfish to point the way to the lost presents. Once retrieved, the party can go on and the sad child is made happy by her sister's good deed.

Still other stories have a blatantly social responsibility moral. There is the new child in class who cries every night because he has no friends, until one day a wonderful friend appears to say, "Hello, I would like you to play with me. What is your name?" And what is the name of the child who made that sad little boy so happy: "It is me, _____ (your child)!"

Through such stories we encourage children to develop action-oriented plans, to take the initiative, to be the focus of attention, to be assertive and independent yet always responsible. Their imaginative involvement in these confidence-building scenarios is rewarded by the other fantasy characters and also by the storyteller. It can be part of your shyness prevention program, or an effective way to teach social skills to your already shy child, as well as to give that child some self-esteem boosts.

We mentioned earlier the value of mixed-age socialization in which older shy children play with younger ones. Let's review briefly the recent research which supports the conclusion that a powerful and simple way to "rehabilitate socially withdrawn children" is by creating mixed-age play groups.

A team of University of Minnesota psychologists (Wyndol

Furman and Donald Rahe under the direction of Willard Hartup) studied twenty-four preschool-age children in seven day-care centers. From over two hundred children they had observed, twenty-four were singled out as "social isolates," those who talked or played with their peers less than a third of the time. These isolates were paired with a same-age peer, or a younger partner (by twelve to twenty months). If assigned to the control group, they were without a partner. The pairs were brought together for ten play sessions, each twenty minutes long, scheduled over a period of four to six weeks.

The classroom behavior of these children as well as all the others in the seven classes was then observed for a month. Neither the teachers nor the observers knew which children had been designated as social isolates.

Playing alone with a same-age peer increased the isolate's subsequent interaction in class. However, the big effect came from giving the shy children an opportunity to play alone with younger playmates. This doubled their frequency of interaction, which then reached the same level of social interaction as the nonisolate children.

The researchers conclude that the special ingredient was the one-on-one nature of the play situations with younger playmates that offered the opportunity to be socially assertive. They were allowed to practice leadership skills that were met with success from their nonthreatening and often openly approving younger admirers.

Parents can help their shy children by inviting a younger child of the same sex over to play, and then slowly progress to include older children of the same and opposite sex. It is not advisable to invite a bunch of kids over, put them into a room or backyard together and hope your shy child will play with them. The social competitiveness is too great and the situation requires more complex social skills than the shy child is likely to have. Think small and the shy child will stand taller.

The Preschool for Your Child

Without question, we recommend a preschool experience to help children develop social skills early in life. Here are some guidelines you might find useful in selecting the right school with an eye toward minimizing its shyness-eliciting potential for your child.

Observe the children before school starts, at recess, and when they are leaving school at the end of the day. Do they greet one another, smile, laugh, seem relaxed and to be enjoying themselves? Are there children on the periphery of the action, not drawn into the circle of friendship and play? Do children seem to be helping one another, playing in groups, or engaged in solitary activity?

Look for Structure

Too much structure stifles independence, too little is chaotic and scary for the shy child. A moderate amount of structure gives the child a predictable environment in which he or she has a stable role and where following the rules brings desirable rewards.

• Is there a lesson plan scheduled for each day?

• Are there small group activities and one-to-one pairings as part of structured team play and projects?

• What are the class rules and what happens if they are broken?

• Is the classroom environment well prepared to stimulate the child's curiosity?

• Is the teacher in control of the class?

• Do the children have an activity to begin as soon as they enter class rather than sit and wait for something to happen?

• Are children given choices of activities from a reasonable set of alternatives?

The Teacher

If your child is shy, you are going to want him or her to have a teacher that is sensitive to shyness and whose manner is one that will draw your child out. Here are the guidelines one such sensitive teacher furnished us with:

• The teacher should greet each child *individually*, using their names, as they come into the classroom. She should ask them how they are and comment on anything new about their looks. This gives the child some positive attention and makes him or her feel important. It also gives the teacher a chance to find out which side of the bed was jumped out of on that particular day.

• The teacher should make eye contact with each child when greeting them, and when speaking to one of them in class. Not only is this a way of giving positive attention, but it teaches a child by example to make eye contact with others.

• The teacher should get down to the children's level when talking to them. She should squat or sit in a small chair to make her more their size.

• She should be relaxed and should smile often.

• The sensitive teacher will invite, rather than order, the children to participate.

• She should allow the children to watch in order to warm up to a new situation.

• The teacher should generate a sense of warmth and respect, and be in control of the class.

• The teacher who is sensitive to the feelings of children, especially shy children, will not single out a child for criticism; she will also know when it is and isn't appropriate to single out a self-conscious child for any reason—even positive attention—in front of his or her peers.

• On the other hand, share time is one occasion when most children like attention and don't mind being singled out, as first, each child participates, and next, usually self-consciousness melts away when a child has something that he or she truly wants to share.

• The teacher should not reinforce shy behavior by giving a child too much attention when he or she is alone—the child may then behave shyly as an attention-getting device.

• The teacher should be sensitive to a child's need for special attention, and draw him or her out slowly, gradually easing the child into the group and then giving the child reinforcement for participating or responding to the other children.

Easing on Down the School Road

Once you have decided which preschool is right for your child, describe the school to him or her and then arrange for your child to visit at least once before starting school. Give the child a chance to roam around and inspect the school, the toys, and the play equipment, and to watch the other children at play. One mother who did this told us that her child protested rather vigorously when she asked him if he'd like to go to preschool, but after she took him to visit he couldn't wait to start, begging her daily to take him back.

Give the child as much information as possible about the basic rules and rituals necessary to start out on the right foot. For example, does a school bell signal line-up time; do you line up with a partner? The teacher might assign an older child to serve as a "peer advisor" for that first day. Also establish with the teacher the best plan of action if your child cries, clings, and pleads not to be abandoned. Should you stay each day for a shorter time or go "cold turkey," leaving the teacher or assistant teacher to take over?

Plan a special treat for every night of that first week of school. Hang up any school work the child brings home in a conspicuous place—for example, with magnets on the refrigerator door. Reinforce the process of trying, of attempting new things—not merely acceptable products.

The following questions may give you some insights into situations that may contribute to your child's feelings of shyness:

• Are you doing what you can to make your child feel secure, be independent, and take responsibility?

• Are your expectations realistic?

• Are you sending off the child each day dressed differently from his or her peers?

• Do you reward shy behavior by equating quietness with goodness?

• Does the *teacher* reward shy behavior for the same reason?

• Is some other child picking on your child? Ask the teacher.

• Is there some activity that may be making the child feel inadequate—something he or she doesn't feel he or she can do well?

• Does the teacher encourage your child to try new things? And does she reinforce the child for doing so?

• Is the teacher sensitive to shyness? Does she make attempts to draw your child out slowly?

• Do you get your child to school on time? Sometimes children feel very self-conscious when they usually come into class late.

• Is there something over which your child feels shame?

If you can determine that there is some situation in the classroom that is keeping your child's pattern of shyness in force, bring this to the teacher's attention. If someone is picking on your child, for example, the teacher may be unaware of it, so you need to tell her so she can put a stop to it.

You should talk to the teacher in any event. If your child is shy, the teacher needs to know this, and you need to have her cooperation in gently drawing your child out and helping to build up his or her confidence.

CHAPTER SIX

Dear Old Golden
Rule Days (from 6–12)

No matter what you've done thus far to give your child feelings of security and high self-esteem, the one fact of any child's life that can be a determinant in how confident he or she may be is *school*. Thus, what is really needed to conquer shyness is cooperation from the school and the people to whom we daily entrust the care of our sons and daughters.

There are, we have learned, some wonderfully sensitive teachers who go out of their way to make children feel good about themselves and minimize that barrier to learning—*shyness*—at every turn.

One teacher who was kind enough to write to us and describe how she tries to help her shy students told us: "I go out of my way to make sure these children feel important and well liked as individuals in their own right." She does it quietly, without making them feel different and without creating a sense in the other children that the shy ones are her favorites.

Each day, she told us, she makes a habit of speaking to the more reticent of her students individually, asking casual questions about what they did over the weekend or complimenting them on a new pair of shoes, a dress, or a shirt. And she's careful to avoid topics that could be threatening, to insure that these small conversations are positive.

This teacher knows how to draw out her shy ones by arranging for them to participate in lessons or activities with peers who are understanding and accepting, and she encourages other children to include them in their playground games.

She gives her shys plenty of praise and reinforcement whenever it's appropriate to do so.

Another teacher, sensitive to shyness, told us, "If a child is doing poorly with the lessons because he or she is too shy to ask questions, or too lacking in self-confidence to venture an answer—even on paper—I offer help privately. I also tell shy students to see me after class, under the pretext of their having left a sweater or lunch box behind. In time, the student will ask for help during class time."

In one third-grade class we observed, there were twenty-five students, and only one was obviously shy—and he was a Japanese boy who spoke very little English. When we commented on this absence of shyness in the classroom, the teacher told us that there were no major problems and what problems had existed at the start of the year had all but disappeared.

Not surprisingly, competition in this class was deemphasized, while helping each other and consideration for other people was emphasized.

The class was arranged in the old-fashioned style with the teacher leading the discussion from her desk at the head of the class. All of the children eagerly participated, and the teacher commended even those who volunteered wrong answers, which encouraged the students to take part with little risk of being embarrassed. The teacher also tried to make the shy students feel more comfortable about participating in class by giving them extra help in preparing a speech or presenting a project before the class.

With a gold-star teacher such as this one, it is no wonder that the only obviously shy student was the Japanese child, new to this country and struggling with language problems. And it's our guess that before the year's end, this teacher will draw that child out too.

"If it makes a child feel self-conscious, don't do it, is my rule," a male teacher of second grade told us. "If it is humiliating, demeaning, or puts a shy child in the limelight when he or she can't handle it, I back away. Nor do I force the shy child to get up and give a speech unless I have prepared that child and am sure he or she can be relatively comfortable, experiencing only a normal amount of stage fright—which I explain is something *everyone* experiences."

However, despite all the positive things we observed in classrooms, there is no question that school can be a breeding ground for low self-esteem, and hence shyness. In their outstanding book, *A Child's Journey*, psychologist Julius Segal and author Herbert Yahraes point out that the course of a child's development is dramatically affected by his or her emerging self-image, and that the child who feels confident and masterful will mature differently than the one who feels unsure and inadequate. They say that while it is true that many of a child's self-doubts arise from within, they "can either be reinforced or reduced by the outside world and other childhood anxieties might never take root were it not for the ego-destroying messages that key adult figures so cavalierly deliver to the young." And it is *in school*, say the authors, that "children's perceptions of their capacities and competence take hold."

"The power of a teacher to influence that image," they write, "is awesome." Many psychological forces are at work: the burning need to please an authority figure; the need to receive attention and reinforcement; the fact that the child is in a subservient role; the system of rewards and punishment that is perpetually evident. It is this combination of factors that exists in the classroom, the authors explain, that can mold a child's self-concept.

The power of the teacher is awesome. It is awesome, in part, because for the prime time of each weekday the teacher is a parent substitute, and as such, the young child looks to him or her for security and support.

How does a child cope then, when the anticipated source of

support turns out to be precisely the opposite? There are good teachers, we have noted, but there are also some teachers in any school system who simply are not well tuned to the needs of young children.

And whether a teacher is good or bad, the elementary school experience is one of constant evaluation and comparison, and a time when, in the name of order and conformity, spontaneity flies out the window—and childlike behavior can be translated into "bad" behavior. In *The Myth of the Happy Child*, psychologist Carole Klein says that children are continuously attacked in school for being a "baby." The contempt, she says, attached to the term fosters a child's own contempt for being what he or she is.

Furthermore, asking a child to do more than he or she is able to and then criticizing him or her for their helplessness, not only teaches that child to be ashamed of who he or she is, but undermines what the child feels capable of becoming. Klein writes, "Not only in its oppressive demands, but also through constant criticism that's so often a function of the role of a teacher does the school become a particular arena for experiencing shame."

And most important of all, school is where a child must learn to deal with the peer group. The child who has gone to preschool has an advantage in that he or she has had the opportunity to develop some social skills and learn to get along with others. However, many children start elementary school not knowing anyone else in the class, which can be rather frightening. And if a child has difficulty forming friendships, he or she is bound to be lonely and, quite possibly, if he or she is seen as different from the other children, the object not only of rejection but of ridicule.

A case in point that illustrates how the combination of forces can come negatively together, is Suzy. When she was in the first grade, her mother told us, this once outgoing child became very shy. Where once Suzy would bring a friend home to play, or play with neighbor children after school, she fell into a pattern of coming home from school and going directly to her room, shutting the door behind her. Often, Suzy's mother found her sprawled across the bed crying. When her mother would ask her what was wrong, Suzy would simply say, "The kids don't like me."

Shortly after Suzy fell into this pattern, her teacher telephoned Suzy's mother and told her that Suzy was failing in school and suggested they get together for a conference. It was at the conference, after the teacher showed Suzy's mother the poor work her daughter had been doing, that she told the mother, "And you've got to do something about her thumb sucking. I'm doing everything *I* can here in school." She then explained that several weeks before when she caught her sucking her thumb, she began to bring Suzy up to the front of the class every day and put her in a chair facing the rest of the children who were instructed to remind Suzy if she forgot and sucked her thumb. The reminding, Suzy's mother learned, came in the form of "Suzy is a baby, born in the *navy*," and "Suzy," who wore thick glasses, "is a four-eyed thumb sucker."

Suzy's mother was aghast. But the riddle of Suzy's behavior was solved. She removed Suzy from the class, after complaining to the principal, and set about reversing the self-esteem-robbing process that had been set in motion by Suzy having been held up to ridicule, and scorned and rejected by her peers.

We'd like to tell you that Suzy's story ended happily at that juncture. But in the new classroom, Suzy's shyness continued to interfere with her ability to concentrate, and she had little confidence that she could do any of the work. Sometimes she wouldn't even try to answer the questions, while other times, so unsure of the answers she put down, she'd erase them until the paper was all but torn. And she never asked for help. After much talk about holding Suzy back, she was promoted to the second grade.

Shortly after she entered the second grade, another parent-teacher conference was called, and Suzy's mother was informed that in order for Suzy to catch up she would have to receive some special education. And, in the state of California, for a child to be placed in a special education class, the law requires that he or she be classified as "educationally handicapped."

By the time Suzy was in the third grade, she was desperately shy. She bore the label "educationally handicapped" perfectly demonstrating daily that indeed she was. Suzy was different. She wore glasses; everyone remembered that she had sucked her thumb and although she didn't any longer, she continued to be teased about it. And, Suzy was "a dummy."

To us, this is a tragic case of the erosion of a child's self-esteem that so easily could have been avoided. Suzy was, and is, one of those fortunate children who comes from a stable and loving home and whose only "physical defect" has been that she was nearsighted. A pretty child, she even looked pretty wearing glasses. And, in fact, the very children who, at the encouragement of Suzy's first-grade teacher, had come to call her "four eyes," had originally complimented her when she first got her glasses. The power of a teacher to erode a child's self-confidence is overwhelming. And the power of a teacher to turn otherwise nice children into tormentors is frightening.

However, the power of parents to repair the damage ultimately can be inspiring. Suzy is in high school now, and she doesn't have a shy bone in her body. And, she's no longer "educationally handicapped."

The Golden Rule

Added to all the potential ways to damage a child's self-esteem that can lead to shyness is the very real fact that shyness may be fostered by some teachers (and parents) who value the quiet, nonaggressive, passive child. Consider this teacher's memo: "Adam's first test grade was C+, but because he was talking during the second test he received an F. I'd appreciate your help on this to be quiet (sic)."

Silence can be so golden to some teachers that they truly do value it more than academic performance. Adam had been behind in math and had studied hard for his exam. His goal was to make an A in the class. After that experience, he lost interest in math.

Naturally, teachers must maintain order in the classroom so they can teach, but *teaching* and *learning* ought to be goals that have a higher priority than absolute silence, and we question the justice of giving a low academic grade for deportment, rather than for performance in a subject.

Often the need (or reverence) for silence in a classroom is such that it conveys the old messages, familiar to us all, "Children should be seen and not heard," and "Speak only when spoken to." And in most instances, it is not balanced by periods when children can speak freely and conversationally. They speak when spoken to *by the teacher*, and generally only when they raise their hands and happen to be called upon to do so.

Recalling her experience when she started the first grade, a high school senior told us, "I remember precisely what started my shyness. I had dropped my pencil and was asking my neighbor if she could reach it when this harridan in a pink suit swooped down upon me, yanked me out of my seat, and shook me 'for talking.' I was absolutely mortified. From that moment on, I knew that to stay out of trouble meant you stayed quiet. So I did just that."

For the already shy child who has been told all of his young life, "Sit still" and "Be quiet," entry into elementary school, at best, continues the original program; at worst, depending on whether or not a child has other attributes that set him apart from his peers, it intensifies it.

Silence in elementary school is a golden rule that combines with other golden rules to formulate, or define, the ideal schoolchild: quiet and well behaved; responsive but not assertive; bright but not precocious; and physically attractive. Often, elementary school is like solitary confinement: There are long periods of enforced silence, of "heads down on desks" for unwanted (and impossible to achieve) naps. Children's almost boundless energy is severely constrained in the interest of order. They listen to the teacher give orders or instructions but are given little training in listening to their peers and in carrying on intelligent and interesting conversations. This pattern, cut in elementary school, forms a social straitjacket that becomes tighter with each year of schooling through college.

The Future of a Child's Present

Perhaps unintentionally, traditional schooling prepares most children to become followers, to obey authority without question and become cogs in the political and economic machinery of the nation. The goal of turning out "manageable students" is further facilitated by a subtle form of conditioning. One of the major, unheralded achievements of education is the transformation of a child's time sense. Most young children are present-oriented. They feel and act in response to experiences in the here-and-now. They live in the present moment, with all its spontaneity, impulsiveness, and unpredictability. Much of the charm of youth resides in that "expanded present" temporal orientation. Schooling suppresses the present in favor of the future and with due respect paid to the past. Elementary school children must learn to delay gratification, to do boring tasks because of the desired consequences of work successfully completed.

Intrinsic motivation—the joy of doing something for its own sake—is destroyed by imposing a system of extrinsic rewards for doing what someone else wants to have done, when and where they want it. Working to earn gold stars for rote learning of multiplication tables is mental preparation for working later on in life to earn a salary for doing a repetitive, uninspiring job in a factory or business office.

This future-oriented time sense poses a special problem for shy people. Even as children, they live too much in a world of "what will happen if I do X?" Anxiety, social or otherwise, is characterized by a dread of anticipated—future—consequences for one's acts. Shy people are unable to enjoy the pleasures of the moment because they believe someone will have to pay the piper, and guess who that will be? Their excessive concern for social approval focuses their attention on what means must be used to gain desired goals.

Teaching a child future-orientation is obviously a necessary part of mature development. However, we object to its over-reaching sphere of influence that deprives children (and us grown-ups too) of the ability to laugh at nothing, to see beauty in a ladybug's ambling, or exquisite delight in just being close to one's best friend. Shy children need to have their sense of the present expanded rather than subjugated to the anticipation of the future. They think too much and act too little. Parents and teachers should recognize the many ways in which, by their language ("What are you going to be when you grow up?"), their actions, and their example, they pay homage to the future and disdain the present. And they should acknowledge the costs shy children pay for this conditioning.

Measurements of a Child's Worth

Equating physical attractiveness with virtue is nothing new, of course. Most of us became acquainted with this prejudice while still at our mother's knee, listening to stories of beautiful Snow White and Cinderella and wicked ugly witches and stepmothers. Illustrating that this is not just the stuff of which fairy tales are made, but instead a human response by adults in the modern world, are the findings of Ellen Berscheid and

Elaine Walster. Writing in *Psychology Today*, they say, for example, that when a group of adults was shown a collection of children's pictures and asked to point out which of them caused a disturbance in the class, they were more likely to point to the least attractive child. Further, this particular child was thought to be more dishonest. How adults might *act* on such a prejudice is seen by the finding that cute children were likely to be dealt with less severely than the ones who were regarded as ugly.

Finally, there were indications that academic grades given to children can be influenced by their attractiveness. "For all the talk about character and inner values," say Berscheid and Walster, "we assume the best about pretty people. And from grade school on, there's almost no dispute about who's beautiful."

After decrying a system to test children's popularity in the classroom, psychologist James Dobson, author of *Hide or Seek*, explains that the children most likely to be popular with their peers turn out to be those who are the most physically attractive. But even more significant than that, he writes, is that unfortunately *teachers* are products of the same society which molds the values and attitudes of everyone else: "They are often repelled by the physically unattractive child and drawn to the cutie. . . ." Sadly then, it cannot be assumed that all teachers will give the children who need it the most support and reinforcement.

In the eyes of some teachers and adults, however, beauty is only one measure of a child's worth and integrity. When we went to observe in third-, fourth-, and fifth-grade classes, it became immediately apparent that even sensitive teachers behaved differently toward those students who appeared to display better-than-average intelligence.

In one class, for example, when the teacher worked with the "enriched group," she stressed creativity, continually reminding the students, "Don't be afraid to respond in a manner different than usual. Allow yourselves to break the barriers." A flying pencil was laughingly dismissed with, "You guys are really getting carried away." Answers that were obviously incorrect were given the benefit of the doubt as the teacher observed, "I never thought of it that way."

In contrast, when the same teacher dealt with the "slow" group, she continually told the children, "Now there is one and only one answer to this question." The atmosphere was generally restrictive and when students spoke out of turn, she admonished, "Now stop it and begin working." Horseplay that might have resulted in a pencil flying across the room was neither tolerated nor laughed at.

In all but one of the classes in which we observed, we also found that those children the teachers perceived as being brighter were assigned more prestigious jobs in the classroom, such as room monitor or messenger, while the ones who displayed less intelligence or shy behavior were rarely, if ever, assigned any job at all.

Proving that there are no absolutes when it comes to how shyness is seen in the classroom is the simple fact that there are some teachers who seem to foster it as a means of controlling children and keeping them quiet, and still others who value assertive displays of intelligence. In any event, all of the teachers observed during this particular study labeled the *less* intelligent members of their class as *more* shy.

Making matters worse for the shy ones is that often teachers don't give any strokes or feedback to them for the efforts they *do* make, and even on those occasions when they manage to break out of their shyness and attempt to participate, they still may be treated differently than the not shys or go unnoticed by the teacher. We found, for example, that in all but one class those children who were not very assertive—and who we felt were shy—were virtually ignored when they were finally able to muster up enough courage to raise their hands to ask a question or offer a comment. We also found that when the children would line up at a teacher's desk to ask for help, all but the most assertive went back to their seats—after being pushed to the back of the line—with their questions unanswered.

Thus we saw not only how shyness interferes with the individual learning process, but also how it can mask intelligence and keep in motion a cycle of nonreinforcement on the part of the teacher.

We believe that otherwise intelligent children may well have been seen by the teachers as not very bright, an idea that wasn't lost on the children, but instead underscored by the teachers' seeming indifference. Such indifference quite possibly could result in children not asking for help in the future and not getting it, and thus falling behind enough to make the teachers' assessments of them come true.

An interesting experiment that showed how teachers can influence a child's self-esteem by their perceptions of individual children's intelligence was conducted by Robert Rosenthal and Lenore Jacobson. Rosenthal and Jacobson gave a battery of intelligence tests to a group of grade school children, telling them that the results would be fed into a computer and then revealed to their teachers.

When the teachers were told which of the students in the class were the brightest they were quite surprised because most of those so identified were very ordinary students. Nevertheless, they accepted the outcome of the test.

This new information created a dramatic change in the attitude of the teachers, who now showed respect for the "brightest" students and were more confident that the students would succeed. The result of the respect and confidence the teachers displayed was remarkable. In a follow-up study, it was revealed that these formerly ordinary students' I.Q.'s were substantially higher than those of the other students.

The experimenters then told the teachers that no computer had been used, that the test had never been scored, and that the "brightest" 20 percent had been *chosen at random*. The stunning change in the students' performance then must have been a result of the way the teachers viewed them and conveyed to them what was expected because they were bright.

This is a fascinating example of the power of prejudice, to be sure. It is also a fascinating example of the ways in which a teacher can *elicit* displays of intelligence and how those elicitations can foster feelings of self-confidence that ultimately positively affect a child's performance, which in turn results in more feelings of self-confidence. All of this raises the interesting question: If a teacher's positive evaluation of a child can produce positive results, then what sort of results do a teacher's negative evaluations produce—poor performance? the low self-concept that leads to shyness?

Once Over, Not So Lightly

The worst form of negative evaluation is physical abuse. Publicly punishing a child may stop his "allegedly undesirable behavior" but it also has some long-term, even more undesirable consequences. The side effects of this aversive control include development of a negative attitude toward school, teacher, or learning in general; truancy; vandalism; humiliation before one's peers and shyness.

It is generally assumed that corporal punishment in our schools is administered rarely, and then with a light hand, to older students whose disruptive behavior is a threat to the teacher and classroom order. Recent research evidence declares these to be false assumptions. The primary targets of physical abuse by teachers are little boys in grades one through four. Their punishment is often severe, including beating and even kicking.

Some Recommended Tactics

On the basis of these studies and our observations we recommend the following tactics:

• Don't label your child as "shy" to the teacher (and others), but as "cautious," "a deep thinker," "respectful of others' opinions." A quiet child can be immensely valued as a *good listener*—a prize for every actor. Let the child see you listen well to his or her opinion or description. Listen critically, then make explicit how you assumed a "posture of attentive listening" by leaning forward a little. You made eye contact much of the time, looked away occasionally to think about what you heard. Approval was conveyed without interrupting, using nods, simple gestures, "hmm, hmm," "really," "that's interesting," (or more in vogue) "awesome." Advanced good listeners paraphrase what they've heard to be sure they've understood well, summarize, ask a question that will show they've paid attention, and also encourage the speaker to speak on. Finally, a good listener ends with a compliment that will make the talker eager to come back for more, "I really enjoyed hearing what you think about that." Even an elementary school child can be taught how to listen well and to do so with greater discrimination as he or she matures.

• Teach your child how to compliment the teacher, one stroke every week will win over most teacher's hearts. "The time goes so fast when we're having so much fun in your class" said a not-shy second-grader to his beaming teacher. "You read stories in such an interesting way," said another child to her delighted teacher. Ask your child what the teacher did, said, or how he or she looked, that the child thought was good. Then turn it into a compliment that the child practices on you—and delivers when appropriate in private to the teacher.

• The whole world loves an honest compliment and few of us ever get enough of them. Compliment your shy child whenever you can do so, solicit them in return and reinforce any attempts of the child to compliment others: "Jenny, you paint so nice," "I like your tie, Brian," "Tina is the best dancer in ballet class." And of course, when a compliment comes the child's way, "Thank you" is always the most simple and appropriate recognition of its existence. (In later chapters we'll outline suggestions for advanced compliment giving and receiving.)

• Decide whether or not you want to allow a teacher to beat your child in school. If not, make that decision clear and in writing to the teacher and the principal. Or at least you should state necessary conditions such as, never publicly, only when adequately forewarned and the reason for the punishment explained. There are many alternatives to physical punishment, among them, loss of privileges, private conferences, class discussion of acceptable standards of behavior and shared responsibility for discipline. Of course, most "discipline problems" vanish under the warm gaze of attention by the teacher—or parent. They also diminish with interesting curricula, challenging activities, and reasonable rules fairly enforced. Punishment reflects the adult's failure to create the right conditions for a given child to act in effective, desirable ways.

• And what makes punishment in school a "no-no," as far as we are concerned, does so for the same reasons at home. When you hit your child you are admitting you've lost your ability to control his or her behavior using positive incentives and rewards. A child who learns to be fearful of being physically abused by a parent may be untrusting of all authority—a hallmark of the shy person.

Sometimes the Solution May Be Part of the Problem

There are, no doubt, many reasons for "learning difficulties," and we know that shyness is one of them. Typically, as we have seen, shy children don't ask for help when they need it, don't volunteer information, don't take risks, and often their shyness causes them difficulty in concentrating on what's going on in the classroom.

Whatever the cause of a child's learning disability, many of the steps taken to help a child who is falling behind cannot fail to have a negative impact on his or her self-image, making an already shy child shyer—or, possibly setting shyness in motion in a not-shy child.

For example, research on retention (or nonpromotion) has shown that holding children back from the next grade is generally ineffective as a means to helping children "catch up." Numerous observers have found that not only doesn't retention help, it can make it even more difficult for children to move on to the next grade. G. G. Malinson and J. Weston found that children who are not promoted tend to achieve less than they would have had they been promoted. They are less motivated and tend to be more maladjusted. Studies conducted by Philip E. Kraus seem to indicate that children who are held back today are likely to be tomorrow's dropouts. Obviously, holding a child back can be damaging to his or her self-esteem and can set in motion a program of continuing failure that causes that self-esteem to continually drop. As one mother of four girls told us, "I would never allow any of my children to be held back. I was held back, I never caught up, and I never got over it. I've felt inadequate and shy most of my life because of it." The mother of a now grown son told us that she allowed her child to be held back in the seventh grade. "He is shy, and I don't know for certain that it's because he was held back. But he *is* shy, and he dropped out of high school in his junior year."

An alternative approach is to promote a "slow-learning" child, but provide him or her with special classes or help. As we have seen from the example of Suzy, in some school systems, to facilitate this requires selecting an appropriate label—"educationally handicapped," "hyperkinetic," "hyperactive," "emotionally disturbed," "dyslexic," "learning disabled," "retarded," to name just a few—terms, says psychologist Dr. Louise Bates Ames of the Gessell Institute of Human Development, "that are vastly overused." And, according to Julius Segal and Herbert Yahraes, used incorrectly.

Furthermore, say Segal and Yahraes, there can be negative side effects. Children, they argue, are the members of society most likely to become victimized by labels. "In the schools especially, our young are too readily branded as 'retarded,' 'disturbed,' 'delinquent,' or worse." Such labels, they continue, are often stigmatizing to the child, and begin a process by which the child may be removed unfairly from normal social contacts with other children. "Worse yet, labeled children may ultimately incorporate into their self-concepts the brandings affixed to them and may come so to believe in their validity that life becomes a self-fulfilling prophecy."

Shyness and Sensory Defects

Recent studies in New York City public schools have revealed that a sizable number of children placed in special classes for the retarded turn out not to have a learning disability, but rather a sight or hearing defect that has gone undetected. It is easy to understand how a child might appear to be unintelligent if he or she couldn't follow instructions or decode the problems to be solved because they weren't seen or heard properly.

It has been called to our attention that a similar distortion occurs between shyness and sensory deficits. Youngsters, or even adults who are hard of hearing in one or both ears, may miss out on names during introductions, or key comments in a discussion. If they are aware of their hearing they might nevertheless be embarrassed to admit this "defect." But the consequences are worse when others mistakenly judge the hearing deficient person as disinterested or slow, and the person finds it awkward to request that something be repeated. In a number of instances such a process has contributed to the development of shyness and avoidance of social situations.

In recalling his childhood shyness, a brilliant radio engineer we spoke with told us that he became shy because his vision was so bad that he was never certain that his perception of written material or what was written on the blackboard was correct, so he didn't participate much in class. He explained that he didn't want to display his "stupidity" by comment or asking for clarification. We would imagine that a child with deficient hearing might react similarly and become not just self-conscious over a hearing problem, but self-conscious over a "learning problem" as well.

Shyness itself poses a handicap similar to those physical handicaps that interfere with learning. We know shy children of average intelligence who are judged to be "slow," "unmotivated," or "distractable." They appear so to teachers because they are often preoccupied with negative, anxiety-based thoughts, fears of being put on the spot, and so forth. To the extent that they are focusing on such internal messages, they cannot attend as completely to incoming sources of information. In this way, shyness limits the information-processing capacity of the child. Then, realizing that they should know the answer to a math problem, or must *"repetez s'il vous plaît"*— but can't—their communication apprehension increases even more. It is thus important for teachers and parents to recognize the ways in which shyness may give a false view of a child's ability or motivation.

A different perspective on labels comes from the People's Republic of China. Psychologists and educators who visit Chinese schools and inquire about classes for "retarded children" are told that there are *no* retarded children. In China, they are told, there are of course children who need more attention from the teacher, or who require special lesson plans better synchronized to their optimal learning pace. But the *children* are not retarded, it is the educational system that does not recognize this truth, that is retarded.

The message for us is clear. Don't be so eager to put negative labels on the child. Not only do they set the child apart as "different," they also blame the child for the problem behavior while taking the school system, the family, or the society off the hook for their contribution to the undesirable behavior. In other words, ask not what your child has failed to do for the system, but how the system has failed your child.

Another way children get labeled by teachers is through their permanent records that follow them through school. For instance, a kindergartener may be a difficult child for a particular teacher, so the teacher enters onto the child's record that he was "hard to handle," "inattentive," "overactive," "shy," or some other negative description of his behavior in her class. This follows a child and he or she never really gets a chance to start fresh with a new teacher, because before he or she puts one foot into the new teacher's class, very likely that teacher will have already formed an opinion of that particular child. And it just could be that the child really is not all that the previous teacher has cracked him or her up to be, but instead that this teacher and this child had bad chemistry. And even when the teacher's assessment is correct, it doesn't take into account what else might have been going on in a child's life that may have elicited this behavior, and the situation could be, the next year, altogether different.

Parents should request the right to inspect their children's permanent records periodically, and to have deleted from them comments injurious to their children's progress in school.

Because of the damage that negative labels can cause, whenever possible, do not allow your child to be labeled. If this is necessary for a child to be put in a remedial class, get another opinion. One mother of a sixth-grader told us that agreeing to having her son labeled "educationally handicapped" was the worst mistake she ever made. "I definitely think it contributed to his shyness," she told us. "And long after the label no longer applied, he still thought of himself in those terms, often referring to himself as 'a dummy' or 'a loser.' " An alternative suggested by this mother who wished she'd chosen it is private tutoring. But all too often, well meaning parents become their child's worst enemy by applying one little label that sticks to the child. Consider the following example:

"I have a problem with my teen-age son, Dr. Zimbardo," said an executive at NBC-TV. "He's terribly shy with girls, even though he's a good-looking kid. He doesn't have many close friends and spends a lot of time alone, even though he's a swell guy once you get to know him. I wonder if I had something to do with causing his problem. You see, when he was around nine or ten, for some reason I can't remember now, I had this nickname for him—'Dummy.' It's not as bad as it sounds, because I didn't mean it that way. It was just a term of endearment. But then his brothers started using it and it kind of stuck."

Would you believe an allegedly intelligent, loving parent could do such a thing, allow it to continue, and then wonder whether being called "Dummy" by dear old dad and the big brothers could damage one's ego? Unfortunately, it happens more often than it should.

Children's television programs further validate the use of labels to designate someone as inferior or different. Even the usually sensitive writers of "Sesame Street" occasionally slip and someone gets called "stupid." Your child should be made to be vigilant in reporting to you the use of such "bad words"—who said them, about whom, and in what circumstances. One by-product of this surveillance of negative labels is your child will be less likely to use them on others, or when thinking about him or herself.

We are in the process of collecting evidence to demonstrate that children who described themselves as shy are more likely than not shys to see the causes of a variety of problems as the fault of people rather than the result of situational factors. In this way they become more intolerant of others (and of themselves). For example, would your child pick the *a* situational option or the *b* intolerant option:

1. Mary lost her coat. Why?
   a. Somebody else took her coat by mistake.
   b. Mary is forgetful.
2. Jimmy dropped the dishes. Why?
   a. The cat suddenly ran in front of him.
   b. Jimmy is dumb.
3. Sally slipped and fell down. Why?
   a. There was water on the ground that made her slip.
   b. Sally is clumsy.

When the labels come from other children, you really *can* do something about it. We parents are told so often not to get involved in our children's battles that we forget what that really means and how to apply that rule. It is one thing to continually protect a child in an evenly matched squabble, but quite another to jump in when a child is being treated as a scapegoat by several other children. The first question a parent should ask when this happens at school is, "Why is this being allowed?" It should be asked of the teacher and possibly even the principal. And then either or both of them should be told it won't be permitted.

For example, if several children are calling your child a name such as "four eyes," "fatso," or "ugly," those children should be reprimanded by the teacher—or, by the principal, if necessary. And, if necessary, the matter should be brought to the attention of the parents by either the teacher or the principal.

That it is being handled by the school takes it out of the category of parental overprotection and interference. And being told by teachers and principals that ganging up on a child won't be permitted carries tremendous impact.

It benefits everyone involved. The child who is being taunted is not only relieved of the torture, but reinforced by knowing he's protected from unfair attack (which can have the added benefit of teaching a child respect and trust of authorities instead of fear); and the children who are doing the taunting receive a lesson in values.

But the major point we want to emphasize here is: Don't allow anyone to negatively label your child, and don't do it yourself, and of course, don't allow your child to be labeled as "shy."

Paradoxically, in a book on shyness, we would like our readers not to label others as "shy." It is too global, too vague, and too negative. It is also not something that is observable, but inferred from what you do see. Better to describe accurately how the child responds to particular situations than to use shyness as an umbrella to cover up all that is happening. For example, "You don't look people in the eye when you are talking to them, and that makes them feel uncomfortable." "When you go into a new situation, you don't say 'hello' or ask if you can join in the game with the other children. It would be good to do that." In this way, we help prescribe the cure as we give our diagnosis.

The Silent Prison of Shyness

> Heaven lies about us in our infancy!
> Shades of the prison-house begin to close
> upon the growing boy (and girl).
>
> —*William Wordsworth*

All too often, it seems as if that charming, cute, lovable baby who could do no wrong becomes transformed into a grade school child who can do no right. Does the child change or do our demands and standards change? Obviously both, but it appears to most adults that the child has done the changing for the worst—despite our best efforts to the contrary.

Observations of parent-child and teacher-child contacts over these years of rapid change make us aware of the major responsibility the elders must bear for what their child becomes, over and above the developmental changes that govern the transition from infancy to boyhood and girlhood. We are less loving, or at least less openly expressive of our positive feelings toward the child than we were toward the baby. We become more punitive and threatening, shouting, deriding, complaining, and hitting as the child becomes more independent and less helpless.

If the "twos" appear "terrible" to parents, imagine how "sorry" life appears from the "six and over" years to children. Parents become prison guards who are constantly making up and enforcing rules to limit the child's freedom. "Don't do this," "You can't do that," "How many times must I tell you you will be punished if . . . ," "loss of privileges for a week," and the litany goes on. Parents speak to their own children in terms and tones they would not think of using on any other human being! Indeed, it is not excessive to use the prisoner-guard metaphor to characterize the parent-child (and later teacher-pupil) relationship. Rules replace reason and discussion, roles replace personalities, commands replace democratic negotiation, and punishment for rule violation replaces incentives of love.

Consider the analogy of the "good prisoner" to the shy child who grows up in a psychologically coercive prison. Prisoners don't volunteer information, don't initiate contacts with authorities, are suspicious of others who are different in any way, come to rely upon a highly structured environment and feel uneasy in permissive settings, and they usually obey orders.

A checklist of what teachers have told us to look for when observing a child in class or other social settings includes a number of items which describe the shy child as comparable to the prisoner. Is your child:

• reluctant to initiate conversation or activities, add new ideas, volunteer or ask questions?

• reluctant to impose structure on situations that are ambiguous, by means of questions, rules or physical rearrangement of the elements?

• reluctant to talk as much as not-shy children with classmates, allowing more silent periods to develop, and interrupting less than other children?

• unable to handle permissive situations, such as dancing?

• more likely to have special problems when the guidelines are not spelled out?

• less likely to use hand gestures than others?

• more likely to spend time in his or her seat, and less likely to wander around and talk to other children?

• more likely to obey orders without question and rarely be troublesome?

Imagine you are heading a prison reform commission and you must observe how humanely your child is being treated in your home and in school. Try distancing yourself to be as objective as possible. How often is the child made to feel inadequate and inferior instead of competent and desirable? How much coercion is used to elicit specific responses from the child instead of making requests with explanations of why? How frequently is the child ignored and not spoken to directly instead of being given a fair share of the conversation?

From this perspective of "detached concern," we'd like you to evaluate how much and in what ways the school is contributing to your child's shyness versus other forces at home and in the neighborhood.

Up Against the School Wall

First of all, ask your child what he or she thinks of the teacher: Does he or she feel comfortable with the teacher? Is the teacher friendly? Is the teacher friendly with your child? Does your child feel the teacher is helpful?

And then, from your observations in class, answering the following questions will help you to evaluate how sensitive your child's current teacher is to the needs of children, and how sensitive he or she may be to shy children in particular.

1. Does the teacher single children out in ways that appear to make them feel self-conscious or ill at ease? For either criticism or praise?

We have learned, from talking to a number of students, that children may experience feelings of shyness when being singled out for *any* reason—even when being complimented. One college student, for example, told us that her second grade teacher consistently held her up to the class as a model of what a good student is. Not only did this make her feel shy, she said, but "It was a double whammy because I could tell that the other kids resented me for being 'teacher's pet.' "

Notice when a teacher singles out a child for punishment, or makes a spectacle of him or her, as did Suzy's teacher. If a teacher does this with a child other than yours when you're in the classroom, it's safe to speculate that he or she would do it with *your* child when you're not there.

2. Does the teacher make comparisons between a student and his or her "brighter" brothers or sisters that the teacher may have taught in previous school years?

It's bad enough to make comparisons between students in a classroom, but still worse is the sort of comparisons that are sometimes made by the same teacher having taught more than one child in a family. One woman told us about the problems this created for her younger sister: "My sister Mary was not the 'bright, genius type' that I was . . . and the poor kid not only had to follow in my footsteps, but had the same teachers throughout grammar and high school. She'd get, 'And your sister, Joan, did so well. What's wrong with you?' Now *that* makes a person go into a shell faster than anything. Mary, not surprisingly, is quite shy."

When a teacher does this, obviously, he or she is not at all sensitive to a child's self-esteem or the problem of shyness.

3. Does the teacher make an effort to decrease the number of unessential and potentially painful activities, such as the distribu-

tion of valentines or party invitations, when all children are not included?

Unless parents and teachers are especially sensitive to this, the most attractive and popular children in a class will receive the most valentines, while some children will receive only a few—or, none at all. No doubt, long after the fun of the party has been forgotten by the more popular kids, those who are less popular will carry the pain of one more unhappy piece of evidence that they aren't worthy. The same goes for distributing party invitations in class when all but a few children are being invited.

4. Is the teacher able to control the class?

We think it is important to children's feelings of security that the adult who is responsible for them—be it parents *or* teachers—be in control. When he or she is not, children being children will take advantage of the situation, which really isn't good for them, to say nothing of the fact that it interferes with the learning process. In short, the teacher who is able to control his or her class is the one who inspires confidence in his or her students.

5. Is the teacher given to displays of temper?

You may never witness a loss of temper firsthand, but then again you may. We have been told of a teacher who arranges her class in a circle and when a child speaks out of turn he is sent to a chair in the middle and subjected to a rampage from the teacher. On other occasions, this same teacher throws chairs across the room when a student acts up. Needless to say, this practice makes the children very nervous. As one eleven-year-old told us, "You just never know when it's going to be you. And sometimes you think she might break your arm or something."

6. Does the teacher have realistic expectations of each child?

In the *Myth of the Happy Child*, psychologist Carole Klein tells the story of six-year-old Robert. It seemed that Robert couldn't tie his shoelaces without the teacher's help. But six-year-olds, the teacher maintained, are "supposed" to be able to tie their shoes. If enough of them in Robert's class could demonstrate that they had mastered this skill and it was important to the teacher, Robert couldn't fail to see it that way too—and his inability to accomplish this task as evidence of incompetence. In Robert's case, his teacher responded to the situation by heaving heavy and exaggerated sighs, and in a tone of abject weariness meant to imply utter disdain, she would call on another child to help tie Robert's shoes for him. Robert would then sit and suffer the giggling and jeering of his peers. As Klein points out, "So powerful a force can school be in a child's response to his own development, that it can take precedence over the family's more sympathetic atmosphere." Although Robert's mother laughs and kisses him when he confesses his failure, saying, "Who cares about such a silly thing?" and "I promise you by the time you go to college you'll know how to tie your shoes," Robert is not comforted—for "as surely as Robert knows his name he knows that the boy named Robert will never be smart enough to go to college."

Such humiliations remain with children long after they have managed to reverse the "failure" that inspired them, and there are no rewards in accomplishment when the motivation has been to avoid disgrace, which in Robert's case, wasn't avoided. By singling out this child, the teacher may well have set in motion a pattern of shyness that would follow Robert throughout his time in elementary school.

7. *Does the teacher allow children to taunt or tease other children in hurtful ways, such as making fun of them for physical differences? Does he or she allow several children to gang up on one child?*

When a teacher lets this happen, as Robert's teacher most certainly did, not only is he or she insensitive to *shyness*, but that teacher is insensitive, period. Furthermore, the classroom should be a place where our children learn something about values and social skills. Clearly, this is not the way they learn about either.

8. Does the teacher encourage free expression and encourage all of the children to participate by democratically responding when they raise their hands to ask a question or offer an opinion? Or does he or she seem to recognize the same students over and over again?

It stands to reason that if a child is frequently recognized by the teacher and reinforced, the child who is infrequently, or never, given the same recognition isn't. That child can quite easily internalize a sense that what he or she has to say isn't worth listening to.

On the other hand, when a teacher encourages participation of all of the children, he or she creates an environment in which the children feel comfortable and feel that what they have to offer is important.

And certainly when a teacher doesn't respond to the needs of children who need help with the lessons, he or she is not teaching, let alone doing anything to help draw the shy ones out.

9. A difficult question to answer is: Is there a classroom scapegoat?

If, after observing several times in class, you notice one child being criticized or reprimanded and sense that the teacher doesn't like him or her, the chances are this child is the teacher's scapegoat. A *good* teacher who has bad chemistry with a particular child will recognize it and may temper the temptation to pick on that child; however, one teacher told us that the healthy answer to such a problem is to level with the principal and have the child put in another class. "I couldn't take the chance," she told us, "that I wouldn't pick on one boy in my class simply because our personalities clashed. So I did us both a favor. His new teacher says she thinks he's a great little guy."

We tend to feel that when a teacher, given the choice, chooses to allow a child he or she dislikes to remain in class, it may be because that particular teacher *needs* a scapegoat. Studies into the dynamics of child abuse reveal that the one dangerous thing about people who need scapegoats is that if they lose theirs, they find another. Know that in the classroom, *your* child may be a potential target—especially if shyness makes him or her vulnerable.

Your answers to these questions, hopefully, have given you insights into whether your child's current school environment is one that inspires confidence or fosters shyness. If you feel that it is the latter, we advise arranging to have your child put in another classroom, if possible. We also advise that you observe the new class *in advance* of your child's move.

We appreciate that the size of the class pretty well determines how much a teacher can help those children he or she has identified as being shy. In a class of fifty or sixty students, children can easily get lost in the shuffle, the shy ones can recede further into the background, and there are fewer opportunities for children to practice verbal skills through participation. And there are more people to laugh when a mistake is made than in a smaller class, say, of twenty. The large classroom, increasingly prevalent in our public schools, may not only make it harder for our children to do well scholastically, but may foster shyness which, coming full cycle, inhibits the learning process, fostering more feelings of low self-esteem.

Perhaps when all is said and done, the best we parents can hope for is that teachers will pay close attention to the sage advice offered by a sixth grade boy. When Philip Kraus asked children to answer in writing, the question, "If I were a teacher . . .," this child wrote:

"My class rules would be:

1. Let them have a talking period twice a day.

2. Don't be cruel with them they are only children.

3. Don't only teach them but have fun with them.

4. Let everybody be one big happy family. Don't let anyone be put out. Remember everyone is a life itself and everyone wants to be wanted at school and at home. Thank you."

Dealing with Teachers

After talking with a number of parents it became apparent that many parents see teachers and other school officials as absolute authorities who know more about children in general, and *their* children in particular, than parents possibly can. So, regardless of what a parent may feel, there is a tendency to defer to the "experts," and let a teacher's pronouncements overrule a parent's better intuition and judgments.

Making matters more complicated is that some parents, especially with their first children, are intimidated by school personnel. As one mother remarked, "When I first started going to parent-teacher conferences, I felt like I was six years old. My daughter's teacher was *my* teacher, the principal of the school was *my* principal, and I'd better behave myself. It didn't help that I sat in a tiny chair, while the teacher sat at her desk, looking down at me." And she, like many parents, said she worried about being evaluated as a mother, which she felt put her at a distinct disadvantage.

It helps, in your dealings with teachers and other people at the school, to be aware of the fact that they can arouse such feelings of anxiety, and then remind yourself that a teacher can't possibly know more about a child who is one of thirty or more and been in that teacher's class for only a few weeks or months, than the parent who has been living with the child from the moment of birth. You know your child better than anyone else does. And if you've been raising children for a number of years, your experience qualifies you as an expert in that area.

What the teacher *can* do is give you information about your child's performance and conduct in the classroom, and tell you how your child gets along with his or her peers.

Keep an open mind when talking to teachers, but don't let worry over evaluation of yourself interfere with getting information or trusting your best instincts. The first rule in dealing with problems that crop up with schoolchildren is: *Do not ac-*

cept a teacher's pronouncements as absolutes; and if you have questions, ask them.

• It is helpful to write out your questions and comments in advance on an index card, then be sure to ask each one in turn. This tactic is useful when dealing with doctors, lawyers, or other busy experts. It shows you are prepared and your anxiety won't interfere with getting your points across. Often the teacher or authority person will say, "Are there any other items on your list we haven't covered," so don't feel your "shopping list" will make you look silly—to the contrary, it will get you better results. It has been our experience that parents who come so prepared are respected for making that effort.

• Don't fall for the gambit of "What seems to be *your child's* problem?" There is a problem your child is facing, but it may be "the school's problem," or "the teacher's problem." You don't want to start with the handicap of apologizing for your child's shyness problem. Instead of saying, "Why does my child have a problem making friends," ask, "Why are the other children in this class not more friendly toward my child?"

• Separate a teacher's conclusions and global evaluation from a descriptive statement of the behavior in question and the context in which it occurs. You need to know as specifically as possible what your child does say or do (or fail to) that is not desirable and under what circumstances it happens. "Troublemaker," "underachiever," "socially anxious," "hyperkinetic," "shy" are broad concepts that can mean quite different things to different people. You want to know what the behavioral evidence was which generated those abstract attributes.

Forces Other than School

If you are, after observing in the classroom, convinced that your child is shy and still cannot quite pinpoint anything that is in the school environment that may be feeding his or her shyness, answering the following questions may give you some clues.

1. *Do other family members single out this particular child for criticism or teasing, resulting in the child's apparent self-consciousness?*

Often, as most parents know, siblings are the guiltiest of parties. While it is unwise to take sides in siblings' battles, any parent has a right to put a stop to an unfair fight or one that may be obviously damaging to a child. Furthermore, parents have an obligation to teach their children not to demean others or call them names—even if those "others" happen to be brothers and sisters.

And if one parent makes it a practice to demean a child, the other has an obligation to point this out and even intervene. While presenting a unified front is important, it is only important when it is beneficial and not detrimental to the child. As one shy student told us, "My father constantly told me I was worthless and wouldn't amount to anything, and my mother never said a word. As far as I was concerned, her silence meant that either she didn't care about my feelings or she agreed with him."

We heard a mother call her shy ten-year-old daughter "a fat slob" in response to the child's knocking over a glass of milk while passing a plate at dinner. Father comforted the crying child with "That's all right, honey. Daddy loves you." But the message that gets through is "Daddy loves you even if you are a fat slob." Father was acting the good guy role, not confronting mother so as to prevent future abuse, while being kindhearted to the child. Such public violation of a child's dignity should never be tolerated in a family.

2. *Does the child have something over which he feels shame—such as bed wetting?*

Do *not* add punishment or admonishment to a child's sense of shame. *Do* consult a pediatrician and ask for help for the child.

Often the problem will go away as the child matures, when you are patient and understanding. But again, consider that the "problem behavior" may be a side effect of something more serious that needs to be discussed, such as the child's not feeling loved or accepted by family members or peers. Or, there could be some physical problem that calls for medical attention.

3. *Do other family members use this "secret shame" as a weapon?*

One shy child we spoke to told us that his sister always threatened to tell all of his friends that he wet the bed unless he'd do whatever she told him to do. Parents need to be sensitive to this sort of emotional blackmail and put a stop to it the same way they would put a stop to other unacceptable behavior. Not only do you come to the rescue of the victim, but you can teach a few values to the blackmailer at the same time.

4. *Do you or other members of the family label the child as shy? Or do you negatively label in other ways that can be damaging to a child's self-esteem or create feelings of shyness?*

Most certainly, by now, we have made the point that labeling a child anything negative can have far-reaching consequences, so don't do it, and don't allow anyone else to do it.

5. *Is there some adult relative, family friend, or neighbor who the child sees frequently who may be doing something to contribute to his or her shyness?*

The best way to find out if this may be the case is to ask your child. One mother who assumed that her child's shyness was her fault, finally did just that.

Mrs. B was summoned to the school by seven-year-old Paul's teacher who told her that Paul was becoming shyer by the minute. The teacher explained that he became quite agitated when asked to read aloud—something that hadn't bothered him at all in the past. But lately, the teacher said, Paul would blush, stammer, lower his head, and then silently refuse to even try. After much soul searching, accompanied by the weighing of her every word to Paul, Mrs. B finally asked him what she was doing to make him feel so shy. When he told her she wasn't doing anything, she asked him why he didn't like reading anymore, and he said it was because he couldn't read as well as other people. She then asked where he had gotten such an idea.

As it turned out, every day after school Paul went to a neighbor boy's house to play. The friend's mother would then sit the two boys down and have each one take turns reading aloud from a book. After each reading, this mother would praise her son and tell Paul he couldn't read nearly as well as her child and that he was a terrible reader—and not too bright to boot. This apparently had been going on without Mrs. B's awareness for many weeks.

On being told of this, Paul's teacher put the pieces together, adding a new dimension. The neighbor boy was also in her class and she'd had many dealings with the mother. She told Paul's mother that this woman was extremely ambitious for her child and had taught him to read early and tutored him constantly. The books she had the two boys read from were several grade levels beyond a typical second-grader's capability, and because she had tutored her son he could read the words. Paul, on the other hand, couldn't, and that fact, coupled with the ambitious mother's harshly negative evaluation of him, caused him to feel inadequate to the point that he felt he couldn't read the books that were used in his class. What Supermother was doing was bolstering her child's self-esteem and her own at the expense of a young child.

Paul's mother told us that it took nearly two years to undo the damage that had been done to her son.

Things To Do with and for Your Shy Child

Some of the suggestions offered below will have a familiar ring, but in *this* chapter they are tailored specifically to the school-age child. Some of those that apply to children of all ages are repeated here for completeness—*and* as reminders.

• Try to see the child's social situations from his or her point of view. At times, physically "get down on the mat" with the child to see eye to eye, rather than talking down.

• Talk about what you feel, think, value, and what you've done while the child was at school, and encourage an exchange of such information from the child. It is amazing how little children (regardless of their age) know about their parents.

• When you ask a question, wait for an answer, don't answer it yourself. Parents who have a short fuse for quick replies tend to discourage shy children from attempting to formulate answers to what come to be seen as rhetorical questions. In our shyness clinic, the therapists have had to endure the painful learning experience of waiting up to several minutes before any one of the eight shy adults would venture a reply to a simple question. Shys seem to have an infinite tolerance for silence that drives others "up the wall." If you wait attentively, the reply will come and subsequent ones will come more frequently.

• Remember the first response, the first step, taking that first action is very difficult for the shy child. However, barriers that make it difficult to initiate responding can be weakened by practice and rehearsal.

• Enroll the child in drama or dance classes, if you think he or she might enjoy it.

• Encourage the development of physical skills that can be used in team sports.

• Help the shy child step out of his or her shy role to be a different person. Stage simple puppet acts, use masks, exchange roles (you be the child), have shouting contests, be totally ridiculous for a half-hour, dress up in unusual costumes. Play the "Which puppet is shy?" game to discover your child's views about shyness.

• Share with your child some of your own frailties as a child—what you couldn't do or were afraid of and how you overcame them.

• If you are still shy, enlist the child's counsel for how you might react differently in shyness-provoking situations.

• Pretend that you are the child's grandparent for a weekend and notice the ways in which your relationship changes.

• Help the child practice making eye contact while talking and listening.

• Notice how often your child smiles, and do *all* you can to get the whites of those teeth showing! It is important to start smiling early before the braces are installed and embarrassed children talk without revealing any teeth at all.

• Encourage your child to laugh at funny things, to have a sense of humor and perspective about his or her own shortcomings or frustrations.

• People who smile, laugh, display a sense of humor, and make eye contact are judged to be more desirable by others—and rarely seen as shy. Model these behaviors yourself and point out positive instances in others.

• Teach and display listening skills: Assume an attentive, forward-leaning open posture. Use eye contact; nod; make reinforcing gestures; and use words like "yes," "hmm," "very interesting." Ask questions for clarification, or to follow up on implications of what was said. Paraphrase main points to be sure you understand what was communicated. Indicate that the conversation (or lecture) was enjoyable and valuable.

• Encourage children to talk loudly enough and clearly enough to be heard and get their message across. Let them practice using the telephone for information and have them order their own meals in restaurants, talk to salespeople in stores, and so forth.

• Teach them to take phone messages properly. "Hello, this is Billy Williams. . . ." (*wait for reply*), "No my mother can't come to the phone right now. Can I take a message for her?" . . . "Thank you. . . ."

• Teach your friends and relatives to talk to your child and not treat him or her as if he or she had no existence except as your messenger. Shy children will react favorably to adults who show a genuine interest in them—in a nonthreatening manner. But most adults don't take the integrity of children seriously enough to accord them the respect they deserve.

• Teach the child how to interrupt politely and effectively with "Excuse me," "I have a question," "I'd like to say something about that." Reinforce them by stopping to allow the interruption when it is done correctly, but not otherwise.

• Give compliments whenever possible to the child and other family members; make it clear that *you* like getting compliments in return from them. "That was a delicious dinner" makes all the preparation time worth it—but people need permission to give compliments. Phil has to tell his students, for example, that it is okay to say if they liked a lecture, and not only to complain if they don't. Assume the whole world needs more strokes.

• Don't make the child feel different or separate from his or her peers by dress or by making him or her get to school late.

• If you drive your child to school, arrange to take another child, even if it means going a bit out of the way. Ditto for having another child over to your house occasionally, or taking them to the movies or circus.

• A younger playmate will help a slightly older shy child practice social skills and be more assertive.

• Watch how your child plays with other children to detect inappropriate behavior, such as being too bossy or possessive, or initiating excessively, or not compromising or complimenting.

• Where other children clearly reject your child, go to the source and ask them why. Do so using the wording we've found to work with shy adults in our clinic: "What could (*my child*) *do so* that you would like to play with him (or her) more next time?" You are seeking constructive feedback about behavioral changes required to bring about a desirable consequence. You don't want the other children to document, or even continue to think in terms of your child's faults or past faux pas.

In general, your plan of action is to improve your child's basic social skills and to reduce anxieties about being evaluated (and rejected) by others. You do so through modeling the behavior yourself, through verbal instruction, and by creating opportunities to practice being a sociable person. At the same time, you must continue to build the child's self-esteem and security base of "being loved no matter what."

I Love My Child, But There's No Time to Help

Preventing or overcoming shyness involves a major commitment of time, energy, and attention to the most basic aspects of personality development and socialization. Each parent must decide how much they are able to do and "give at home" without feeling guilty about how much more they might be doing.

One-parent families present a particular problem for that working parent to find time to do anything more than cope with his or her family's survival needs. But the 12 million American children currently living with one parent are the ones most likely to need and benefit from our recommendations for combating shyness.

Nearly one-fifth of all children under the age of eighteen today are living with one parent. Among black families, half of the children live in one-parent families. Since 1967 the number of one-parent families has increased by one million every year. Ninety percent of these families are headed by females—that is ten times the increase in two-parent families during the decade from 1967 to 1977. The Census Bureau estimates that 45 percent of all the children born today in this country will spend at least a year living with only one parent. Most one-parent families have come about through separation or divorce, but recently

unmarried women have begun keeping their children and raising them themselves.

A recent study conducted by the National Association of
Elementary School Principals was conducted of 18,000 elementary and high school students from one-parent families. It concludes that children need much more attention and help from
the school than they currently receive. As a group, they show
lower achievement and more discipline problems than their
two-parent peers. They are absent more, late to school more,
and show more health problems.

Although not reported in the study, we would suspect that
these children would also have more problems with social adjustment, loneliness, and shyness.

Heads of one-parent families need to do all they can to promote the sense of self-worth and sociability of their children.
Giving the children responsibilities for which they are praised
(rather than chores which are taken for granted) alleviates the
burden on the parent and builds a sense of self-reliance and
sharing. Make whatever time available for social contact "quality time"—to talk, laugh, and exchange ideas, feelings, fears,
not just to complain and command.

It is important to increase the opportunities for socializing by
having group potluck dinners that include children, and weekend outings with other one-parent (and two-parent) families.
The child needs to feel part of a communal system. In our ever
more alienating society, that is often difficult to achieve—even
when there are two parents. For single parents it becomes imperative to create an extended family of friends, neighbors, and
relatives. For such parents, following the spirit of the recommendations we are proposing may be sufficient to combat
shyness when there is not time to follow the letter of the
prescriptions.

CHAPTER SEVEN

The Best Years of
Their Lives (from 12–17)

We believe that the pain and pressures of the teen-age years are considerably greater for today's young people than they have been for most previous generations. First of all, society is in a state of great transition, there are so many freedoms without attendant responsibilities.

Then there is the structure of the educational system. When we were growing up, we went to elementary school until the eighth grade, and graduation marked an important rite of passage, after which we looked forward to high school as a milestone. Adjusting may have been difficult, but we only had to do it *once*. Most of today's teen-agers must do it *twice*.

They leave the relatively secure environment of elementary school *two years* before we did, when they are just changing from being children to adolescents. "It's a *big* step," one seventh-grader told us. "You go to seven different classrooms, have seven different teachers, and it's confusing and scary. There are some different kids, and other kids have changed a lot. It's enough to make *anyone* shy."

One former junior high school teacher, Roy Nehrt, describes this as "the worst period in a kid's life." Nehrt, now an official with the National Center for Education Statistics, says the junior high school student "is under all kinds of pressures from all sides and he can't cope with them." If it is a bad time generally for all adolescents, one can safely assume that it is far worse for the shy ones.

Then no sooner have they made their adjustments and presumably gotten through junior high school, then they graduate again, and must adjust to high school. Here, according to several counselors we interviewed, "They can very easily get lost in the shuffle just because the student bodies are now so large."

And underlying all of the environmental factors, the tendency to be shy is probably the greatest during the early teen-age years, according to David Elkind, a developmental psychologist, in that the turmoil of adolescence is due to newly attained thinking capacities as well as emotional changes. In his study, "Understanding the Young Adolescent," Elkind proposes that the super-high degree of self-consciousness that we see in youngsters around their early teen years is a result of the teen-ager having developed an ability to think about what *other* people may be thinking.

Ideally, this ability has the virtue of enabling the teen-ager to take the role of the other person, thereby being able to better sympathize with others and find a common ground for relationships. However, Elkind goes on to note, this new achievement is often marred by an "inability to distinguish between what is of interest to others and what is of interest to the self." This preoccupation with the self leads teen-agers to believe that everyone else is as concerned with their behavior and appearance as they are. Their imaginary audience is conceived as one that holds up all of their thoughts and acts to close scrutiny and judgment.

"When you believe that everyone is watching and evaluating you, you become very self-conscious," Elkind explains. Over time, a more realistic balance is achieved with the teen-ager's awareness that often others don't notice or even care what he or she is thinking, feeling, or doing. Such knowledge lowers self-consciousness, yet offends the narcissistic desire to be noticed as a special person. This dual view of social reality is observed over and over again in shy adolescents and adults: "I want to be on center stage, the most noticed of people, but I don't want to risk being evaluated for fear of rejection."

The Importance of Being Popular

To be popular is everything—even more important, according to a survey of Colorado high school students, than getting good grades or "being in the newspaper or on TV." In fact, according to a UPI account, school officials said that getting good grades ranked only ninth—slightly ahead of "being smiled at"—on a list of fifteen types of recognition that high school students would like to receive. Being popular was first among the fifteen choices offered.

And the key to popularity is being just like everyone else, only perhaps just a touch more special. For the already-shy child who doesn't feel that he or she is like everyone else, and may feel special only in that he or she is *inferior*, this is a time when things can easily go from bad to worse. And our research has shown that during these early teen years, this is truer for girls than for boys.

It takes so little for adolescent girls to really suffer. A teacher at Jordan Middle School in Palo Alto told us that a trivial remark, or someone looking at them the wrong way often is enough to set a girl off for the entire day. Girls, more than boys, he said, were reluctant to ask a teacher for clarification during class, or even go up to him or her afterward for fear that the other kids would see them and think they were stupid. And as sensitive as they are, he said, the girls were far more cruel in their stinging remarks to other students than were the boys. In fact, he emphasized, it is the girls who create most of the painful experiences for the other students, boys included. So, even though they can be hurt at imagined insults, on a daily basis they usually wind up being devastated by each other.

Why might girls be so much meaner than boys at this age? True, they are often cranky because they are going through the trauma of having their bodies transformed by maturity. True, the pressures—as they are for boys as well—are greater than ever before. But, on top of everything else, it may be that the need to be popular in school and be attractive to the opposite sex is programmed more forcefully into our teen-age girls than our boys. At the same time, generalized sexual feelings have become more specific.

Regardless of their fears, however, the girls' desire to be attractive tends to result in great concern over the way they look. And unfortunately, adolescent girls, like everyone else, tend to hold themselves up to cultural ideals, unfavorably comparing themselves when they fall short of looking as great as Olivia Newton-John—and at a time when skin eruptions and weight problems are not that rare. One shy thirteen-year-old explained her seventh-grade miseries this way:

"Why does everything happen at the same time? You start junior high and you're so scared you can't sleep the night before. Then you get your period, clothes don't fit, your skin breaks out, you get braces on your teeth. I have to wear headgear fourteen hours every day—and it hurts and looks dumb. I have to go to the speech therapist because my tongue doesn't work right and if I don't do my speech exercises three times every day, my teeth won't straighten. I'm on a diet, and I've got a ton of homework all the time. My mom makes me give my face a treatment every day. And none of it helps because I still feel like a dog and don't know how to act. I just know I will never be popular or have any friends—especially boyfriends—because I'm such a weirdo."

And some of the things that can turn one into a "weirdo" would be laughable were it not for the fact that the pain that is felt is so genuine. One mother told us that after her husband had bought their daughter a new lock for her bike, she found the girl in her room, crying in despair. When she asked what was wrong, her daughter told her, "Mom, it's the bike lock. It's not the kind the other kids have. I can't use it, so I can't ride my bike, and now I have to walk to school, and I'll have to think of something to say if someone asks me why I'm walking. And please don't tell Daddy because he'll just get mad." A bike lock. It has created a complex and multifaceted problem, simply because it is different and has the potential, therefore, to set the girl apart from her peers in what she considers to be an important way.

The length of one's pants can be of equal importance. If, for example, a boy consistently wears pants that are a trifle short, he's teased about wearing "floods," and depending on anything else that might be "weird" about him, he may earn for himself the label "fag," "nerd," "turkey," or "scuzz," and even long after he has stopped growing and therefore has a wardrobe that fits properly, he's still known by one of the labels his too-short pants earned him. In some cases, even kids who really do like him will reject him simply because liking and hanging around with a fag or a scuzz is a socially unwise thing to do—only the very secure can afford the luxury of that sort of loyalty. Thus, he can consider himself lucky if he manages to have one or two friends at school, and certainly he can never hope to be popular.

It almost seems as if it isn't enough of a punishment for an adolescent to know in his or her heart that he or she isn't popular, but that this fact must be forcefully and publicly driven home by measuring each student's popularity in an institutionalized fashion, such as is done in one of our local junior high schools each year. The method of measurement is an event called "Flower Day." The way it works is that each student can pick up a number of blank "orders" and fill in the names of everyone he or she would like to have a carnation sent to during the course of the day.

On the average, each student receives five or six flowers, but always there are those who receive more or fewer. One year one girl received fifty-five, another received forty-two, one boy received thirty-five, and a handful of kids received one or no flowers at all (we are told, by the way, that it's worse to receive one flower if it's from a teacher or counselor than to receive none at all). This is not a happy event for everyone, obviously. The kids who get one or no flowers are provided with more than enough evidence that not only are they unpopular, but no one at all likes them.

One boy who received no flower managed to bravely hold back his tears until he reached the safety of home and his bedroom where he remained the entire weekend. Another who received only one had been, before that day, very excited about a Memorial Day weekend his parents had planned for the family. But on the trip, he picked one fight after another with his fourteen-year-old sister, verbally abused his parents to the point where they lost all patience with him, refused to join them for meals in restaurants, managed to get lost once, and had a generally miserable time—along with his exhausted parents and sister. Needless to say, by the time the trip was over, whatever feelings of low self-worth this boy brought with him on the trip were far lower because of the way he'd behaved—reinforcing his sense of worthlessness with virtually every word and deed.

And how did the girl who received the fifty-five flowers feel? Absolutely miserable! She was so embarrassed by all of the attention that by day's end she was in tears. Tears of embarrassment, and tears over a very realistic fear that she would be resented by many of the other kids. And quite possibly, suggested a member of our research team, a few of her tears were for the kids who were so painfully and publicly reminded that they were truly unpopular.

One observer, Louis Fine, sums up the sad lot of the troubled or lonely teen-ager this way:

"Abnormal or pathologic adjustments exist when an adolescent is friendless, has poor peer group ties or is sexually promiscuous. Frequent or solo drug use almost always indicates significant adjustment problems.

"The peer group is so important to the psychological development of the adolescent that it is fair to say an adolescent without friends is an adolescent in trouble and in need of professional help."

A number of high school students we surveyed said that they believed some kids would do absolutely anything to be popular or have friends. When we asked specifically if they felt that teen-age girls would use sex, some of these students said yes. One said, "To be popular in this school you have to be a slut."

We do not, however, have any hard data to support this view. Because it is prohibited by California law, we were unable to question students about their personal sex practices, so we were unable to learn from individual students whether they themselves were sexually active and if so, why. It is our guess, however, just from living in the real world, that there are, as the students suggested, girls who, lacking other attributes, will use sex. One woman, recalling her teen years, told us that the one thing that affected her life more than anything else was that she was not pretty: "I've always wondered," she said, "what it would have been like to be pretty—wondered if I really would have wound up in the back seat of cars with boys I really didn't like, having sex I didn't want."

In our view, sexual promiscuity is still seen as deviant behavior, and with this exception, generally there is no greater conformist than a teen-ager—at least with respect to his or her particular group or the group he or she wants to be part of. Ask anyone who grew up during the fifties and started smoking in high school how he or she got started. If the group we ran with smoked and drank beer, only the very strongest and most confident members of the group resisted the pressures to conform—we didn't want to be different or square. We wanted to be cool and belong. One shy extrovert told us, *"Peers are your worst enemy . . . unless they're honor students and don't like smoking,* drinking, and screwing around." And Louis Fine notes, "As peer group loyalties develop, friends become very important, seemingly more important than parents. . . .

"The peer group provides the self-conscious, emotionally unsure and anxious adolescent with needed psychological support in his attempt to establish a 'separate' identity. The identity achieved . . . is separate only in reference to parents and other adults; it is very conforming in regard to peers."

While it is true that a teen-ager need not be shy to conform to the group, we have reason to believe that those who are shy are more vulnerable to social pressure. In our high school survey, for example, twice as many shys felt that other people put pressure on them to drink or take drugs than did the not-shys. Furthermore, that shy people have a deeper need to be accepted and have more difficulty standing up for their rights or stating their opinions, makes them more apt to be followers than leaders.

But there is still another possible reason for shy teen-agers to use drugs or alcohol. Twice as many shy teen-agers as not-shys said they used drugs or alcohol at dances or in other social situations to make them feel more at ease, confident, less shy, and more like part of the group. A number of shy adults have also told us that they use alcohol to combat shyness. One of them, now a recovered alcoholic, provides us with a good illustration of the connection between shyness and drinking:

"I was a teen-age alcoholic. I started drinking—mostly beer—when I was about fifteen just because everyone I hung around with drank. But the one thing I noticed right away was that after I had a couple of beers my feelings of self-consciousness would fade. Sometimes I even experienced genuine feelings of self-confidence—feelings I couldn't ever remember having had before. So, every time I was about to get into a situation that I knew would make me feel shy—like going to a dance—I'd have something to drink beforehand."

As time went on, his tolerance to alcohol built up, so one drink wasn't enough to put him at ease—to keep him from blushing and trembling and feeling embarrassed over his symptoms, while melting away his inhibitions. Soon it took two, and then three, and so on, until ease and drunkenness arrived at the party together.

A most insidious side effect of using alcohol, drugs, or sex, either to overcome feelings of shyness or gain popularity is that these behaviors result in feelings of guilt and a vicious cycle of feelings of inadequacy and worthlessness, which may lead to more of the same behavior—and more shyness.

When viewed in light of a teen-ager's need to be popular or have friends, sexual promiscuity is perhaps better understood. And drinking and drug use, either to conform or cope with feelings of shyness, can be seen as something other than rebelliousness against parents.

Fear of the Opposite Sex

Even though statistically more girls than boys are shy during the teen-age years and do seem to have a rougher time of it, boys, especially the shy ones, have their problems too. In fact, many shy male adults who have written to us have said that their shyness began during those painful years when some were self-conscious about being shorter than the girls, their voices were changing, they saw themselves as different, and they were just discovering the opposite sex.

Virtually all of the teen-agers we surveyed (including junior high and high school students), whether they labeled themselves as shy or not-shy, said they felt shy in situations involving contact with the opposite sex. Interestingly enough, our survey revealed that once they are in high school, and presumably have weathered the freshman year, some of the girls shed their general shyness. However, and this was very surprising to us, we found that among students who said they were not shy, more females than males admitted to fear of the opposite sex. But when it came to those students who labeled themselves as shy, more males than females admitted to this fear. Thus, we must conclude that with respect to boys, girls feel more anxious at an earlier age—probably because girls generally mature sexually about two years before boys do—so some adolescent shyness appears to be a phase some females at the junior high level go through and later overcome. And since a number of not-shy males and females say that they are shy with members of the opposite sex, we must further conclude that a certain amount of shyness is normal and nothing to worry about. We do suspect, however, the reason more not-shy females express fear of the opposite sex than vice versa is due to traditional programming and the fact that girls have been conditioned to "not be forward with boys."

In any case, shyness is, obviously, more intense and more prevalent in the beginning—at the first dances at junior high school where the kids generally go stag and girls frequently end up dancing with each other, while the boys shuffle their feet and think about getting up the courage to ask one of them to dance. The words of one counselor after the first dance of the season describe such an event very well: "The room was filled with pain."

The situation does improve with time—at least for some teen-agers. Eventually some of the boys ask some of the girls to dance. But even they, and the girls they ask, experience shyness, while those who don't get asked and those who get turned down feel rejected and unwanted—and, of course, self-conscious. And if they feel that way often enough, and are embarrassed by sitting on the sidelines, publicly exposed as rejects, they'll stop going altogether. As one teen-age boy told us:

"When I was twelve years old, I went to my first junior high school dance. I was really scared that none of the girls would dance with me. I didn't ask any of them, for fear that they would say no to me. Looking back, I realize that it wouldn't really have mattered much if they had said no, but I was so scared that I didn't give them the opportunity to. I also realize that very few of them actually would have rejected me, if I had just taken the risk. But I didn't take the risk, and spent the night sitting in a corner with some friends. None of us was dancing, we were just talking about the dance, putting down the girls, putting down the disco, and just generally being bored. We all felt pretty bad because of all the people dancing and having fun while we were sitting there doing nothing. Finally, we broke up and I walked home alone. I was so depressed by that dance that I didn't go to another dance for two years."

And once boys and girls start dating, it can never be easy for anyone—except perhaps those who are confident and very popular. As with the dance, the boys ask for dates and fear rejection, while the girls sit and wait, fearful that they won't be asked. And yes, women's liberation notwithstanding, for the most part, the dating ritual remains unchanged.

Even casual social encounters with the opposite sex can be painful for a shy teen-ager. As one seventeen-year-old boy told us:

"Last summer, I was downtown and I met this girl from school. We were pretty friendly in school, but we never had any contact outside of school. She hailed me from down the block and ran up to meet me. By the time she reached me, I could hardly talk, and I mumbled something stupid about how I had to run—although I actually wasn't going anywhere—and said I'd call her later. As I walked away, I kept thinking of all the things that I should have said, and I realized what a perfect ass I'd made of myself. I never did call her, because I was so ashamed of the way I had acted. I figured she'd never want to talk to me again."

And yet, for all this boy might know, the girl he was talking about could have felt precisely as did a girl who described a similar encounter:

"I was in the drugstore buying some binder paper when I saw Alan, who is in my history class. He's a real fox, and I like him, and I thought he liked me a little because he was always nice. I went up to him and started talking about the history assignment, and other things—just to make conversation. He mumbled something at me, and said he had to get home, but he'd see me later. I guess I was wrong about him liking me, and now I'm so embarrassed that I made a fool out of myself by forcing myself on him."

Helping Your Shy Teen-ager

If you ever tried to give a teen-ager advice, you know how well received it is. Even parents who have kept the lines of communication open have difficulty simply because a natural stage of development during the teen years is to separate from the parents. To do this requires that the teen-ager view his or her parent as some sort of a dim-witted throwback to the Dark Ages who neither knows what's really happening nor has anything to say worth listening to.

And they can throw a parent off guard because sometimes they bring their troubles home, sometimes they want to talk, sometimes they ask what they should do, and sometimes they even treat you as if you have some intelligence. And then the very next day, because of a hormonal surge, you find yourself put back firmly in your place. Even shy teen-agers, as most parents know, can be most aggressive when their parents "get out of line."

One mother told us that one day her fifteen-year-old daughter came home and told her, "Mom, you're so understanding, and you really are smart. And you always tell me the truth, so I'd never lie to you." The next day the mother drove up in front of the house and saw her daughter standing on the sidewalk with her friends. She spotted a cigarette sticking out of her daughter's pants pocket. When she asked her about it, the daughter said, "I don't have any cigarettes." When the mother reached over and touched it, pointing it out to the daughter, the girl told her, "Well, I didn't put it there. Someone else must have." You will be gratified to know that this mother responded by grounding her child for "insulting my intelligence."

Even people who are not the parents of the children who need help have difficulty in reaching them. At one junior high school in Palo Alto, for example, a shyness clinic was set up, and only seven kids were interested. Of the seven, all but one denied they were shy. When explaining why they were participating, they said they were there because they each "had a friend who was shy and wanted to help." These youngsters were shy about being shy, quite obviously.

Because of the difficulty adults have in reaching young people, chapter 9, "The Student's Shyness Handbook," is designed to give junior high, high school, and college students the tools to work through their shyness by themselves. Parents can best help by referring their children to this material and then, depending on the ages of the children, working indirectly to make their children feel secure and have fewer things over which to feel self-conscious.

The first rule to remember when you want to help a shy teen-ager overcome this problem is *not* to say, "Don't be shy." Besides labeling the child, you must remember that nobody ever got rid of a phobia by being told to. But the child can be encouraged to *act as if* he or she were not shy.

Now then, since one's personal appearance can play such a dramatic role in whether he or she is self-conscious, and since this is something parents *can* help a child with, we shall begin by working from the outside in.

Personal Appearance

If you weren't born beautiful, you may remember how it felt to have features over which you felt self-conscious. Can you remember the pain? Can you remember wanting to hide in your room? One woman, illustrating the painful shyness she had because of her bad skin, told us, "I had to go to school, but when I had a choice I stayed in the house—on weekends and after school. I remember the summer after I graduated from high school, I scarcely ever left my bedroom."

Skin

Next to the myth that all teen-agers will grow out of shyness is the one that they all will grow out of teen-age acne. Some do. Some people *never* do, and continue to be plagued with skin problems all of their lives. But whether the angry eruptions magically disappear or not according to some schedule has little bearing on the damage they can do to a sensitive and self-conscious teen-ager. And you can't get your mind off a skin problem because: a) the itching and burning constantly remind you that you have it, and b) people keep asking you about it or telling you which of the useless over-the-counter remedies you should try.

Dermatology has come a long way, and in most instances, acne problems that range from mild to severe can be alleviated altogether with creams, vitamins, or antibiotic therapy—in some cases, just correcting a thyroid imbalance will do it. It is a myth that uncleanliness is the root cause of acne, and adults and others who insist that a clean face promotes a clear one only add insult to injury while the problem remains. A child with skin problems should see a skin specialist at the first sign of trouble.

Weight

Either overweight or underweight can be a source of self-consciousness. There is a right and wrong way to deal with a teen-ager's overweight. This letter illustrates the wrong way:

"I was 12 years old and in the seventh grade. My Mom, Dad, and I were sitting in the back yard. I was going through the awkward first months of having my period—trying to stay a 'tomboy' and yet wanting to be a 'girl.' I was overweight to the point of being ugly. Words I remember were my father's to my mother, '*Do* something about her, will you? She's fat as a pig!'

"That's all I needed. I ran to my room to hide and cry."

The right way is to:

(a) Take your son or daughter in for a physical examination and have your family doctor or pediatrician talk to him or her and put the child on a diet.

(b) Keep low-calorie nutritious snacks on hand.

(c) Don't nag because it reinforces a person's sense of ugliness and may cause frustration that can only be appeased by a Twinkie orgy.

(d) Set a good example.

Teeth

The good news is that most kids eventually see a stint with the orthodontist in a positive light. Tin is definitely in these days and braces have become a status symbol of sorts. Wearing braces says, "I've got a problem, but I'm solving it." Not only is it fashionable to wear braces, but it usually turns out to be a lesson in responsibility. And when those braces come off, people feel great about themselves. No one should have to go through life with teeth that look like a Japanese fan or ones that Dracula would envy. It is expensive, to be sure, but most orthodontists have no-interest payment plans that aren't as painful as those for buying a car, and the investment in your child's self-esteem is invaluable.

Grooming

When you don't nag a child about his or her bedroom, you have saved up to nag about important things—such as personal hygiene. Nag, if you must, for daily showers and regular shampoos, and clean clothing.

Clothing

Remember that teen-agers are the ultimate conformists. Provide them with enough nice clothing so that they will look good according to *their* code. Don't insist that your daughter or son wear something that their peers wouldn't be caught dead in. For example, it comes as no surprise that one of the shyest girls in the seventh grade at Jordan Middle School is impeccably dressed. She wears beautiful pleated skirts, with coordinated blouses, sweaters, and knee sox, and highly polished oxfords. Her peers, by comparison, look pretty tacky—worn jeans, T-shirts, down-filled jackets, and whatever tennis shoes are in fashion (it varies from month to month). Obviously, this girl's parents mean well, but for all their efforts they may just as well deck out their daughter in a gorilla costume. We may personally abhor the current conformity, but we must maintain an awareness of its importance to adolescents, and how appearing different from their peers can set them up for shyness.

It is a trivial thing, and yet one woman, now the mother of two teen-agers herself, recalls that she became much shyer during the teen-age years when her mother forced her "to wear those little-girl dresses with sashes in the back when all of the other kids were wearing skirts and sweaters."

Hair

It should be clean and in some current style. No crew cuts for boys just because Dad had one twenty years ago, no fluffy bouffants because that's Mom's preference. And don't argue about length—length is determined not by Vidal Sassoon, or even the president of the United States, but by what is deemed acceptable by the peer group.

Helping Your Child to Feel Secure

Even though they may resist it at times, seize those opportunities when your teen-ager wants reassurance and demonstrations of your affection. Touch them while you can, for soon they will be grown and out of reach, and then look at some of the following suggestions for other ways you can make them feel secure.

Privacy

While privacy is always important to all children (yes, we know, except for their parents' privacy), at no time is it as important to a young person's sense of security as during adolescence. Again, for the most part, their rooms, desk, drawers, diaries, and mail should be seen as off limits.

For the most part. There are exceptions to every rule, and while it is true that parents ought to respect their children's privacy, a notable exception is when you *genuinely* have reason to believe that your child may be doing something that is damaging to his physical or emotional health, such as using drugs. Before searching without a warning, we suggest talking to your child. But if talking nets you nothing and you still believe that your child may be doing something that is self-destructive, then you have a responsibility to find out if that's the case. And if searching a room or a drawer is the only way you can accomplish that, then view this as something that is justifiable to do under the circumstances.

Set Limits, Make Rules

One of the new myths is that adolescents want and respond well to total freedom. The fact is they don't have the experience to know how to deal with it. A part of that myth holds that virtually all children can make their own decisions about such matters as drinking or having sex, among many other things. This myth, says psychiatrist Dr. Helen DeRosis, is reinforced by many contemporary TV shows. "The problem is posed," she says, "and parents on TV shows then tell their youngsters that they must find their own solutions. Television kids then do just that, and it all ends very happily. This scenario gives both parents and teen-agers the idea that children can make their own decisions, which is absurd given the fact that the teen-agers don't have the experience to do so. And when this is the message they receive, they are terribly insecure and terrified. The burden this places on young people is enormous."

"Parents must make the rules," says Dr. DeRosis, author of *Parent Power/Child Power*, "and in the end often they must make the decisions that their children are not yet capable of making."

One teen-ager who has no limits may boast that his folks don't mind if he stays out all night ("That's his decision"), and a friend might express envy, but according to a number of young people we spoke to, those envious friends may be secretly glad their parents have imposed a curfew because they then know that their parents really care. And fair and reasonable rules *are* evidence of caring—even though they are often met with resistance. Ask the person who has no rules to abide by—chances are he or she will tell you they feel unloved because of their absence. From time to time a letter appears in Dear Abby or Ann Landers that speaks to this need. Here's one that was written to Ann:

Dear Ann Landers:

Every now and then some teen-ager complains about his folks treating him as if he were still in rompers. He resents being asked "Where are you going?" "Who with?" "When will you be back?"

Well, my folks never ask me any of those questions. I am free to come and go as I please, and I don't like it much. I have the feeling if they really cared about me they would make some rules. But when rules are made, somebody has to enforce them—and that means work. It's easier to let kids run wild.

How I wish my mother would say, "No you can't go ice-skating with that cold." But she never would. She always says, "It's up to you." I feel frightened and alone because I have too many decisions to make.

I hope those kids whose parents ask a lot of questions and do a lot of bossing know how lucky they are. It means that somebody loves them.

—On my Own in Bridgeport, Conn.

This letter brings us back to security, and how important it is for a child to have it. One psychiatrist who specializes in the problems of adolescents told us that adolescents without limits can be likened to your "walking across the Golden Gate Bridge and discovering that the railings are missing. With no limits, these kids are terrified." And, quite obviously, insecure.

Rules Need Reasons

If you are going to warn a teen-ager about the dangers of pot smoking, tripping out, or venereal disease, Dr. Helen DeRosis advises, "Do your homework." In other words, make sure you know what you're talking about, and tell your child the truth. Not only does this give the child a good reason to avoid doing certain things, it also builds in him or her a trust of the parents.

And, if you give a teen-ager a reason for your rule against pot smoking, for example, and that reason is based on *facts,* when someone else attempts to pressure your child to go against your rule, your child will have complete information when it comes to making a decision in the matter.

Preserving Dignity

Don't laugh when your teen-ager makes a mistake or does something foolish. Don't talk about his or her blunders to other people. And don't lightly dismiss those things that he or she may feel strongly about by saying something like, "Oh, that's nothing to worry about," when that teen clearly thinks that he or she has plenty to worry about—and has shown confidence in you by discussing it with you. It is better to nod sympathetically, or simply say "I know, I know," and reinforce your "I knows" with some physical affection.

And while no one expects a parent to tolerate abusive treatment or obnoxious and disruptive behavior, confrontations should be private—and, most decidedly, never in front of a child's peers.

A basic rule might be to try to treat teen-agers the same way you would treat adults you respect.

Keep the Lines of Communication Open

A good listener can learn a great deal about what makes a particular teen-ager tick. A good way to shut them down is to use sweeping generalizations such as "You always," and "You never," when correcting an adolescent. And when you're not correcting, but instead conversing, really listen to the mundane complaints and chatter. When offering criticism to your teenager, try saying, for example, "I think you'd look good with your hair cut in that new style I've been seeing," instead of "Your hair looks terrible that way," or "You'll make a good impression when you go for your college interview if you wear conventional clothing," instead of "Don't dress like a bum."

"Active listening" is similar to understanding that the teenage girl who tosses her clothing around the room in the morning does so for reasons that aren't readily apparent to the harried mother who sees her daughter turning her room into a disaster. She isn't intentionally going against her mother's standard, but instead is searching for something to wear that will make her more socially acceptable. In any case, active listening means that you listen with an ear that hears *all* the words, and what might lie back of them. It is tuned to picking up the small clues that the person doing the talking is bothered by something he or she is not talking about explicitly.

An example of this is the mother of a thirteen-year-old girl who had, as a special graduation present from elementary school, completely redecorated her daughter's room only to have her child say she hated it. "I couldn't figure out why Linda didn't like the room. She had wanted it done in tones of green, and I'd gone out and done all the leg work to find samples of wallpaper, carpeting, and fabrics. I had picked out five or so of everything, and then let her choose her favorites. When the room was finished it was beautiful and all of Linda's friends were dazzled by it."

As it turned out, there were six words buried in the barrage of complaints about the room that Linda's mother heard: "I don't want to grow up."

"I almost didn't hear her, and I surely wouldn't have had I been dwelling on how ungrateful Linda was for all my efforts. It dawned on me, in a flash, that in redecorating her room, I'd forcefully driven home the point that, like it or not, Linda was growing up. Where once the room had been a child's room, it was now a young lady's room. And Linda was in mourning that her uncomplicated childhood was gone forever. Instead of berating her, I got all her stuffed animals and put them on the bed. And then I listened, as she tearfully complained about how awful it all was and how scared she was. She needed to be able to say that—and I needed to know she felt that way."

Prying vs. Privacy

When we discussed with a group of shy junior high school girls problems they were having, "prying by parents" was a near unanimous selection. As we probed further, it became clear that what they were objecting to was their parents' attempts to find out what they were feeling and thinking at a time in life when they were in the process of developing a private self, of having secrets shared only with "Dear Diary," of becoming a unique person. Their parents were distressed because the transparency of childhood was now clouded and murky. No longer could they tell just by looking at their child's behavior "what was up," since public actions did not necessarily correspond to the private world of the child's imagination.

While these youngsters may have been overreacting to their parents' concerns (over the loss of innocence of their children and the emerging gulf between them), nevertheless, parents of teen-agers should change the access routes to their children if they sincerely want them to talk to them about what they really want, need, feel, and fear. Replace the interrogating style of Grand Inquisitor with an invitation to discuss some issue of parental concern where self-disclosure is first initiated by the parent. But there will still be those fantasies that are reserved for one's self alone—and the independence of thought the teen-ager's fantasies reflect should be honored.

Give Praise

At a time when there's so much to criticize, parents have to look hard for times when they can offer praise and reinforcement. So, even if it is his or her regular chore to take out the garbage, mow the lawn, or do dishes, use it as an opportunity to give your teen-ager recognition for efforts. And remember to give them compliments when they look nice.

Continue to Imbue a Sense of Responsibility

Some liberal parents take the view that whether a teen-ager does his or her homework is a personal decision. We feel that a more sensible view is expressed in the words of one father who told his son, "I have my job, and I do it every day. Your job is to go to school and *learn*." The caring expressed by this statement makes a teen-ager feel secure. And it teaches responsibility at the same time. Furthermore, the child who is allowed to cut school and avoid doing homework and ultimately makes very poor grades or even flunks out of his or her classes can't possibly have a very good self-image, and self-image is one of the things this is all about.

A teen-ager is perfectly capable of maintaining his or her own room (even though many resist doing this), establishing study habits, doing his or her own laundry, and getting to various appointments on his or her own. Some responsibility to the family itself is in order: doing dishes, taking out the garbage, running errands, and doing other chores that need to be done are not too much to ask, and are things that ultimately make a person feel better about himself or herself—even though he or she may complain every step of the way.

Participating in the Educational System

While it is useful to observe your child in elementary school, doing so in junior high or high school is possibly the worst thing a parent can do. However, parental involvement at other levels can prove beneficial not only to your child, but to others as well.

Possibly because of constant exposure to teen-agers, some teachers and school officials become rather insensitive to the plight of their students. Thus, an involved parent can do a bit of reminding and encourage the development of a climate in school that is structured, as much as possible, in ways to minimize shyness.

A good place to begin is with contests that have no winners. As we have seen from the example of "Flower Day," both the least popular and the most popular seem to suffer from humiliation.

Certainly not all winners are unhappy about winning. Some

kids *have* to win—they are driven to be winners, sometimes by inner forces and sometimes by parental pressure or the need for abundant approval from their parents and their peers. However, we question the value of popularity contests when the stakes are as high as they are for those kids who don't like to be singled out and are, through no choice of their own. Is it necessary to have an event that is *supposed* to be pleasurable when any pleasure at all seems to be at the expense of someone else's self-esteem?

Parents who are concerned about the negative effects of such popularity contests need to band together and do what they can to call a halt to them. There will be strong opposition: It will come largely from parents for whom their children's popularity is inordinately important to them; it will come from extremely popular kids who need the adulation of their peers and who aren't concerned about the resentment that comes their way.

But in the end, if more parents would look for ways to establish equality, and forcefully identify these ways for teachers and other school officials, they would not only be helping the shy and unpopular kids, but those who are neither shy nor unpopular, but are pressured by their parents to win every contest as well.

Something else parents can have a voice in is the very structure of the school. In some cases, the chickens have come home to roost for the liberal educators whose dreams of academic freedom have turned into a nightmare. One high school we visited, for example, changed their tight structure to give all students a choice in the matter of what classes they would take and how many, and opened up the campus so that the students could come and go as they please. As it turns out, not all students are mature enough to make the right decisions, and some have as many as three free periods a day that are normally spent in nonconstructive, self-esteem-robbing ways: drinking coffee at a nearby restaurant, smoking, taking dope. At some point they receive the news that they may not have enough credits to graduate, which hardly reinforces a person's self-image. And some of the teachers and counselors complain that their jobs are made tougher because they simply have no control when the structure is this loose. Shys need a structured environment in which to function most effectively.

Whether our kids go to private school or public school, we parents are paying for it, and we have every right to participate enough to insure that we are getting our money's worth. So for the sake of your child's education and self-esteem, make some noise.

Combating Shyness with a Sense of Purpose

A fundamental problem teen-agers have is threefold: First, they are neither children nor adults, and the younger ones in junior high school have the added confusion of being in a state of physical and emotional transition—along with a very real sense of having no control over their destinies; next, while young children are generally cherished, teen-agers are routinely disparaged—everyone at least pays lip service to the children-are-wonderful school of thought, while viewing teen-agers with disgust is a socially acceptable pastime; finally, teen-agers have difficulty finding any purpose to their lives. This is because, increasingly, they have no roles. Here in Palo Alto, for example, we have lived in a rather protected environment until recently; where once there were many schools, we have now, in the interest of economy, shut down a number of schools and consolidated them. The result is that there are many more students in all of our schools and the number of roles available for them remains finite. There is only one student body president, one officer for each class, one student council, and one varsity football team. The competition is stiffer than before, the alienation greater than before. It's a blueprint for shyness.

Working together, parents and teachers ought to explore some ways we can give our young people some roles that have meaning. A fringe benefit would be that when teen-agers make contributions to the community or the school, there becomes less justification to disparage them as a group, or for what they are.

So, what can we do beyond encouraging our children to develop a specific skill?

Perhaps we can begin by giving them fewer choices. For example, a social studies teacher might advise a class that there's going to be a fund-raising walk to fight world hunger and ask his or her students to volunteer. An alternative to merely announcing and recruiting is to have as a class assignment the organization of such an event, with each student having a job and each one of them required, as part of the assignment, to also participate in the walk.

Other assignments could include participating in a club or serving on some school committee, and giving boys and girls the choice of which one they will do—not the choice of not doing anything. This is no more undemocratic than the requirement that all students take math, history, physical education, and science.

We need to encourage our children to help others and help find ways for them to do so. Focusing attention on another is one way a shy person can set aside self-consciousness and feel good about himself or herself. And whether shy or not, finding ways that children can help others can provide them with important roles. At one of our local junior high schools, a program exists that involves kids with community projects. The idea is a sound one—but only the scholastic cream of the crop can participate. As it turns out, these A students are also, for the most part, very popular, confident, and not very shy. It seems to us that recruiting some shy, less popular kids would serve more than one purpose: It would provide more volunteers; it would help shy kids feel better about themselves and give them the opportunity to forget about themselves, while meeting new people.

If you're looking for ways to give your children a sense of purpose, this might be just the time for parents to do some volunteer work in a political campaign or for a worthy cause and take their kids along with them.

CHAPTER EIGHT

The College Years (from 17 on)

Getting into college marks an important milestone in the lives of our young people: the transition from adolescence to young adulthood. Most of the time it signals a change from dependence on parents to greater independence. Often it means moving out of one's family home and living in a dormitory with one's peers. This is true, to some extent, even when students go to a community college as they still spend less and less time at home.

For many students, the freshman year, especially the first part of it, is very depressing. It is a letdown to realize that they aren't particularly special, but just one of thousands of "look-alikes"—some of whom are bound to be brighter than they are. One student described his feelings this way:

"All my life, my parents' dream was that I would go to Stanford University, so it was my dream too for as long as I can remember. I used to think, 'Boy, if I can just do that, I'll have it made.' And when I was accepted, I was on a natural high for days. But now that I'm here, I feel like I'm surrounded by people who are smarter than I am, and hundreds and hundreds of people who, obviously, because they got in, are just as smart as I am—so I'm not the exceptional person I was led to believe I was."

Another student who made it into a top college on a scholarship agreed, and added, "Instead of feeling like I'm special in a positive way, because there are so many students whose parents are famous or rich, I feel special in a negative way—poor."

The transition to college from high school is far greater than moving into high school from junior high, not just because it spells a time for greater personal independence, but the environment is dramatically different. Because of the sheer size of the campus and the size of the classes, no matter how good a student may be, he or she can get lost among the sea of students. There are just so very many students, and so very many large classes that often students find themselves submerged in the mass of mass education. For example, the 680 students who take Phil Zimbardo's introductory psychology course constitute a greater number than the total enrollment of most prep schools and even that of quite a few high schools. At large state colleges, such as the University of Minnesota, there may be as many as 2,000 students in a single lecture course, part of whom watch the professor profess via a TV screen.

At this point, students who got through high school by studying hard and because they had some easily recognizable talent, ability, intellect, or because teachers showed a special interest in them, will find that this simply isn't enough in college. Most of their peers are in the same boat, so they will have to do more than study, if they are to distinguish themselves in the eyes of their college teacher. If they do not, they will be stampeded over by those who do. It is the rare college that is geared for students who remain reticent, not very assertive, not very independent, who don't participate or take initiative. In short, *the shy of the world most often recede even further into the background in college.*

It is instructive to note the two major problems that students need psychiatric help with during their college years. The first has to do with intellectual performance, the second with social performance. A failure to meet the standards of their ego ideal causes disappointment and a lowering of self-esteem among the largest number of candidates for professional counseling.

For years, parents, relatives, and teachers have defined them (labeled them) as "A students." Their self-worth has been wrapped in that precious "A" quality wrapper. Indeed, some students follow the lead of overzealous parents, and set for themselves the impossible standard of *being perfect*. In a world of imperfection, filled with competitive others who also aspire to be Numero Uno, there will surely be a lot of fallout on those who cannot maintain such a lofty status. For many, the illusion carried through high school where they were the barracudas among the minnows. In college (or later in graduate and professional school) they discover that they are swimming in a tank filled with great white sharks. For example, among the 1,600 entering freshmen in the class of 1984 at Stanford University, the *average* high school GPA was 3.8—where 4.0 is perfect. Thus, there are probably more students with straight-A high school grades than any lesser grade. We might add that in addition to a person perceiving he or she is no longer so intellectually special in this more rarefied atmosphere, because of the selection standards, other attributes also become more common and less distinguishing, such as athletic and musical ability, and looks, for example. To the extent that a student has come to believe that he or she is conditionally loved and respected based on performance and appearance, then that student will become depressed when failing to measure up to the unrealistic criteria internalized in his or her younger days.

Of nearly equal importance as a contributor to psychological distress among college students is a sense of failure in establishing meaningful relationships with peers. All too many students seek therapy for loneliness, or for the inability to make friends and have friendships develop into close personal contacts. The sense of "being out of it" is more acute in a setting so full of opportunities to be "in it," especially where students eat their meals together and have a social life outside of classes. Unlike high school, where students often hold dual citizenship of friends in the neighborhood as well as school chums, in college it's usually all-or-none at school. For that reason the friendships that develop can be intense and lasting. But for the shy students, there is more at stake in making or failing to make friends in college.

Shyness Changes Over Time

Our research has revealed that for about one-third of the students their level of shyness didn't change during the college experience: They were not shy when they went in, didn't have problems with shyness in college, and weren't shy when they graduated; or, they were shy when they went in, while they were there, and they came out possessing the same degree of shyness. So, for this group of students, the college years had no effect whatsoever on their shyness.

One study revealed that at the start of a new semester, shy college students were found to score higher on a scale of loneliness than their peers who were not shy. As might be expected, over the course of the term, the loneliness levels of both groups decreased as they got acclimated to the novel situation. However, when their loneliness was again measured the next term, the shys were still significantly more lonely. The authors, J. M. Cheek and C. M. Busch, point out that the passage of time alone is not enough to offset the tensions and inhibitions characteristic of shyness. This personal factor in loneliness can lead to enduring problems in social adjustment.

Another 25 percent of students in our research have reported that the time they spent in college made them more shy. One shy student, now a senior, whose college experience has caused her to become increasingly shy—and miserable to the point that she periodically says that life isn't worth living—has changed schools three times in hopes that a new environment will minimize her shyness. Possibly it could if she would recognize that the campus is only a stage, and she's still the star of her own show and what she needs is a new act.

With each new opportunity to start fresh, to leave her shy image behind her, this young woman does the same things that have consistently reinforced her shyness and made it worse: She refuses to live in a dormitory unless she can have a room all to herself, and thus misses the social opportunities inherent in dormitory life. Like many other students we've observed in the cafeteria, she comes in and heads straight for an empty table, sits down, and then constructs a barricade out of books, dishes, and coats on the table and any empty chairs. The message is clear: Do Not Approach.

Not surprisingly, she signs up for no seminars and does not involve herself in any campus activities. In effect, for all of her spoken desire to lose her shyness, she reminds us of the person who burns to become a concert pianist, but hasn't quite realized that to do so requires not just knowing the keyboard and how to read music, but *practice, practice, practice*.

We fear that she, and other students who are this shy and reinforcing their shyness daily, will probably become increasingly shy and socially inept after college simply because the opportunities to meet people, get to know them, and practice social skills will diminish considerably in the outside world. They will find that they simply have to put much more effort into making an acquaintance in the adult world, let alone a friend. These are the people who are more likely to lead lives of quiet desperation than those who decide to do something about their shyness during the college years.

The good news is that even with all of its alienating qualities, the college experience provides abundant opportunities for overcoming shyness. We were delighted to discover that 40 percent of college students do, in fact, seize the opportunities to become *less* shy, and they *are* successful in combating their shyness. For these students, the college experience makes them more open, more outgoing, more able to enjoy the company of other people, more able to put their best feet forward, and more able to show themselves off in the best light—and they wind up being better able to appreciate what other people have to offer. *These are the joys of not being shy. They amount to an ease and delight in making the human connection.*

Thus, shyness can alter the quality of a college education in significant ways, so much so, that it becomes a different experience for the shy student than it is for the not shy. The inhibiting aspect of shyness that holds one back from social contacts deprives the student not only of friendships, but also the learning that comes from informal association with others from diverse backgrounds. Moreover, college friends are potential lifelong "contacts" who may help one's later career through their influence, status, or advice.

We have done extensive research with college students on campuses throughout the United States and in a number of other countries in the world, and this is what our research, and the students themselves, have told us about the interference of shyness in their lives.

• Shyness interferes with the social lives of students in various obvious ways; they don't make as many friends as they would like, they don't take the initiative and approach other people with whom they feel they might have something in common—as friends or partners for class projects and term papers.

• The nearly chronic sense shy people have that they are being evaluated causes them to react inappropriately in a number of situations. Worry over performance and evaluation makes it difficult to process incoming information. As a result, shys can give the impression of being rather inept, in the classroom, or in an interview situation (for postgraduate work, college recruitment by industry, for example).

• Shy students tend to be more conforming, less willing to defend their beliefs, less willing to express their opinions publicly, and more willing to go along with others than to hassle or argue. It's easier for them to be compromised, seduced, unwillingly cooperative, to end up doing chores for other people that are not in their own best interests, and to go along with the group whether or not it is good for them to do so.

• In many cases, shy students have particular difficulties meeting the opposite sex, dating, and establishing intimate relationships. In part, this is because many of them have been bookworms or intellectuals who have spent a lot of time hitting the books or working on projects alone. Many college students have gone to single-sex high or prep schools and just haven't had as much experience with the opposite sex as they should. Forty percent of all of the shy students we surveyed told us that being alone with a member of the opposite sex is a situation guaranteed to trigger off feelings of shyness. And because they have learned to anticipate that this is a situation that will make them feel shy, they often avoid it.

In comparing shyness of eighteen- to twenty-one-year-old students across eight different cultures we find that the prevalence of those who consider themselves to be currently shy is lower in Israel (31 percent) and Mexico (39 percent) than in the United States (44 percent). It is about the same level as the United States among those surveyed from Germany (43 percent), Newfoundland (44 percent), and India (47 percent). In Taiwan (55 percent) and Japan (57 percent) we find the highest incidence of college age students labeling themselves as shy. The universal nature of shyness is revealed in the fact that over 75 percent of the students in each of these cultures reported that at some time in their lives they considered themselves to be shy.

The primary shyness elicitor among U.S. students, "being the focus of attention before a large group," is also the most powerful in all the other countries except Israel and India. In Israel, most people experience shyness when in situations where "I am vulnerable, e.g., when asking for help," while in India opposite sex, one-to-one interactions contribute most to shyness. Other prominent elicitors of shyness across these diverse cultures are situations requiring assertiveness; of being in a lower status, as when speaking to superiors; and when being evaluated or compared, as in an interview; and finally new situations in general. Strangers, authorities, and members of the opposite sex all serve to create a fair degree of shyness in people throughout the world.

The two most characteristic behaviors of the shy American are silence (reported by 74 percent of those surveyed) and inability to make eye contact (48 percent). The clues to shyness are also seen in a low speaking voice among Israelis, Mexicans, and Indians; and in stuttering among Mexicans; and to a large degree among Indian students. Blushing is a key sign of shyness in all these cultures except India.

The following table outlines the major negative and positive consequences of shyness as perceived by students from these different cultures. It is obvious from inspection of the data that shyness poses problems for many students regardless of their cultural background. Virtually all people recognize the existence of negative consequences that attend shyness, while fewer report positive consequences. It should be noted, however, that the most often reported virtue of being shy is that it provides a kind of social-emotional detachment which allows one to observe others and then act more wisely rather than act on impulse. About a third of those surveyed in each country also note as a plus for shyness the modest, appealing impression it is possible for the shy person to project.

In our attempts to modify shyness, it should be our goal to maintain as many of these positive features as possible while getting rid of the negative consequences. Thus, for example, while we strongly urge the shy student to take more responsibility in initiating social contacts as well as asking and answering questions in class, that does not imply rushing in where angels fear to tread. As you examine the chart, you may become aware of some other interesting culture-bound effects that fit or challenge your stereotypes (for example, were you aware of the powerful role that shyness appears to play among German youth?).

Cross-cultural Dimensions of Shyness
in Eighteen- to Twenty-one-year-old Students

	U.S.A.	Israel
Prevalence of shyness	44%	31
Shyness is a problem	63%	42
Negative consequences (yes)	97%	92
Causes social problems	76%	53
Creates negative emotions	61%	33
Assertion difficulties	68%	30
Others make wrong evaluation	53%	20
Excessive self-consciousness	53%	15
Cognitive and expressive problems	41%	29
Prevents positive evaluations	36%	20
Positive consequences (none)	18%	19
Observe others, act carefully, intelligently	48%	31
Creates a modest, appealing impression	36%	33
Avoids negative evaluation by others	27%	30
Provides anonymity and protection	24%	22
Avoids interpersonal conflicts	14%	23
Allows one to be more selective in interactions	22%	17
Enhances personal privacy	23%	13

The student must take responsibility for becoming a known entity by participating in seminars, requesting tutorials and independent reading courses, by going to faculty office hours to ask questions and make comments. And the student must show sufficient interest in the subject matter by personally requesting additional information beyond what is required of

Mexico	Germany	New-foundland	India	Taiwan	Japan
39	43	44	47	55	57
79	85	76	83	60	75
97	100	100	80	93	97
70	84	86	45	64	86
55	72	47	40	43	47
45	74	90	53	52	90
22	61	57	33	29	55
21	61	45	30	32	40
50	63	43	27	58	39
25	56	39	20	38	39
42	45	30	24	17	24
32	45	45	41	35	34
25	30	34	26	29	39
13	34	36	20	25	20
9	19	23	23	23	23
19	7	15	35	23	27
20	26	19	32	25	20
9	13	15	27	21	14

everyone in order to stand out as a serious scholar, one worthy of being a research apprentice.

But many shy students manage to do just the opposite; they avoid taking seminars because they are expected to talk, participate, share ideas, comment on the ideas of others, and offer appropriate criticism. They shy away from the seminars because of a lack of confidence and a lack of practice in conversational exchange. And they miss what is truly *best* in college—the give-and-take among students who really do have something to say, and the sharing of ideas and experiences between them and their teachers.

Because shy students may spend four years anonymously in large lecture halls, a number of professors find that many of their students remain unknown to them. This becomes apparent when a student who is about to graduate comes to the professor's office to ask for a letter of recommendation. The professor is at a loss to say something personal about the candidate (for a job or advanced training) because their contact has been, at best, impersonal. To be effective, letters of recommendation must go beyond the candidate's test scores and grades to comment on character, motivation, maturity, stability, and the suitability of this individual for a particular placement. Unless the candidate has previously established himself or herself as a unique individual to at least three professors, supporting letters for even bright students will be politely positive, but not passionately enthusiastic. And to move up the ever narrowing ladder of career advancement it is such personal endorsement that is essential. But how can a teacher go out on a limb to say "Take this candidate, I back him 100 percent," or "She can't miss," when the candidate is just another face and GPA in the crowd?

So even when shyness is not so great that it prevented these students from making it into college (while it was a detriment to some of their high school peers), nevertheless, it can be a barrier to further success.

We mentioned in an earlier chapter that among West Point cadets shyness and leadership effectiveness don't go together. Positions of responsibility and those with high visibility go to those judged to be the most effective leaders. A positive spiral effect emerges in which those who get chosen for the better jobs have greater opportunity to display their ability, and then are judged as more competent than those given less demanding routine jobs. Similarly, in private industry we have found shy employees to be more dissatisfied with their jobs and to have lower morale because they feel passed over for promotion and not recognized for their accomplishments. And indeed, they are not recognized—in comparison to not-shy coworkers who don't hide their light under a barrel. The not-shys have learned an important lesson of success: Talk and the world listens sometimes; be silent and the world listens never.

Interestingly enough, those who appear to be very bright may simply be very eager and socially adept, as evidenced by the observations made by a young woman who told us:

"I really won't ask a question or make a comment in class unless I'm pretty sure I'll sound intelligent. And one day, just for the fun of it, I decided to pay very close attention to the quality of the questions being asked and the comments being made by some of the more assertive students—one in particular. Some of the questions and comments were so dumb that I could hardly keep a straight face. But, they were well received, seemingly, by the professor and the other students. I think that's because what was said reflected a command of the language and the delivery was good."

In short, it's not what you say that counts, but how you say it, which may not be a good value, but it turns out to be a useful ploy. And it may mask a lack of knowledge and comprehension, just as silence can mask intelligence.

Thomas Harrell, a professor at the Stanford Graduate School of Business, has been studying what it takes to be successful in business. In a series of studies that predict how much business school graduates will earn five to ten years after graduation, Harrell and his associates have shown that "personality does matter for business success." High earners are the socially bold extroverts who talk the most. It is those men with high levels of health, energy, and self-confidence who, when they were in school, enjoyed such activities as "making speeches" and "interviewing clients." To be a successful business manager, then, requires being an effective communicator. But a moment's reflection will tell you why this is so. We tend to judge other people's intelligence largely from their speech. In addition, those who speak first and most get to direct the domain of the conversation to areas they already know most about, thus they seem more knowledgeable. Finally, advancement in business is more often associated with one's being persuasive and effective in dealing with other people than for one's technical skills. It is little wonder then that Dale Carnegie courses geared toward "How to Influence People" are heavily subscribed to by corporations eager for their junior executives to become more socially poised and interpersonally effective.

What Do You Say to a Shy College Student?

There may not be much advice left that parents haven't already given to their shy children by the time they are of college age. There may not be much advice an eighteen-year-old is willing to accept from his or her parents—even if the student knows he or she could use some good counsel. In the next chapter we will offer specific recommendations for shy students to act upon (or reject) on their own. At a more general level, here are some key points you, as a parent of a shy college student, may wish to get across in your "farewell to the troops" message:

• Shyness is common among college students; your child will be in good, though quiet, company among the 40 percent of other shy students.

• It is possible to change one's degree of shyness at any time, assuming there is a strong personal commitment to invest the effort to do so.

• Does the child really want to be less shy?

• As a new student in college, the shy person is a stranger in a paradise where he or she has the freedom to be whatever he or she wants to be. By acting *as if* they were not shy with others who haven't already pigeonholed them, they will be judged as not-shy.

• In order not to be seen as shy, all a student has to do is: smile, make eye contact, introduce him or herself by name to strangers in a voice loud enough for them to hear it, say "Hi!" in passing, listen attentively, ask a question, make a comment, offer a suggestion, and give a compliment when it is deserved.

• To be accessible to others, a student should start by not dressing in ways that turn other students off (too rich, too sloppy, too weird), or by erecting a buffer zone of books and paraphernalia around one's seat in the cafeteria or in class.

• A person should recognize the importance of listening to what other students have to say in class and out.

• It's best to enjoy the *process* of learning, for its own sake and not just for the grades. Intellectual risks should be taken, and a student should be open to new experiences and challenges.

• Convey the idea that failure is part of every genuine risk; that failure is a learning experience when it tells us what to do differently next time.

• Your child is loved unconditionally regardless of his or her success or failure experiences—all you can expect is a good try.

• Suggest that your son or daughter be willing to ask for help when necessary from fellow students, teachers, counselors, and staff. It is not a sign of weakness, but a recognition of the human condition to seek—and to give—help when needed.

• Tell your teen to expect to feel lonely at first, and from time to time again in that new school, until those faces and places become familiar enough to be comforting.

• Let your child know he or she can expect to feel inadequate at times, to be less sharp or witty than the next student or not as worldly as another. The best term paper may get shot down in a severe critique and A's will not always be waiting at the end of every course. But out of such experiences emerges a more realistic appraisal of one's strengths to be relied upon and weaknesses to be remedied.

• Ego and performance (intellectual, athletic, social) are not interchangeable items; ego is not to be put on the line every time performance is sub par. You have nothing to lose by trying. As we learn from the Israelis, "If you have nothing and ask for something there are only two outcomes. You will be refused, and then nothing is changed—so there is no loss. Or you will get what you want so everything is changed for the better. Therefore, ask until you get what you want."

• When there is a conflict with another student or a teacher, it should be discussed, negotiated, bargained. A person shouldn't capitulate reluctantly without stating his or her point of view in objective, unemotional terms. And a disagreement should never be resolved by simply *assuming* one is wrong and turning one's anger inward. There is always an advisor, ombudsman, pastoral counselor, or parent to turn to before a person becomes a victim.

• Make it possible to say: "I love you. I miss you. I hope you are happy and enjoying yourself."

What Parents Ought Not to Do

• Don't give too much advice based on how things were when you were eighteen. Times have changed.

• Don't have unrealistic expectations that amount to demands for what your child must achieve. Phil Zimbardo had a student, Mark David, whose C average prevented him from gaining admission to medical school, but who was delighted working in the Peace Corps in Africa. The student's father, however, was furious that all his planning was for naught. "You see I named my son Mark David so that he would have an M.D. before and after his family name!"

• Accept your child's limitations, values, and interests by not pushing him or her in unwanted or unattainable directions.

This of course assumes parents know their child well enough to be aware of liabilities and assets.

• Don't add to the already high level of competitive striving by putting on more pressure for top grades when you call or write. Assume your child knows by now you would rather see A's than C's—don't be redundant. Use some of that time to explore your child's feelings, opinions, worries. Also remember that you are a person beyond your parenthood—start being someone your adult child might like to have as a friend.

• Resist the temptation to say, "If you would just apply yourself more. . . ."

• "Don't treat me like a baby" is a sad lament from a young adult to momma and poppa that is heard in various versions in our colleges. Shy students, more than the others, must learn to feel self-reliant, need to have their self-esteem boosted not sagged by being tied down to apron strings. An outstanding woman basketball star was chided by her father during his weekly phone calls for not scoring enough points and doing all the things he taught her. She's a big girl now who takes direction from her college coach who wanted her to be a playmaker and not a hotshot. Dad only made her feel confused and inadequate.

• Hold back on the criticism, be loose with the praise. Be a security port for your shy child in these times of sailing in frightening waters. Remember there is a long life after college and your son or daughter will want to visit with you, will choose to maintain a close, loving relationship if you've been a beacon of support rather than one of the hard places to avoid.

CHAPTER NINE

The Student's Shyness
Handbook

He's essentially a shy person and a quiet man. I'm not sure I ever fully understood what made him overcome that shyness. It's absurd he's so shy. There may be a bit of Dale Carnegie in all of us, but to overcome shyness by becoming President of the United States is a little much.

> —*Gary Schneider,*
> *advisor to Jimmy Carter*

If you are in junior high school, we don't have to tell you that this is probably a tough time for you and that any feelings of shyness you've had in the past are at their most intense. What you may not know, however, is that there are plenty of other students in the same boat. Much of what you're feeling will pass with time. But shyness, even though it may diminish, rarely will go away all by itself.

If you've moved on and are in high school, you know all that. If you are just starting out and are having trouble adjusting, you may be frustrated and discouraged, and may feel that everyone else is having a far easier time of it: that Fate has singled *you* out for misery. These feelings are understandable, and when you think you are somehow different, try reminding yourself that you aren't, that probably half of all of the other students in your school are going through precisely the same thing, you can survive this too, and can even reduce your feelings of shyness and anxiety.

If you've made it to college you may have packed up your old familiar feelings of shyness and brought them with you. Or, if you're like many students, you weren't shy until you stepped on campus and realized with a shock that college can be a huge, isolating, and frightening place to be.

Whatever your age, your level of shyness, or when and where you acquired it, if you're willing to work, your shyness can be reduced or even conquered entirely.

Step Number One: The Decision to Change

Part of getting over shyness *begins with the decision to do so.* For some people, shyness is a safe haven and something to hang onto. It can be an excuse—to avoid taking risks, to remain dependent, to not see people you'd rather not see, to avoid doing things you'd rather not do. We know, for example, a student who is very shy. Being shy means that she receives a number of benefits. People feel sorry for her and offer to do things for her because she seems so afraid to do them for herself. People spend time with her because her sad shyness makes them feel guilty. In social situations, in exchange for their kindness, they receive stony silence. The trade-off for receiving without ever giving is never knowing the joy of giving or the richness of deep friendships.

If this sort of prison is not for you, then take that *first important step:* Decide that it isn't for you and that you don't want shyness to continue to intrude on your life. Demand a parole.

Step Number Two: Learning About Your Shy Feelings

Do not label yourself as shy. Instead, tell yourself that you experience shyness in certain situations. Now make a list of what those situations are, ranking them in order of the amount of shyness felt.

After making your list, compare it to the following:

where I am focus of attention—large group (as when giving a speech)

large groups

of lower status

social situations in general

new situations in general

requiring assertiveness

where I am being evaluated

where I am focus of attention—small group

small social situations

one-to-one interactions with opposite sex

of vulnerability (need help)

small task-oriented groups

one-to-one same sex interactions

Now make a list of all of the types of people who make you feel shy.

Compare your list with the following:

strangers

opposite sex

authorities—because of their knowledge

authorities—because of their role

relatives

elderly people

friends

children

parents

What we have found, through surveying over ten thousand people, is that those situations and people most likely to arouse feelings of shyness—to set the heart pounding, or the cheeks blushing—are essentially the same for all people whether they label themselves shy or not-shy.

So color your basic feelings of anxiety "normal," and get

ready to move on to ways in which they can be reduced and managed, beginning with doing something about that breeder of shyness—low self-esteem.

Step Number Three: Building Self-Esteem

Here are some exercises designed to bolster your self-confidence and help you master some of the situations that make you experience feelings of shyness.

1. Make a list of all of your very best qualities. Include personality traits, your values, special talents, and skills, such as: kindness; honesty; sense of humor; athletic ability; musical, artistic, or writing talent; carpentry, typing, cooking, or sewing skills.

2. Now make a list of your most glaring flaws, and call that list, "Things That Need Improvement." Then determine which of those can be improved, along with the importance of each item on the list. Then set *realistic goals* for change, and *one at a time,* set about doing what you can to whittle down your list of "Things That Need Improvement." *Be sure to give yourself enough time for each item on the list.*

3. While you are working on your personal improvement program, focus on one of your strong points and develop it further, charting your progress in writing (in a journal or in your diary). Note any setbacks and write how you feel about them and work out ways to make your plan work better for you. Remember this: Even if you fail at something you are attempting to do, it is not failure—*genuine failure* comes from being afraid to try.

4. Remember that when taking *any* risk, part of being realistic is to be prepared. In other words, when you are about to do something that you want to do, but are very afraid of failure, be sure you have done everything you can to be fully prepared. If you are going to try out for the soccer team, for example, don't do it before you've given yourself the time to

practice and develop your skills; similarly, if the debating team is more to your liking, make sure you know your subject.

5. Because most people need concrete reasons to feel good about themselves, make it your rule to behave in such a way that you build up your self-respect and avoid doing things that will tear it down.

6. Resolve to avoid doing things that make you feel guilty.

7. Try to do one thing either each day or each week that will make you feel good about yourself. Here are some ideas to get you thinking:

> Start an exercise program.
> Bake some cookies.
> Put photographs in a photo album.
> Clean your room.
> Repair a possession that is broken.
> Straighten out your bookshelves.
> Reorganize your work area.
> Write an overdue letter to a friend.
> Paint or paper one wall of your room.
> Return your library books.
> Paint a picture, string some beads, do ceramics.
> Do any small chore you've been putting off.
> Do your homework without being told to do so.
> Read a book.
> Write a poem.

Think of other things you can do to make you feel good about you. Make a list of them and a list of things you *should* do—and do them, and ultimately delight in the joy of crossing some "shoulds" off your list.

Step Number Four: Your Personal Appearance

While we do not subscribe to the idea that good looks are the measure of the person, we do know that when you look as good as you possibly can, you will feel less self-conscious. Evaluate your personal appearance and if it can stand improvement, take action.

Make a list of all of the ways in which you can improve your physical appearance.

If you have skin problems, crooked teeth, a large nose, floppy ears, or any one of a number of physical things that you feel set you apart in an important way—a way that makes you feel self-conscious—*tell your parents about it and tell them how you feel*, and enlist their aid in doing all that can be done to correct whatever you may feel is a *physical* situation that is contributing to your shyness.

At the same time, *you* can do certain things by yourself to insure that your appearance is the best you can make it:

1. Are you neat and clean?
2. What about the clothes you wear?
3. Take a good look at your posture. Is it erect and proud? Or do you slouch, reflecting your shy feelings?
4. Are you overweight?
5. Are you underweight?
6. Could you use a new hair style?

It is easier to get your parents to help you if you make an effort to help yourself. So, start your diet, wash your hair, take care of your clothes.

Step Number Five: Learn to Be Your Own Best Friend

Henry David Thoreau once wrote, "I never found the companion that was so companionable as solitude. We are for the most part more lonely when we go abroad among men than when we stay in our chambers." Lucky fellow, Thoreau—he knew who his best friend was.

The pleasure of our own company is something we all would do well to enjoy. But, as we discussed in previous chapters, shy people have more trouble than not-shy people in simply being alone.

Not to be able to enjoy one's own company is to be dependent on others for entertainment—and dependence is an important component of shyness. Furthermore, if you don't enjoy your own company, who else will?

A change in attitude then, is the first step toward enjoying your solitude—or, your own company. View it as an opportunity to use time creatively, while you establish a measure of independence. Start by making a list of the sorts of solitary activities you would enjoy if you saw solitude more positively. Here are a few ideas to get you started thinking:

working on a hobby

reading

playing a game of solitaire

listening to music

sunbathing

planning or organizing a project

any of the activities listed by you, or suggested by us, for
     making you feel better about yourself by doing some-
     thing constructive

The discomfort of being privately alone is as nothing compared to the discomfort of being publicly alone. Not-shy people don't worry about it, but shy people feel self-conscious about it—it's as if they are broadcasting to the world the evidence of their unworthiness: No friends.

Once you have learned to be comfortable with yourself privately, it's time to work up to behaving like a not-shy person in public. It will help you if you remember that other people are quite unlikely to occupy their thoughts with why you might be alone in a public place. Here are some suggestions for "going public," again, just to get you started thinking:

Walk down a neighborhood street, enjoy the scenery, and
     turn off thinking about yourself.

Run errands.

Go shopping, window shopping.

Run, jog.

Bicycle.

Go to the library.

Browse in a bookstore or record store.

Have a cup of coffee at a lunch counter.

Have a glass of beer if you're old enough.

Practice, practice, practice, and while you're at it, learn to smile at strangers on the street.

Step Number Six: Practice Social Skills

If you don't know how to behave in social situations, one of the best ways to learn is by watching other people who are socially skilled. Look at what they do, listen to what they say, and practice following their example. If you observe not-shy people in social situations, typically, this is what you'll find:

• For one thing, not-shy people smile often and make eye contact with other people. Practice doing both.

• When listening, people who aren't shy demonstrate their attentiveness; they lean forward, nod, and say such things as, "Interesting," "I never knew that," "Tell me more," "How come?" So, respond with your words, and with your eyes, and when appropriate, your smile.

• Not-shy people not only smile often, they *laugh*. When someone says something that's funny, they grin. So practice grinning. It makes people feel good when you show appreciation of their sense of humor. The other side of that is to show that *you* have a sense of humor, which is something you convey by laughing at people's jokes and telling a few jokes of your own.

• People who aren't shy control the domain of conversation and the situation they are in. One way they do this is by being the *first* to raise their hands in the class, make a comment, ask a question, tell a joke, or make an interesting observation. The advantage to the shy person who follows this assertive example is that when you are *first,* you don't suffer the anxieties in going over all the different scenarios in advance and the anxiety that builds up while you work up your courage to say something. Furthermore, if you wait too long, what you wanted to say will be said by someone else, so you ought to say it first so you will "own" it. You need not be verbose or manipulative, just simply appropriately assertive. So, think about what you're going to say, plan it, plunge in, and be the first to ask the question or make the comment.

• Not-shy people are also appropriately discriminating. They don't like everyone or everything, nor do they dislike everyone or everything. So when asked your opinion of something—a book, a play, a movie, a lecture, some food—look at it from all sides. What did you like about it? What didn't you like about it? What was unusual about it? What was mediocre about it? More often than not, shy people tend to react more simplistically, saying they either like or don't like something. Few things in the world are that simple. But, the double bind for many shy people is that they don't want to draw attention to themselves for fear of negative evaluation, and even when they transcend that fear, there is a tendency to worry about hogging the conversation and uncertainty that people really want to hear what they have to say. In short, they fear imposing on others or making asses of themselves. Well, sometimes, you just have to run the risk of making an ass of yourself or being a blabbermouth. To date, nobody has died from making an ass of themselves.

And this is as good a place as any to point out that most people are not that intensely focused on *you,* and even when they are listening to you, they are concerned with the impression *they* are making.

• When not-shy people find themselves in a setting with other people who have superior knowledge, special talent, or are outstanding in any number of ways, they tend to see this as an opportunity for broadening their horizons, adding to their store of knowledge, making useful contacts, and improving themselves. Shy people, on the other hand, typically make unfavorable comparisons between themselves and "superior" people, viewing the talents of others as evidence of their own personal inadequacy. What they—and you—need to do instead is to begin to look at life not as a series of tests in which you are competing with every person you come in contact with, but rather, see this part of life as a sort of pre-season training program where you learn from and are enriched by every encounter you have. Therefore, you *do* want to be with people who have things to offer that you don't have because once you are with them you will have some of that to offer someone else. You do this by kicking the habit of thinking in terms of *you* or *they* and *better* or *worse*, and getting into the habit of thinking in terms of what you can learn from other people.

• A key aspect of the not-shy person is a concern for social responsibility—a concern for other people, for making other people feel welcome or comfortable, and for recognizing the identity of other people. These are all of the things that the shy person wants from other people, but doesn't readily give to others.

• People who aren't shy know how to accept compliments gracefully. They smile and say a simple thank you when someone tells them they like what they are wearing. A compliment on a comment made in class may be received by a thank you, and a further discussion of the subject may follow, further bridging social gaps that may exist between people who don't know each other well.

• Not-shy people do favors for other people and ask other people to do favors for them. Shy people, on the other hand, don't offer to do favors, and don't ask for help. And you are going to be in desperate trouble in school and in life unless you are super-brilliant and resourceful and never have to ask for help. Don't project an illusion of being a know-it-all, never asking for help when you could use it. People don't like know-it-alls, but beyond that, people *do* like to be depended on and needed. Ask somebody for their class notes, saying you have difficulty taking good notes. In the bargain, you also pay someone a compliment for their note taking. Or, if you need a ride, ask someone you know is going in the right direction to give you one. On the other hand, if you have a car or a motor scooter and someone needs a ride, offer it. Offer to pick up something for someone while running errands for yourself. And *do* accept favors when they are offered to you.

• Something that not-shy people do that our shy introverts don't do often is give strokes to other people. They give compliments. They say, "How nice you look today." It doesn't matter what you give compliments on, but *do* give them, and do it as a natural course. Anything you like you should compliment. When you are free with your compliments to others, you'll receive more of them than you do now.

A rule to remember is to be friendly and show interest in other people. Some of the shy students we've worked with really do not contribute much in a social encounter, but toss the ball into the other person's court time after time without showing any sign that they wish to have an exchange. They may say "Hi" or "Hello," but forget that there's supposed to be a middle and an end. A typical conversation goes like this:

NOT-SHY: Hi, how are you?
SHY: Fine.
NOT-SHY: What have you been doing lately?
SHY: Studying.
NOT-SHY: What's new?
SHY: Nothing.
NOT-SHY: Well, see you around.

The not-shy person, obviously, must give up just because the response is so limited, and the shy person is left with a feeling of having been rejected—which in some cases serves to feed his or her sense of unworthiness. The shy person must take some responsibility and at least hold up his or her end. A better social encounter, which shouldn't prove too difficult, would go like this:

NOT-SHY: Hi, how are you?

SHY: Fine. How are you?

NOT-SHY: Pretty good. A little tired, though.

SHY: How come?

NOT-SHY: I've really been hitting the books.

SHY: I know what you mean. It really can get exhausting, can't it?

NOT-SHY: Yeah. And boy, that history teacher of ours is really something else. Say, what's new with you?

SHY: Oh, nothing much. Been playing a little tennis, going to the movies. How about you?

NOT-SHY: Same old stuff. Got in a little skiing a week ago.

SHY: Oh? Where'd you go?

NOT-SHY: Squaw. Ever been there?

SHY: No. What's it like?

As you can see, in the first exchange the shy person asked no questions and showed no interest. In the second exchange the shy person was friendly and showed interest by asking a few questions—the *same* sort of questions *he* was being asked. The point is, you don't have to go to a Dale Carnegie seminar to learn to say to people, "How are you?"

Just do it. And practice your conversational skills and gestures in front of a mirror, and talk into a tape recorder and play them back. Then assume the posture of a critic, and jot down notes on the ways in which you can improve both your delivery and timing.

A fringe benefit in being sociable is that when you remain silent in a social encounter, it tends to make *you* just as uncomfortable as it does other people. This feeds your self-consciousness because you then dwell on it. Your mind becomes filled with negative thoughts about yourself and truly absurd fears about the various ways you will make a fool of yourself and be rejected by others. On the other hand, when you show interest in another person and *listen* to what he or she has to say and at least try to respond, the reverse is true, as it gets your mind off yourself.

If you think you have absolutely nothing to contribute to a conversation, then take the time to learn about things that are of interest to the people you come in contact with. Read the newspaper, books, magazines, school publications; listen to the radio, go to the movies. One socially successful fourteen-year-old we know is a walking *Guiness Book of World Records,* and most entertaining.

Make a list of the things your peers are interested in. Then pick those things that interest you too and make it a point to gain at least enough knowledge to make conversation and ask questions.

Another way to gain knowledge and practice social skills is to become involved in a worthy cause. What's going on in the community or on campus? Are there chapters of national organizations such as NOW, ZPG, Save the Whales, the Children's Rights Crusade?

There is no better place to meet new people with whom you will have something in common and be able to develop friendships than when working in a cause you care about.

When going to a meeting (or seminar, party, class), *be on time*—or early. When you walk into a group situation late, people suddenly turn to look at you. You will be noticed, but only because you're different—you're late. You'll be feeling anxious and self-conscious. Also, there is a sense that you are an intruder. Look at the students coming into class late, for example. The sheepish expressions on their faces reflect their feelings of embarrassment, and perhaps even guilt.

On the other hand, if you are the *first* on the scene, you have a distinct advantage in that when the next person comes in, you can strike up a conversation with him or her. It is natural to do so when you are waiting for something to begin.

To be socially adept takes practice, so practice wherever you can. When you go to the store, the library, or the cafeteria, for instance, instead of treating the people who wait on you as functionaries, treat them as people. Greet them, ask how they are, say it's a nice day, or comment on the lousy weather. Look for opportunities to give someone a compliment, by looking at what they're wearing, what they look like, the color of their hair and eyes. And say thank you when you've been served or waited on. The point is, be nice. And notice something about the person that you can comment on favorably.

Step Number Seven: Dealing with the Opposite Sex

Developing your basic social skills will give you the *foundation* for dealing with members of the opposite sex. Here are some basic rules to keep in mind:

Warming Up

1. Members of the opposite sex have feelings too—uncertainty, anxiety, fear of rejection.

2. Do not automatically view a member of the opposite sex as a potential romantic partner. Look upon him or her as a person that you'd like to get to know instead of an object.

Asking for a Date

1. Asking for a date is frightening, so work up to it slowly. Ask the person out for a cup of coffee, or over to your place to

go over class notes, listen to a new record, or see something new you have, *when the time is right*. The time is right when you feel comfortable doing so, and the other person has been responsive enough that you've gotten the impression she likes you as a friend.

2. When finally you are ready to ask for a date, have something specific in mind: a concert, a play, a movie, a party. If you've gotten to know the person well enough to ask her out for coffee, you should feel comfortable inviting her out for the day or evening. *Be sure to ask well enough in advance so she doesn't feel she's being asked at the last minute*. About one week in advance for dinner or a movie, about two weeks in advance for a big event, such as a prom or a concert.

3. If you fear you will get tongue-tied, write out a script and practice it, and then do your asking over the telephone. Be friendly and specific. For example:

> You: Hi, this is Tom Smith. How are you, Susan?
> Her: Fine. How are you?
> You: Fine, thanks. Say, the reason I'm calling is that I have two tickets for a rock concert and wondered if you'd like to go with me. The group playing is the BeeGees and you mentioned that you liked their music.

Improvise: Just as you are not really going to say you are "Tom Smith," you will use your own language to get your message across.

4. Prepare yourself for rejection. If she says "No," don't assume immediately that it's because she doesn't want to go out with you. There are many reasons for a turn-down—a person may not feel well, may have a prior commitment, or even have personal problems and be anxious or depressed. If she doesn't give a reason (which is unlikely), don't press it. The one thing you need to remember is that you were able to ask someone for

a date and neither the doing so nor the rejection proved fatal. *Give yourself credit for taking the risk* and now that you've done it, resolve to do it again—with the same person (unless she says "No" three times in a row) or someone else with some regularity.

5. Now, if she says "Yes," be sure to be specific about the time you will pick her up, and how she should dress.

6. Be on time, but *don't be early*. Although being on time is important in most situations, this is one time when it is better to be a few minutes late than to be early because when you're early for a date it puts the other person on the spot—especially if she has to answer the door in her bathrobe with her hair not yet dry.

7. On the date: If you have followed our advice and have something specific planned, you should have something to talk about beforehand, something to do during, and something to talk about afterward.

At the end of the evening, let your date know you enjoyed yourself, take her hand, perhaps kiss her on the cheek, depending on what sort of signals she sends out. If she's tense and stand-offish, don't force any issues. Even if she is warm and relaxed, don't come on too strong. Many shy people make this mistake when they are eager for romance. Don't rush things. Timing is everything.

How to Respond to an Invitation

1. If someone you want to go out with asks for a date and you want to accept and can, thank the person, make sure you have the time and date right, and ask, if he doesn't tell you, whether you should dress up or keep it casual.

2. When the time comes, show interest in the person—what he's doing, trips he's taken—and in the world around you.

3. At the end of the evening, thank the person, and if a little romance is appropriate set the tone by expressing warmth. But

do not feel that you have to pretend affection that isn't there or "make-out" because someone spent money on you or because it's the thing to do.

4. You might want to strike a blow for equality and fair play by offering to share expenses. Or if you like each other and will continue to date, you can reciprocate—with *you* doing the asking, planning, and paying.

5. If, on some occasion, someone asks you out and you really don't want to go with that particular person, you are under no obligation to accept. But *do* be kind when you turn someone down. Remember, he probably had to work up quite a bit of courage to ask you.

A Special Message for First-Year College Students

While your primary goal is to do well in your classes and finish college, this is a time to consider what else the college experience can do for you. Specifically, what it can do for your shyness, and your ability to interact with other people.

The opportunity is probably greater in this four-year period for all sorts of social contacts than at any other time in their life.

Furthermore, your fellow students are going to be the future's lawyers, doctors, politicians, businessmen and businesswomen. And the student who isn't shy will establish important contacts during this time, while the shy person will have fewer contacts which ultimately minimizes chances for future success in life. Once you finish school, the opportunities to meet people for either social or professional reasons will be drastically reduced.

So, knowing that once you finish college the opportunities that are now before you will dwindle, *now* is the time to make the decision to get the most you can out of these years. It *is* possible, regardless of whether or not you consider yourself shy, to stop being shy. It is possible to put your shyness on the back burner—to step into the role of a not-shy person and seize the opportunities instead of letting them pass you by.

Remember, nobody knows you are shy. You are, essentially, a New You, if you are starting college. Our research has revealed a strange contradiction you may already be aware of: *that most shy people are less shy when dealing with strangers than they are with people they know.* Since you are now living in a world full of strangers, who you will *get* to know but who have no preconceived notions about you, the first step you put forward can set the tone for those that will follow, so make it a not-shy one. Let that be the very first impression you make on each new person you come in contact with.

Play a role. Play yourself. You know the lead character in your life script. Who is this person? What are his or her qualities? Does this person have a sense of humor? Does this person like people? Is this person intelligent? Play everything that this person is *without shyness.*

You begin to step into your not-shy role by following the steps we have set down for learning social skills. But you will do more, and even be able to distinguish yourself academically, if you avoid hiding out in large lectures and sign up for some seminars and participate. If you feel you need to prepare for this, you can go see the teacher and ask what the game plan of the seminar is. In passing, you might want to tell the teacher that you have been troubled in the past with shyness, and therefore might find it difficult to participate, but that you'll try. When the teacher realizes that shyness is a problem to you, he or she won't put you on the spot and will certainly be more appreciative each time you respond. Over and above that, *be the first person to make the first comment.*

When you don't do this, but instead drop back into the last row of the large lectures and classes, most of what you learn you could learn just as well, if not better, by simply going to the library and reading books. When you don't participate, you don't learn about yourself, nor do you learn to appropriately assess the quality of your own thinking, your imagination, or your ability. You don't learn one of the things that college ought to be preparing you for—to be able to talk intelligently with other people and feel comfortable doing so.

For students who manage to keep a low profile, going through college is, as some students have told us, "beating the system." By taking only large lecture classes where you are anonymous, you are not singled out by your professors and are able to remain safely in the background. Theoretically one can even go all the way through college and be a straight-A student without ever having spoken a single word to another human being. However, when you're about to graduate, and are applying to a graduate school or trying to get a job and you need a letter of recommendation from a professor, don't be surprised if one is not forthcoming simply because the professor can't say anything about you beyond what your grades were—information that would be obvious from the transcript.

Once you get out of college there are few times you are going to be asked to take a written test—for many people, nothing beyond a driver's test or a civil service exam. But you *are* going to be asked to talk, to comment on world affairs, the economy, the coming election, or even a movie you've seen. And, of course, most likely, you're going to be interviewed for potential jobs and be evaluated on what you say and how you say it. In short, personality *does* count in business as well as in social situations.

Begin now to be the personality you know is best for getting what you'd like out of life.

CHAPTER TEN

The End of Shyness

To wipe out the pain of low self-esteem and shyness in large numbers of people we must raise the coming generations with a high sense of morality, humanity, and concern for others. We must give them integrity and enough conscience to know that the difference between good and bad depends on how you regard other people, and not on getting straight A's, being an athletic star or a homecoming queen. It means wiping out bigotry and replacing it with a reverence for human beings, cherishing their uniqueness, being compassionate for the blows life deals people, and imbuing in our children the sense that they are not immune to misfortune, in order that they can feel another's vulnerability to pain.

Even children who are set apart from their peers in what some adults would consider a positive way run the risk of being shunned into shyness. Albert Einstein was, as we know, noted for his brilliance. He was also noted for his shyness, which we would guess started early in life because he was "different," and because his consuming passion for science isolated him, while his advanced intelligence necessarily meant he had difficulty relating to his peers.

Parents, and some teachers of gifted children, may well see such a gift as a prize but, for some who possess it, we suspect that the gift is an albatross because it sets the child apart. Some children, so advanced, we have learned, decide that in order to be "typical" they must hide their giftedness; some who are lonely and out of touch in a classroom setting may even be seen as below average when they don't participate and are bored by the class work that is uninteresting and unchallenging to them.

One mother of a child who has a special talent in science told us that in every evaluation of her son by teachers, she is told, "He is not a 'mainstreamer,' and thus he is a problem." She tells us that rarely, if ever, do teachers speak of his strengths, but instead focus on his "inattentiveness," and see his lack of interest in the class as a personality deficit that ought to be changed. Worse, is that her son has internalized this value, and his self-esteem has eroded, as he sees himself as a failure, and different in a negative way from his more "mainstream" peers.

Shunned in the classroom, the boy acts out, and further alienates himself from his teachers and his peers. As Dr. Charlotte E. Malone, a consultant on the gifted, noted in an interview, the child who does this is saying, "Listen to me," "Laugh at me," "Feel sorry for me," "Please like me." An alternate reaction, she says, is simply to withdraw: "These youngsters read an excessive amount and do projects to excess, so far as their time goes by." In other words, they use reading and solitary projects as forms of escape.

One of the most tragic consequences of being gifted and rejected that Dr. Malone has seen among the children she has worked with is the decision to act like everyone else: to, in effect, not be gifted.

So, here we have another example that tells us that we ought to be teaching ourselves and the coming generations that "different is okay."

We can indict a society that reveres conformity, the body beautiful, intelligence, success, and improperly motivates many young people, but when we do, we must own up to the fact that *we* are society. And if we want our culture to embrace deeper values we must first tend our own gardens and next not permit bigotry and cruelty to go unchallenged.

When was the last time you told your child *never* to call someone "fatso" or "ugly"? When was the last time you told your children not to make fun of other people, and not to judge other people on the basis of their appearance or any obvious physical flaws? When was the last time you told a child not your own not to call others by derogatory names? When was the last time you told another adult that you found racial slurs disgusting?

The only way to make unacceptable the sort of behavior that causes people to feel unworthy and shy is to aggressively—not shyly—refuse to accept it ourselves.

We can also learn a thing or two when we look at a beautiful family most of you have probably heard or read about. Dorothy and Bob DeBolt, who live in Piedmont, California, are the parents of twenty children, fourteen of whom are adopted. One of the things that makes the DeBolt children special is that not all of them are sighted or have two perfectly functioning arms and legs. What makes them *so* special is that they are wonderfully normal—they are independent, responsible, confident, and most are not shy. As it turns out, the magic ingredients the parents use include some of our strategies to minimize or prevent shyness; so let's review them in light of the way these parents guide their children:

• *Unconditional love* is a given in the DeBolt household. It serves as the backdrop for everything else that takes place. Every child in this family is imbued with a sense of parental love and acceptance that is not based on performance, but instead is a constant—the anchor that all children need.

• *Expectations* must always be realistic. They are based on what a particular child is capable of doing and are neither too high nor too low. For example, when Karen, a congenital quadruple amputee, was ready to tie her own shoes, using her hooks, her parents were ready to let her do it—no matter how long it took.

• *Touching* is something that is an integral part of the DeBolts' style of living and parenting. There is a lot of *expressed* love and affection in that household.

• *Discipline with love* is basic when you have that many kids. You have to discipline or you have chaos. You have to be firm but gentle, and you have to have rules. And when some of your kids have never before known what it is to have their parents care, discipline becomes evidence of love. It is lovingly and reasonably meted out, and the parents do a lot of *very* active listening.

• *Talking* is especially important in this family. The children need to, and are encouraged to, talk (when they are ready) about how they felt about their lives before they became members of the family, how they feel about their physical problems and themselves, and how they feel about the knocks they get in their present lives. A lot of talking goes on among all of the DeBolts.

• *Paying attention to your child:* The special needs of each child means that each gets abundant attention from the parents—and from other family members. The children talk, the children listen to each other; the parents talk, the parents listen. The climate is there for all of them to do so.

• *Building trust:* Trust is understood from the moment the DeBolt children become part of the family. The basic contract is that the parents trust the children and the children learn to know they can count on the parents.

• *Self-reliance, responsibility:* This is where the DeBolt family truly shines. *Every* member of the family shares the chores. J. R., who is blind, for example, has to do the dishes like everyone else. Oh, he broke a few plates at first because he can't see—but then, how else could he learn, except by doing?

• *The pleasure of their own company:* They are given the tools—encouraged to read, given music lessons, and encouraged to develop expertise.

• *Risk taking:* Risk taking starts with preparing the children for the risks they are about to take. Then, without pressure, the parents assess a child's readiness to learn a new skill, encourage him or her to try it, and then stand back, and let them go—without helping. Dorothy says that the hardest thing she has to do is to *not* do—to not help a child who is struggling to put on a prosthetic device, tie a shoe using hooks. Once, the whole family watched as it took Karen three hours to make it up the nineteen steps of the staircase, and then they cheered like mad when she made it. No one helped her, and the achievement was all her own, and she basked in the glory her family showered on her for her triumph.

The children are taught to cope with "failure," and see it as a necessary process in learning new skills. They are taught to pick themselves up, dust themselves off, and try again.

• *Developing tolerance:* It goes without saying that in a multiracial household, racial tolerance is not an issue. It further goes without saying, since all of the children are so different from each other, they are taught to appreciate individual uniqueness. And, they are not apt to attribute mistakes and blunders to incompetence, but rather view them in light of the circumstances in which they occur. By being taught to be tolerant of themselves, the children are automatically taught to be tolerant of others.

It is clear that the children are also taught to be tolerant of intolerance. When one of them has had a bad experience because he or she can't see or because he or she is "different," the parents explain why some people behave the way they do— usually in very charitable terms.

• *Sticks and stones:* It is enough to say that the DeBolts dislike and refuse to use the label "handicapped" in referring to any of their children. Dorothy DeBolt says that truly handicapped people are those who are incapable of expressing love.

All of us can learn from the DeBolts, a family that has gone through many crises: when a new child comes on the scene, when one becomes ill, when one is hurt by his or her peers, when a child undergoes surgery to hopefully correct blindness.

Wendy, in fact, was not only blind when she joined the family at the age of five, but had also been a battered child. Everyone is aware of the emotional (as well as physical) damage child battering can cause. Modern medicine was able to restore Wendy's sight, but the battering scars that you don't see were healed over by being loved for herself, being made to feel secure with her new family, and made to feel like a worthwhile human being. When someone wants you so much for yourself as your parents do, how can you doubt your worth?

Sometimes when writers write about the DeBolt family, they call the children "the kids that nobody wanted." Well, if these children weren't wanted by anybody else, they certainly went from ground zero to being cherished when they and their parents found each other.

We don't mean to make it all sound so easy. It wasn't, and it isn't. But it is downright inspiring. If Bob and Dorothy DeBolt can give so many children a sense of high self-esteem, we must have the power to do so too. The DeBolts are living proof of the power of unconditional love, and the wisdom of having realistic expectations of our children.

The children of the *future* need to learn values by the examples set by their parents and other adults. If, in the process of helping the children of the *present* conquer their shyness, we teach them the value of love, integrity, kindness, tolerance, and respect for individual differences, these are the values they will hopefully, assertively, convey to others as being worthwhile. Moreover, these are the values they will most likely impart to their own children. If the children of the present learn that there is joy in the process of learning as well as the outcome of achieving, they will learn, as we see in the DeBolt family, that there is such a thing as competition that is *healthy*, that doesn't pit peer against peer, keeping friendships from flowering. Competition with oneself, measuring today's success against that of yesterday's, is the sort of thing that can fill one with a sense of personal pride and a zest for moving on and trying to reach the next plateau in anything—from taking the nineteenth step up the staircase to saying the first "hello" when coming in contact with someone new.

The end of shyness, then, depends pretty much on us. We will continue to plant the seeds and let them grow by perpetuating superficial standards and prejudice with a shy silence that does nothing, and often is seen as acquiescence. Or else, in the process of helping our own children not to be shy, we can weed and make our own corner of the garden as rich as it can be. We can make our garden a breeding ground for the reverence of the uniqueness of every human being, one that allows all of our children to celebrate life and love themselves and each other.

NOTES

Chapter One

page no.

1. Peter Read, "Socialization Research Revisited," *The Sage Foundation Report*, June, 1980.   1

2. P. G. Zimbardo, *Shyness: What It Is, What to Do about It* (Reading, Massachusetts: Addison-Wesley, 1977; New York: Jove, 1978); P. Pilkonis and P. G. Zimbardo, "The Personal and Social Dynamics of Shyness," C. E. Izard, ed., *Emotions in Personality and Psychopathology* (New York: Plenum, 1979) pp. 133–60.   2

3. David Wallechinsky, Irving Wallace, and Amy Wallace, *The Book of Lists* (New York: William Morrow, 1977; Bantam, 1978).   4

4. R. T. Santee and C. Maslach, "To Agree or Not to Agree: Personal Dissent Amid Social Pressure to Conform" (Paper presented at the Western Psychological Association Convention, San Diego, April 1979). Submitted for publication.   6

5. C. Maslach and T. Solomon, "Pressures Toward Dehumanization from Within and Without" (Paper presented at the Western Psychological Association Convention, Los Angeles, April 1976).   6

6. T. Solomon, "Shyness and Self-concept in Grade School Children" (University of California, 1977).   6

7. D. Stockdale, "An Assessment of Shyness in Children by Teachers, Parents and Peers" (Master's Thesis, Iowa State University, Ames, Iowa, 1976).   6

8. *Diagnostic and Statistical Manual of Mental Disorders*, 3rd ed. (Washington, D.C.: American Psychiatric Association, 1980), p. 227.   11

9. J. M. Cheek and A. H. Buss, "Shyness and Sociability," *Journal of Personality and Social Psychology*, 1981. Under editorial review.   18

Chapter Two

1. D. Baumrind, "The Development of Instrumental Competence   29
Through Socialization," in *Minnesota Symposia on Child Psychol-
ogy*, vol. 7, ed. A. Pick (Minneapolis: University of Minnesota
Press, 1973), pp. 3–46. And, "The Contributions of the Family to
the Development of Competence in Children," *Schizophrenia
Bulletin* 1 (Fall 1975), 14:12–37.

2. R. Schicha and P. G. Zimbardo, "The Relationship Between   32
Shyness, Authoritarianism, and Structure" (Stanford University,
California, 1980).

3. M. D. S. Ainsworth, "Social Development in the First Year of   34
Life: Maternal Influences on Infant-Mother Attachment," in *De-
velopments in Psychiatric Research Viewpoints in Review: Essays
Based on the Sir Geoffrey Vickers' Lectures of the Mental Health
Trust and Research Fund*, ed. J. M. Tanner (London: Hodder,
1977).

4. James Prescott, "Body Pleasure and the Origins of Violence," *The*   35
Futurist, April 1975.

5. James Lynch, *The Broken Heart* (New York: Basic Books, 1977).   36

6. G. S. Lesser. Children and Television: Lessons From Sesame   37
Street. (New York, Vantage, 1975).

7. *San Francisco Chronicle*, 8 November 1978.   38

8. G. B. Shaw, *Candida* (Baltimore: Penguin Books 1974), pp.   38
35–36.

9. K. D. O'Leary et al., "The Effects of Loud and Soft Reprimands   42
on the Behavior of Disruptive Students," *Exceptional Children*
(1970), 37:145–55.

10. D. M. Briggs, *Your Child's Self-Esteem* (New York: Doubleday   42
1970; Dolphin, 1975).

Chapter Three

1. E. Kennedy, *If You Really Knew Me Would You Still Like Me?*   54
(Niles, Ill: Argus Communications 1975).

2. C. G. Lord and P. G. Zimbardo, "Mapping the Private World of   60
Shyness Through Template Matching and Q-Correlates" (Stanford University, California, 1980).

3. Dava Sobel, "Solitude Emerges as a Blessing in Research on   62
Adolescents," *New York Times*, (19 August 1980), p. L-662.

Chapter Four

1. E. Goffman, *The Presentation of Self in Everyday Life* (New York: 80
Doubleday, 1959).

page no.

2. R. M. Arkin, "Self-Presentation Styles," in *Impression Management Theory and Social Psychology Research*, ed. J. T. Tedeschi (New York: Academic Press, 1981).   81

3. R. M. Arkin, A. J. Appleman, and J. M. Burger, "Social Anxiety, Self-presentation, and the Self-serving Bias in Causal Attribution," *Journal of Personality and Social Psychology* (1980), 38:23–5.   81

4. J. Brockner, "Self-esteem, Self-consciousness, and Task Performance: Replications, Extensions, and Possible Explanations," *Journal of Personality and Social Psychology* (1979), 37:447–61.   81

5. G. M. Phillips and N. J. Metzger, "The Reticent Syndrome: Some Theoretical Considerations About Etiology and Treatment," *Speech Monographs* (1973), 40:14–24.   82

6. M. Snyder and W. Swann, "Behavioral Confirmation in Social Interaction: From Social Perception to Social Reality," *Journal of Experimental Social Psychology* (1978), 14:148–162.   84

7. A. E. Ellis and R. A. Harper, *A Guide to Rational Living* (North Hollywood, California: Wilshire Book Co., 1975).   85

8. J. Wolpe, "Behaviour Therapy in Complex Neurotic States," *British Journal of Psychiatry* (1969), 110:28–34.   87

9. F. Orr, D. Degotardi, J. Boughton, and B. Crouch, "Social Shyness: An Experimental Clinical Study," *University of South Wales, Student Counselling and Research Unit Bulletin*, no. 15 (1979).   88

10. A. Buss, "Sociability, Shyness, and Loneliness" (Paper presented at the American Psychological Association Convention, Montreal, Canada, 1980).   89

11. W. A. Corsaro, "We're Friends, Right? Children's Use of Access Rituals in a Nursery School," *Language in Society* (1979), 8:315–36.   90

12. Z. Rubin, *Children's Friendships* (Cambridge, Massachusetts: Harvard University Press, 1980), pp. 139–40.   92

13. J. Gottman, J. Gonso, and B. Brasmussen, "Social Interaction, Social Competence, and Friendship in Children," *Child Development* (1975), 46:709–18.   95

14. A. Garner, *Conversationally Speaking: Tested New Ways to Increase Your Personal and Social Effectiveness* (Los Angeles: Psychology Research Associates, 1980).   95

15. *San Francisco Chronicle*, 20 September 1980.   96

16. E. Aronson, *The Jigsaw Classroom* (Beverly Hills: Sage Publications, 1978).   98

17. N. Dennis, *Cards of Identity* (New York: Signet, 1955).   99

18. H. Arkowitz et al., "Treatment Strategies for Dating Anxiety in College Men Based on Real Life Practice," *The Counseling Psychologist* (in press).   101

19. M. Fischetti, J. P. Curran, and H. W. Wessberg, "Sense of Timing: A Skill Deficit in Heterosexually Anxious Males," *Behavior Modification* (1977), 1:179–94.   101

Chapter Five

1. Furman, W., Rahe, D., and Hartup, W. W., "Rehabilitation   127
of Socially Withdrawn Preschool Children Through Mixed-
Aged and Same-Sex Socialization," *Child Development* (1979),
50:915–22.

Chapter Six

1. J. Segal and H. Yahraes, *A Child's Journey* (New York: 134
McGraw-Hill, 1979).
2. M. R. Lepper and D. Greene, eds., *The Hidden Costs of Reward*   139
(Morristown, N.J: Lawrence Erlbaum Association, 1978).
3. E. Berscheid, and E. Walster, "Beauty and the Best," *Psychology*   141
Today (March 1972), pp. 127–8.
4. J. Dobson, *Hide or Seek* (Old Tappan, New Jersey: Fleming R.   141
Revell Co., 1974).
5. R. Rosenthal and L. Jacobson, *Pygmalion in the Classroom* (New   143
York: Holt, Rinehart and Winston, 1968); "Teacher's Expectancies: Determinants of Pupils' IQ Gains," *Psychological Reports*
(1966), 19:115–18.
6. L. A. Hyman, E. McDowell, and B. Raines, "Corporal Punish-   144
ment and Alternatives in the Schools: An Overview of Theoretical and Practical Issues," in *Proceedings: Conference on Corporal
Punishment in the Schools*, ed. J. H. Wise (Washington, D.C.:
National Institute of Education, 1977), pp. 1–18.
7. G. G. Malinson and J. Weston, "To Promote or Not to Promote,"   147
Journal of Education (1954), 136:155–8.
8. P. E. Kraus, *Yesterday's Children* (New York: John Wiley & Sons,   147
1973).
9. C. Klein, *The Myth of the Happy Child* (New York: Harper &   157
Row, 1975).
10. "The Most Significant Minority: One-Parent Children in the   170
Schools," (National Association of Elementary School Principals, Arlington, Virginia, 28 July 1980).

Chapter Seven

1. D. Elkind, "Understanding the Young Adolescent," *Adolescence*   172
(Spring 1978), 13:127–34.
2. "Seventh Grade Can Be Harmful," *Palo Alto Times*, 10 January   173
1978.
3. L. Fine, as quoted in an interview in the *Palo Alto Times*, 1 June   176
1978.
4. Ibid.   177
5. H. DeRosis, *Parent Power/Child Power: A New Tested Method for*   188
Parenting Without Guilt (New York: Bobbs-Merrill, 1974).
6. Ann Landers, Field Enterprises, 4 May 1980.   188

Chapter Eight

page no.

1. J. M. Cheek and C. M. Busch, "The Influence of Shyness on   201
Loneliness in a New Situation," *Personality and Social Psychol-
ogy Bulletin* (1981). In press.
2. P. G. Zimbardo, C. Zoppel, P. Pilkonis, *The Etic and Emic of*   204
Shyness in Eight Cultures. (Stanford University, 1981).
3. M. S. Harrell et al., "Predicting Compensation Among MBA   209
Graduates Five and Ten Years After Graduation," *Journal of
Applied Psychology* (1977), 62:636–40.

Chapter Nine

1. "Hue and Cry," *This World, San Francisco Examiner & Chronicle*,   214
5 December 1976.

Chapter Ten

1. Elaine Smith, "Put-down Pressures on Already Burdened   234
Child," Copely News Service, 25 January 1978.

GENERAL REFERENCES

Ames, L. B. and Chase, J. A. *Don't Push Your Preschooler*. New York: Harper & Row, 1974.

Alloway, T., Pliner, P., and Krames, L., eds. *Attachment Behavior*. New York: Plenum Press, 1977. Especially relevant: Cairns, R. B., "Beyond Social Attachment: The Dynamics of Interactional Development," pp. 1–24; Marvin, R. S., "An Ethological-Cognitive Model for the Attenuation of Mother-Child Attachment Behavior," pp. 25–60; Ross, H. S., and Goldman, B. D., "Establishing New Social Relations in Infancy," pp. 61–80; Simonds, P. E., "Peers, Parents, and Primates: The Developing Network of Attachments," pp. 145–76.

Asher, S. R. "The Influence of Race and Sex on Children's Sociometric Choices Across the School Year." University of Illinois, 1973.

Asher, S. R., Oden, S. L., and Gottman, J. M. "Children's Friendships in School Settings." In *Current Topics in Early Childhood Education*, vol. 1. L. G. Katz, ed. Norwood, New Jersey: Ablex, 1977.

Baumrind, D. "The Development of Instrumental Competence Through Socialization." In *Minnesota Symposia on Child Psychology*, vol. 7. A. Pick, ed. Minneapolis: University of Minnesota Press, 1973.

Baumrind, D. "The Contributions of the Family to the Development of Competence in Children." *Schizophrenia Bulletin*, Fall 1975, vol. 1, no. 14.

Berscheid, E., and Walster, E. "Beauty and the Best." *Psychology Today*, March 1972.

Booraem, C., Flowers, J., and Schwartz, B. *Help Your Children to Be Self-confident*. Englewood Cliffs, New Jersey: Prentice-Hall, 1978.

Bower, S. A., and Bower, G. H. *Asserting Yourself: A Practical Guide For Positive Change*. Reading, Massachusetts: Addison-Wesley, 1976.

Braga, J., and Braga, L. *Children and Adults: Activities for Growing Together*. Englewood Cliffs, New Jersey: Prentice-Hall, 1976.

Briggs, D. C. *Your Child's Self-esteem*. New York: Doubleday, 1970; Dolphin Doubleday: 1975.

Cairns, R. B. *Social Development: The Origins and Plasticity of Interchanges*. San Francisco: W. H. Freeman, 1979.

Cartledge, G., and Milburn, J. F., eds. *Teaching Social Skills to Children: Innovative Approaches*. Elmsford, New York: Pergamon Press, 1980.

Chase, J. A. "A Study of the Impact of Grade Retention on Primary School Children." *Journal of Psychology,* 1968, 70.

Cheek, D. K. *Assertive Black . . . Puzzled White: A Black Perspective on Assertive Behavior.* San Luis Obispo, California: Impact Publications, 1976.

Cheek, J. M., and Buss, A. H. "Shyness and Sociability." *Journal of Personality and Social Psychology,* 1981. Under editorial review.

Cheek, J. M., and Busch, C. M. "The Influence of Shyness on Loneliness in a New Situation." *Personality and Social Psychology Bulletin,* 1981. In press.

Corey, G. *Teachers Can Make a Difference.* Columbus, Ohio: Charles Merrill Publications, 1973.

Corey, G. *I Never Knew I Had a Choice.* Monterey, California: Brooks/Cole, 1978.

Crozier, W. R. "Shyness as a Dimension of Personality." *British Journal of Social and Clinical Psychology,* 1979, 18.

Dahlgren, D., and Buckner, J. *Shyness in Preschool Children.* Senior Honors Thesis, Stanford University, California, June 1979.

David, H. P., ed. *Child Mental Health in International Perspective.* New York: Harper & Row, 1972.

Derlega, V., and Chaikin, A. *Sharing Intimacy.* Englewood Cliffs, New Jersey: Prentice-Hall, 1975.

DeRosis, H. *Parent Power Child Power: A New Tested Method for Parenting Without Guilt.* New York: Bobbs-Merrill, 1974.

Didato, S. V. *Psychotechniques: How to Help Yourself or Someone You Love.* New York: Methuen Press, 1980.

Diekman, J. R. *Get Your Message Across: How to Improve Communication.* Englewood Cliffs, N.J.: Prentice-Hall, 1979.

Dodson, F. *How to Father.* Los Angeles: Nash Publishing, 1974; New York: Signet Books, 1975.

Dobson, J. *Hide and Seek.* Old Tappen, New Hampshire: Fleming R. Revell, 1974.

Dotzenroth, S. "Shyness, Social Self-esteem, and Mental Biases." Ph.D. dissertation. University of Ottawa, Ontario, Canada, 1977.

Egan, G. *Interpersonal Living: A Skills/Contract Approach to Human-Relations Training in Groups.* Monterey, California: Brooks/Cole, 1976.

Egan, G. *You and Me: The Skills of Communicating and Relating to Others.* Monterey, California: Brooks/Cole, 1977.

Elkind, D. "Understanding the Young Adolescent." *Adolescence,* Spring, 1978, 13, pp. 127–134.

Furman, W., Rahe, D., and Hartup, W. W. "Rehabilitation of Socially Withdrawn Preschool Children Through Mixed-Aged and Same-Sex Socialization." *Child Development,* 1979, 50, pp. 915–22.

Garner, A. *Conversationally Speaking: Tested New Ways to Increase Your Personal and Social Effectiveness.* Los Angeles: Psychology Research Associates, 1980.

Gessell, A., Ilg, F., and Ames, L. B. *The Child From Five to Ten.* New York: Harper & Row, 1977.

Girodo, M. *Shy? You Don't Have to Be!* New York: Pocket Books, 1978.

Girodo, M. "Self-talk: Mechanism in Anxiety and Stress Management." In *Stress and Anxiety,* vol. 4. C. Spielberger and I. G. Sarason, eds. Washington, D.C.: Hemisphere Publications, 1977.

Greenberg, M. T., and Marvin, R. S. "Individual and Age Differences in the Patterns of Preschool Children's Reactions to Strangers." Presented at the Southeastern Conference on Human Development, Nashville, Tennessee, April 14–16, 1976.

Greenwald, J. A. *Creative Intimacy: How to Break the Patterns that Poison Your Relationships.* New York: Simon & Schuster, 1975.

Hedrick, S. L. "A Study of Timidity as Related to Intelligence, Achievement, and Self-concept." *Dissertation Abstracts International.* The Humanities and Sciences, September/October, 1972, 33.

Hartup, W. W. "Children and Their Friends." In *Issues in Childhood Social Development.* H. McGurk, ed. London: Methuen, 1978.

Johnson, D. W. *Reaching Out: Interpersonal Effectiveness and Self-actualization.* Englewood Cliffs, New Jersey: Prentice-Hall, 1972.

Kennedy, E. *If You Really Knew Me Would You Still Like Me?* Niles, Illinois: Argus Communications, 1975.

Kiev, A. *A Strategy for Success.* New York: Macmillan, 1977.

Klein, C. *The Myth of the Happy Child.* New York: Harper & Row, 1975.

Kleinke, C. *First Impressions: The Psychology of Encountering Others.* Englewood Cliffs, New Jersey: Prentice-Hall, 1975.

Kraus, P. E. *Yesterday's Children: A Longitudinal Study of Children from Kindergarten into the Adult Years.* New York: John Wiley & Sons, 1973.

Lamb, M. D., ed. *Social and Personality Development.* New York: Holt, Rinehart and Winston, 1978. Especially relevant: Achenbach, T. M., "Developmental Aspects of Psychopathology in Children and Adolescents," pp. 272–303; Asher, S. R., "Children's Peer Relations," pp. 91–113; Conger, J. J., "Adolescence: A Time for Becoming," pp. 131–54; Fein, G. G., "Play Revisited," pp. 70–90; Lamb, M. E., "Social Interaction in Infancy and the Development of Personality," pp. 26–49; Lamb, M. E., and Baumrind, D., "Socialization and Personality Development in the Preschool Years," pp. 50–69.

Lamb, M. E., Suomi, S. J., and Stephenson, G. R., eds. *Social Interaction Analysis: Methodological Issues.* Madison: University of Wisconsin Press, 1979. Especially relevant: Als, H., Tronick, E., and Brazelton, T. B., "Analysis of Face-to-Face Interaction in Infant-Adult Dyads," pp. 33–76; Lamb, M. E., "The Effects of the Social Context on Dyadic Social Interaction," pp. 253–68; Lamb, M. E., "Issues in the Study of Social Interaction," pp. 1–10; Parke, R. D., Power, T. G., and Gottman, J. M., "Conceptualizing and Quantifying Influence Patterns in the Family Triad," pp. 231–52.

Lawson, J. S., Marshall, W. L., and McGrath, P. "Social Self-esteem Inventory." *Educational and Psychological Measurement,* 1979, 39.

Laycock, F. *Gifted Children.* Glenview, Illinois: Scott, Foresman, 1979.

Lenchner, M. J. "The Shyness Workshop: A Possible Solution to a Social Problem." Senior Honors Dissertation. Cornell University, Ithaca, New York, Spring 1980.

Maccoby, E. E., Dowley, E. M., Hagen, J. W., and Degerman, R. "Activity Level and Intellectual Functioning in Normal Preschool Children." *Child Development,* 1965, 36.

Maccoby, E. E. *Social Development: Psychological Growth and the Parent-Child Relationship.* San Francisco: Harcourt, Brace, Jovanovich, 1980.

Mallinson, G. G., and Weston, J. "To Promote or Not to Promote." *Journal of Education*, 1954, 136, 5.

Mayeroff, M. *On Caring*. New York: Harper & Row, 1971.

O'Connor, R. D. "Modification of Social Withdrawal Through Symbolic Modeling." *Journal of Applied Behavior Analysis*, 1969, 2.

O'Connor, R. D. "Relative Efficacy of Modeling, Shaping and the Combined Procedures for Modification of Social Withdrawal." *Journal of Abnormal Psychology*, 1972, 79.

Oden, S. L., and Asher, S. R. "Coaching Children in Social Skills for Friendship-Making." Paper presented at the biennial meeting of the Society for Research on Child Development, Denver, Colorado, 1975.

Patterson, G. R. *Families: Applications of Social Learning to Family Life*. Rev. ed. Champaign, Illinois: Research Press, 1977.

Patterson, G. R. *Living with Children: New Methods for Parents and Teachers*. Rev. ed. Champaign, Illinois: Research Press, 1977.

Pilkonis, P. A., and Zimbardo, P. G. "The Personal and Social Dynamics of Shyness." *Emotions and Psychopathology*. C. E. Izard, ed. New York: Plenum, 1979.

Plain Talk About Raising Children. Periodical published by the National Institute of Mental Health, 5600 Fishers Lane, Rockville, MD 20857.

Powell, B. *Overcoming Shyness: Practical Scripts for Everyday Encounters*. New York: McGraw-Hill, 1979.

Practical Parenting. Bi-monthly newsletter by Vicki Lansky, 15235 Minnetoka Boulevard, Minnetoka, MN 55343.

Radl, S. L. "Why You Are Shy and How to Cope with It." *Glamour*, June 1976.

Radl, S. L. *How to be a Mother—And a Person Too*. New York: Rawson, Wade, 1979.

Renaud, H., and Estess, F. "Life History Interviews with One Hundred Normal American Males: Pathogenicity of Childhood." *Journal of Orthopsychiatry*, 1961, 31.

Rosenthal, R., and Jacobson, L. "Teacher's Expectancies: Determinants of Pupils' IQ Gains." *Psychological Reports*, vol. 19, 1966.

Scarr, S., ed. *Psychology and Children: Current Research and Practice*. Special issue of *American Psychologist*, 1979, 34. Published by the American Psychological Association, 1200 17th Street, N.W., Washington, DC 20036. Especially relevant: Bell, R. Q., "Parent, Child, and Reciprocal Influences," pp. 821–6; Brofenbrenner, U., "Contexts of Child Rearing: Problems and Prospects," pp. 844–850; Hartup, W. W., "The Social Worlds of Childhood," pp. 944–50; Kagan, J., "Family Experience and the Child's Development," pp. 886–93; Kessen, W., "The American Child and Other Cultural Inventions," pp. 815–20; Yarrow, L. J., "Emotional Development," pp. 951–7.

Scharf, P., McCoy, W., and Ross, D. *Growing up Moral: Dilemmas for the Intermediate Grades*. Minneapolis: Winston Press, 1979.

Segal, J., and Yahraes, H. *A Child's Journey*. New York: McGraw-Hill, 1978.

Shaffer, D. R. *Social and Personality Development*. Monterey, California: Brooks/Cole, 1979.

Slater, P. *The Pursuit of Loneliness: American Culture at the Breaking Point*. Boston: Beacon Press, 1976.

Smith, M. *When I Say No, I Feel Guilty*. New York: Bantam, 1975.

Social Change and the Mental Health of Children. Report of the Joint Commission on Mental Health for Children, New York, Harper & Row, 1973.

Sprung, B., ed. *Perspectives on Non-sexist Early Childhood Education*. New York: Teachers College Press, 1978.

Sroufe, Alan. "Attachment and the Roots of Competence." *Human Nature*, October 1978.

Stockdale, D. *An Assessment of Shyness in Children by Teachers, Parents and Peers*. Masters thesis, Iowa State University, Ames, Iowa, 1976.

Suran, B. G., and Rizzo, J. V. *Special Children: An Integrative Approach*. Glenview, Illinois: Scott, Foresman, 1979.

Thevenin, T. *The Family Bed*. Minneapolis: Tine Thevenin, 1974.

Thoman, E. B., ed. *Origins of the Infant's Social Responsiveness*. Hillsdale, New Jersey: L. Erlbaum Associates, 1979. Especially relevant: Bower, T. G. R., and Wishart, J. G., "Towards a Unitary Theory of Development," pp. 65–94; Papousek, H., and Papousek, M., "The Infant's Fundamental Adaptive Response System," pp. 175–208; Stern, D. N., and Biggon, J., "Temporal Expectancies of Social Behaviors in Mother-Infant Play," pp. 409–30; Thoman, E. B., "Changing Views of the Being and Becoming of Infants," pp. 445–59.

Thomas, A., Chess, S., and Birch, H. G. *Temperament and Behavior Disorders in Children*. New York: New York University Press, 1968.

Wassmer, A. C. *Making Contact: A Guide to Overcoming Shyness, Making New Relationships and Keeping Those You Already Have*. New York: Dial Press, 1978.

Watson, D., and Friend, R. "The Measurement of Social-Evaluative Anxiety." *Journal of Consulting and Clinical Psychology*, 1969, 33.

Weiner, D., Frieze, I., Kukla A., Reed, L., and Rosenbaum, R. *Perceiving the Causes of Success and Failure*. New York: General Learning Press, 1971.

White, B. L., Kaban, B. T., and Attanucci, J. S. *The Origins of Human Competence: The Final Report of the Harvard Preschool Project*. Lexington, Mass.: Lexington Books, 1979.

Wrightsone, J. W. *Class Organization for Instruction*. Washington, D.C.: National Education Association, 1957.

Zimbardo, P. G. *Shyness: What It Is, What to Do About It*. Reading, Massachusetts: Addison-Wesley, 1977.

Zimbardo, P. G., and Radl, S. L. *The Shyness Workbook*. New York: A & W Publishers, 1979.

Zimbardo, P. G., and Radl, S. R. "How Teens Can Overcome Shyness," *Seventeen*, June 1978.

Using the Stanford Shyness Survey

This survey was developed as a research tool to help us better understand how people thought about their shyness, its causes, ways of expressing itself, and its consequences. It is a device to focus on areas of personal experience which shyness often affects.

In addition, we have found it to be useful as a means of opening a dialogue about shyness between parents and children. Answering the questionnaire together, a parent and child can begin to discuss and disclose to each other the hows and whys of their own shyness. For some parents, it has proven to be valuable as a shared experience, enabling a deeper level of communication to develop than is usual between them and their children. There are, of course, no right or wrong answers, nor a score to be compared to others. Your answers can be referred to the general body of knowledge about shyness outlined in this book that was in part obtained using the Stanford Shyness Survey.

STANFORD SURVEY ON SHYNESS

Although shyness is a fascinating psychological issue, there has been virtually no research done to increase our understanding of its dynamics and consequences. The present survey represents part of a general research program started at Stanford University (California, U.S.A.) by a team of students and faculty. It is being administered in a number of colleges on the mainland of the U.S.A., as well as in Hawaii, Japan, Mexico, England and Germany. Non-college groups are also being studied in several of these countries.

Please answer all questions as thoughtfully and frankly as you can. We are interested in your experiences, perceptions, and reactions to shyness. The questionnaire is anonymous, so your answers will be confidential.

Thank you for sharing this information with us.

- -

Please circle the number preceding the most appropriate response, or fill in the blank where required.

SECTION A - BACKGROUND INFORMATION

SEX: (7) 1. Male   TODAY'S DATE:
           2. Female

AGE: (8,9) _____ years

EDUCATION: (10)
1. less than 12 years
2. high school graduate
3. some college
4. college graduate

OCCUPATION: (11) (specify: for example, "student," "housewife," "dentist")

_____

MARITAL STATUS: (12)
1. single and never married
2. married
3. formerly married

RACE OR ETHNIC BACKGROUND: (13)
1. white
2. black
3. oriental
4. Spanish-speaking
5. other (specify)

_____

COUNTRY OF BIRTH: (14,15) _____

RELIGION: (16)
1. none, atheist, or agnostic
2. protestant
3. catholic
4. jewish
5. other (specify)

Do Not Write in This Column

Card No.	(1)	_1_
S No.	(2)	___
	(3)	___
	(4)	___
	(5)	___
Nat.	(6)	
(7)		
(8)		
(9)		
(10)		
(11)		
(12)		
(13)		
(14)		
(15)		
(16)		

SECTION B - PERSONAL SHYNESS

Do you presently consider yourself to be a shy person? **(17)**   1. yes   2. no

If you answered "no," was there ever a period in your life during
which you considered yourself to be a shy person? **(18)**   1. yes   2. no

If you answered "yes," was there ever a period in your life during which you considered
yourself not to be a shy person? **(19)**   1. yes   2. no

Do most other people who know you well consider you to be a shy person? **(20)**
1. yes 2. no

Do acquaintances consider you to be a shy person? **(21)**   1. yes   2. no

On the following scale of introversion-extroversion, circle the number which best represents how you would
generally classify yourself. (Note: an introvert is defined as "one whose thoughts and interests are
primarily directed inward." An extrovert is defined as "one primarily interested in others or in the
environment.") **(22)**

Extreme Introvert	Moderate Introvert	Slight Introvert	Neutral	Slight Extrovert	Moderate Extrovert	Extreme Extrovert
1	2	3	4	5	6	7

Compared to your peers (of the same age and sex), how shy would you estimate you are? **(23)**
I am: 1. much more shy   4. less shy
         2. more shy   5. much less shy
         3. about average

What percentage of the general population (from 0 to 100%) would you estimate are shy, that is, would
label themselves as shy persons? **(24-26)** (Fill in your estimate)
_____ %

How desirable do you think shyness is as a personal characteristic? **(27)**

1. very undesirable   4. desirable
2. undesirable   5. very desirable
3. neither undesirable nor desirable

Even if you labeled yourself in general as not shy, both past and present, have you ever experienced
feelings of shyness? **(28)** 1. yes   2. no

Do Not Write in
This Column

(17)

(18)

(19)

(20)

(21)

(22)

(23)

(24)

(25)

(26)

(27)

(28)

Stanford Survey on Shyness (page 3)

SECTION C - DIMENSIONS OF SHYNESS

NOTE: If you have never experienced feelings of shyness, please omit the remaining questions and answer only the last question (Section G), and you will have completed the questionnaire.

If you now experience, or have ever experienced, feelings of shyness, please indicate which of the following situations, activities, and types of people elicit shyness in you. (Place a checkmark next to <u>all</u> of the appropriate choices.)

Situations and activities which elicit shyness in me:

– social situations in general (29)
– large groups (30)
– small, task-oriented groups (e.g., seminars at school, work groups on the job) (31)
– small, social groups (e.g., at parties, dances) (32)
– one-to-one interactions with a person of the same sex (33)
– one-to-one interactions with a person of the opposite sex (34)
– situations where I am vulnerable (e.g., when asking for help) (35)
– situations where I am of lower status than others (e.g., when speaking to superiors, authorities) (36)
– situations requiring assertiveness (e.g., when complaining about faulty service in a restaurant or the poor quality of a product) (37)
– situations where I am the focus of attention, before a large group (e.g., when giving a speech) (38)
– situations where I am the focus of attention, before a small group (e.g., when being introduced, when being asked directly for my opinion) (39)
– situations where I am being evaluated or compared with other (e.g., when being interviewed, when being criticized) (40)
– new situations in general (41)

Types of people who elicit shyness in me:

– my parents (42)
– my siblings (43)
– other relatives (44)
– friends (45)
– strangers (46)
– foreigners (47)
– authorities (by virtue of their role — police, teacher, superior at work) (48)
– authorities (by virtue of their knowledge — intellectual superiors, experts) (49)
– elderly people (much older than you) (50)
– children (much younger than you) (51)
– persons of the opposite sex, in a group (52)
– persons of the same sex, in a group (53)
– a person of the opposite sex, one-to-one (54)
– a person of the same sex, one-to-one (55)

(29) (30) (31) (32) (33) (34) (35) (36) (37) (38) (39) (40) (41) (42) (43) (44) (45) (46) (47) (48) (49) (50) (51) (52) (53) (54) (55)

SECTION D - REACTIONS TO SHYNESS

If you do experience, or have ever experienced, feelings of shyness, which of the following physiological reactions are associated with such feelings? (Check all those that apply.)

- blushing (56)
- increased pulse (57)
- "butterflies in stomach" (58)
- tingling sensations (59)
- heart pounding (60)

- dry mouth (61)
- tremors (62)
- perspiration (63)
- fatigue (64)
- others (specify below) (65, 66)

_____

If you do experience, or have ever experienced, feelings of shyness, what are the overt behaviors which might indicate to others that you are feeling shy? (Check all those that apply.)

- low speaking voice (67)
- avoidance of other people (68)
- silence (a reluctance to talk) (69)
- stuttering (70)

- inability to make eye contact (71)
- posture (72)
- avoidance of taking action (73)
- others (specify below) (74, 75)

_____

If you do experience, or have ever experienced, feelings of shyness, what are the specific thoughts and sensations associated with such feelings? (Check all those that apply.)

- positive thoughts (e.g., feeling content with myself) (6)
- no specific thoughts (e.g., daydreaming, thinking about nothing in particular) (7)
- self-consiousness (e.g., an extreme awareness of myself, of my every action) (8)
- thoughts that focus on the unpleasantness of the situation (e.g., thinking that the situation is terrible, thinking that I'd like to be out of the situation) (9)
- thoughts that provide distractions (e.g., thinking of other things I could be doing, thinking that the experience will be over in a short while) (10)
- negative thoughts about myself (e.g., feeling inadequate, insecure, inferior, stupid) (11)
- thoughts about the evaluations of me that others are making (e.g., wondering what the people around me are thinking of me) (12)
- thoughts about the way in which I am handling myself (e.g., wondering what kind of impression I am creating and how I might control it) (13)
- thoughts about shyness in general (e.g., thinking about the extent of my shyness and its consequences, wishing that I weren't shy) (14)

SECTION E - CONSEQUENCES OF SHYNESS

What are the positive consequences of being shy? (Check all those that apply.)

-- none, no positive consequences (15)
-- creates a modest, appealing impression; makes one appear discreet, introspective (16)
-- helps avoid interpersonal conflicts (17)
-- provides a convenient form of anonymity and protection (18)
-- provides an opportunity to stand back, observe others, act carefully and intelligently (19)
-- avoids negative evaluations by others (e.g., a shy person is not considered obnoxious, overaggressive or pretentious) (20)
-- provides a way to be selective about the people with whom one interacts (21)
-- enhances personal privacy and the pleasure that solitude offers (22)
-- creates positive interpersonal consequences, by not putting others off, intimidating them or hurting them (23)

What are the negative consequences of being shy? (Check all those that apply.)

-- none, no negative consequences (24)
-- creates social problems; makes it difficult to meet new people, make new friends, enjoy potentially good experiences (25)
-- has negative emotional consequences; creates feelings of loneliness, isolation, depression (26)
-- prevents positive evaluations by others (e.g., my personal assets never become apparent because of my shyness) (27)
-- makes it difficult to be appropriately assertive, to express opinions, to take advantage of opportunities (28)
--allows incorrect negative evaluations by others (e.g., I may unjustly be seen as unfriendly or snobbish or weak) (29)
-- creates cognitive and expressive difficulties; inhibits the capacity to think clearly while with others and to communicate effectively with them (30)
-- encourages excessive self-consciousness, preoccupation with myself (31)

- -

SECTION F - SHYNESS, A PROBLEM?

If you labeled yourself as a shy person (either past or present), please respond to the questions in this section.

In general, do you (did you) like being shy? (32) 1. yes 2. no

Do you (did you) consider shyness to be a problem? (33) 1. yes 2. no

In deciding whether or not to call yourself a "shy person," was your decision based on the fact that:
(circle one) (34)
1. you are (were) shy all of the time in all situations
2. you are (were) shy at least 50% of the time, in more situations than not
3. you are (were) shy only occasionally, but those occasions are (were) of enough importance to justify calling yourself a shy person

Do Not Write in This Column
(35)
(36)
(37)
(38)
(39)
(40)
(41)
(42)
(43)

SECTION G - JUDGMENTS OF SHYNESS IN OTHERS

What behaviors on the part of another person would indicate to you that this other person is feeling shy? (Check all those that apply.)

- blushing (35)
- low speaking voice (36)
- inability to make eye contact (37)
- avoidance of other people (38)

- silence (a reluctance to talk) (39)
- posture (40)
- stuttering (41)
- others (specify below) (42, 43)

_____

THANK YOU AGAIN FOR YOUR HELP.
===

OPTIONAL, ADDITIONAL INFORMATION (only if requested)

A.) _____   B.) _____

C.) _____   D.) _____

E.) _____
_____
_____
_____
_____

F.) _____
_____
_____
_____
_____

INDEX